HEAD OF THE CLASS

An Oral History of African-American Achievement in Higher Education and Beyond

TWAYNE'S
ORAL HISTORY SERIES

Donald A. Ritchie, Series Editor

GABRIELLE MORRIS

HEAD OF THE CLASS

*An Oral History of
African-American Achievement
in Higher Education and Beyond*

With an Afterword by
Troy Duster

TWAYNE PUBLISHERS
AN IMPRINT OF SIMON & SCHUSTER MACMILLAN
NEW YORK

PRENTICE HALL INTERNATIONAL
LONDON MEXICO CITY NEW DELHI SINGAPORE SYDNEY TORONTO

Twayne's Oral History Series No. 16

Head of the Class: An Oral History of African-American Achievement in Higher Education and Beyond
Gabrielle Morris

Twayne Publishers
An Imprint of Simon & Schuster Macmillan
866 Third Avenue
New York, New York 10022

Library of Congress Cataloging-in-Publication Data
Morris, Gabrielle
    Head of the class : an oral history of African-American achievement / Gabrielle Morris.
        p.   cm.—(Twayne's oral history series ; no. 16)
    Includes bibliographical references and index.
    ISBN 0-8057-9129-9 (hc : alk. paper).—ISBN 0-8057-9130-2 (pbk. : alk. paper)
    1. University of California, Berkeley—Students—Biography.
    2. University of California, Berkeley—History.   3. Afro-American college students—Biography.   4. Oral history.
    I. Title.   II. Series.
    LD752.M67   1995
    378.794'67—dc20   95–10081
                                                                 CIP

The paper used in this publication meets the minimum requirements of American National Standard for Information Sciences—Permanence of Paper for Printed Library Materials, ANSI Z39.48–1984. ♾™

10 9 8 7 6 5 4 3 2 1 (hc)
10 9 8 7 6 5 4 3 2 1 (pb)

Printed in the United States of America

For Willy

Contents

Foreword

Equal opportunity in education has long been a primary objective in the struggle to make America live up to its pretenses as a land of freedom and justice. Much has been written about segregated schools, about those who stood in the classroom door to bar integration, about civil rights lawyers who pressed the court cases to open the doors, and about the students who at times needed to brave the mob to attend classes. Less attention has been paid to what happened to those who broke through the racial barriers and obtained a decent education, about the impact on their lives and on their community. *Head of the Class* focuses on the first generation of African-American graduates of the University of California, Berkeley, and at their subsequent careers in law, government, business, and other areas. Their stories recall their difficulties at being a small minority within the university, about teachers and others who influenced their thinking, and about their intense determination to learn and to advance themselves professionally. Despite the prejudices that often stood in their way, they exhibit in their testimonies both pride and hopefulness. When considering the lives and accomplishments of these articulate and strong-minded people, it is hard to avoid the description "positive role models."

Oral history may well be the twentieth century's substitute for the written memoir. In exchange for the immediacy of diaries or correspondence, the retrospective interview offers a dialogue between the participant and the informed interviewer. Having prepared sufficient preliminary research, interviewers can direct the discussion into areas long since "forgotten" or no longer considered of consequence. "I haven't thought about that in years" is a common response, uttered just before an interviewee commences with a surprisingly detailed description of some past incident. The quality of the interview, its candidness and depth, generally will depend as much on the interviewer as the interviewee, and the confidence and rapport between the two adds a special dimension to the spoken memoir.

Interviewers represent a variety of disciplines and work either as part of a collective effort or individually. Regardless of their different interests or the variety of their subjects, all interviewers share a common imperative: to collect memories while they are still available. Most oral historians feel an additional responsibility to make their interviews accessible for use beyond their own research needs. Still, important collections of vital, vibrant interviews lie scattered in archives throughout every state, undiscovered or simply not used.

Twayne's Oral History Series seeks to identify those resources and to publish selections of the best materials. The series lets people speak for themselves, from their own unique perspectives on people, places, and events. But to be more than a babble of voices, each volume organizes its interviews around particular situations and events and ties them together with interpretive essays that place individuals into the larger historical context. The styles and format of individual volumes vary with the material from which they are drawn, demonstrating again the diversity of oral history and its methodology.

Whenever oral historians gather in conference, they enjoy retelling experiences about the inspiring individuals they have met, the unexpected information they have elicited, and the unforgettable reminiscences that would otherwise have never been recorded. The result invariably reminds listeners of others who deserve to be interviewed, provides them with models of interviewing techniques, and inspires them to make their own contribution to the field. I trust that the oral historians in this series—as interviewers, editors, and interpreters—will have a similar effect on their readers.

DONALD A. RITCHIE
Series Editor, Senate Historical Office

Preface

Since entering college, I have heard and told stories of the many intellectually talented black youth who—had the world been fair—would have had access to higher education and, with it, would have become leaders in general and leaders of their people in particular.

No doubt every social group has such stories to tell of submerged or denied talent among its members; nonetheless, access to avenues to success such as higher education have not been evenly distributed among all groups. In this contemporary world, fitfully trying to redress the effects of past unfairness through affirmative-action policies and programs, it is important to remember that numerous African Americans have graduated from college. Their experiences are all the more dramatic because there has been until recently little knowledge of the tradition of excellence in higher education that does exist within this group.

As we acknowledge the success stories in this volume, it is important to note that we are celebrating the accomplishments of a highly self-selected group and, equally important, one filtered through the requirements of the dominant society of the first half of the twentieth centtury. The rise of these black men and women to educational and social achievement during that period was extraordinary, and so was the personal cost required. And as we note these stories of success, we must also remember that huge numbers of African Americans were kept distant from even the prospect of higher education. One hope for this book is that it will increase the potential for African Americans to aspire to higher education.

Who were those who "made it" in the early years of this century? Ida Jackson's story is informative here. Before her father's death when she was 10, he father implored her to "Get an education. It's the one thing the white man can't take from you."[1] She carried this lesson from Vicksburg, Mississippi, to Oakland, California, where she became one of perhaps a dozen black students at the University of California at Berkeley. During her college years, she suffered a variety of indignities through which she persisted in her studies.

At Berkeley, she organized the first black sorority and insisted upon participating—alone in her white gown—in the Senior Pilgrimage to visit traditional campus sites. "Of course, I did some foolish things," she recalls. "I told my friend, Oreathial Richardson, we should go."[2]

"She said, 'I wouldn't go. They'll snub you.' My black friends laughed at me for going.

"I said, 'I'm not concerned about what other people think. I want to know what they know. I want to see those places. This is graduation time, and I want to participate in it and see what it's like.' " Rejected by whites, ridiculed by the other Berkeley black students, she moves on, exemplary in her dedication.

Eras of racism seem to have their individual signatures. In the 1920s, Ida Jackson, like her mother and father, took racism for granted. It was vicious but familiar—a predictable demon, loose every day, which daily had to be fought and tamed. One carried the variously healed scars from battle. But the knowledge that racism existed was itself a kind of taken-for-granted wound. What was it like to live in such a world? It required one to be heroic, staunch, and a survivor. And it invited the shadow appellations for these same traits—bullheaded, obtuse, thick-skinned, a sell-out.

Jackson pushed and she gave. Her lone participation in the "white" ritual of Senior Pilgrimage is emblematic of what every black person 60 years of age or more knows about attending predominantly white colleges and universities. It was an enculturation experience. You conceded to speech and elocution conventions, just like an immigrant. Like an immigrant, adoption of new ways could separate you from your grandparents. There were new rituals. There was new music with which to be elevated. You left behind much when you made the deal to be educated in a white setting, at least for the time you were there.

Things are not the same in the 1990s. To set the perspective for my remarks on the contemporary scene, permit me an autobiographical indulgence. It may be useful in describing some of the evolution that has taken place.

Born in Los Angeles in 1935, I was 17 before I entered a white person's home. None was ever in mine until after I completed college. Nonetheless, while Southern California was thoroughly segregated physically, every moment of my education, from kindergarten through graduate school, was integrated. That is, my K–12 school life included a liberal representation of black and Mexican students within a vast majority of whites. The longer I was in school, however, the fewer black students there were in my classes. Through college I increasingly found myself in settings where I was the only black presence. By the same token, practically all black students on campus knew each other.

I will always hold in my mind the picture of a young black man who came to UCLA as an undergraduate in, I believe, political science. I was a sociology graduate student at the time. In my southeast Los Angeles neighborhood, this student would have been known as a "diddy bop." The name had to do with a style that many young black men adopted.

His hair was processed like that of the popular singer Nat King Cole. His speech was authentically what it was: sweet, cajoling, smooth, with a lilt and rhythm completely unrelated to university conversational conventions. His manner was common at my high school but novel on the college campus. (It was important to me in those days to dress and speak as a "graduate student" should.) Later I learned that he graduated with A grades and wrote a significantly original senior thesis. No one in this book was like that stylistically. Everyone in this book knew someone like him.

The point is that something happened in the late 1950s and early 1960s to make how one performed more important than how one was packaged. Debates on the merits of employable English versus black English still show up frequently in the national press. Nevertheless, the question of how a student speaks or dresses on campus has become somewhat irrelevant to his or her intelligence.

I have spent 35 of the last 40 years in the University of California system as student, faculty member, and administrator. Twenty-three of those years I have spent at Berkeley, most recently as vice chancellor for undergraduate affairs. Since 1954 I have been an immediate witness to the gradual changes in campus race relations. Over the past five years I have been somewhat responsible for tending them.

In my estimation what has happened is that the America of the HUAC, beatniks, *Sputnik*, Elvis, SNCC, SCLC, and so forth has, through all those experiences, gradually emerged from its McCarthyite horror of social and political difference and awakened to all the elements that make up the country.[3] Theater, the arts in general, and higher education were the experimental arenas within which the country came to display and reconfigure its repressed cultural elements. Black people figured in the reexamination and were among its prominent subjects. Universities were an important stage for playing out the process. America woke to its social complexity and, gradually, to its diversity.

The civil rights movement and its successful advocacy of black people's rights is, I believe, responsible for our current use of the term "diversity." Every wounded subset of our social mosaic has subsequently sought to use the same tools of protest for redress that other groups use. Unfortunately, almost all have mechanically adopted the victim stance as one of their tools. More important, however, somewhere in the mid-1960s it became OK to be what you were. "Black" replaced "Negro" as the term of choice, and this was self-directed naming, unlike the historic *New York Times* decision to capitalize "negro." Previously, what one was called in America was left to demographers or the bean counters of public-policy evaluation.

At the same time, on many university campuses there developed a dynamic of faculty letting students be and students insisting on being themselves, in ways that were more fundamental than what they were called. Actually, expectations of behavior and dress have reversed. Advantaged black students now struggle to represent themselves as recent denizens of "the hood."

From my perspective, the characteristic injuries of the 1990s for black students are not the clear, vicious racism of the past that hit you in the mouth, called you a hurtful name, and took something irretrievable from your sense of self. What does cause them pain? For many of today's black students, especially those without extensive cross-race contact, it is easy to confuse the loneliness of being 17, the modest slight of fellow students' inattention, or the campus bureaucrat's insistence that you go to window B with the cloudy demon of racism, which they are told exists by everyone who matters to them. I hope that there will be increasing ability to make accurate distinctions in this area.

In fact, at Berkeley, while many African-American students may be noisy about how the campus does or does not fit their needs for role models, few are immigrants awaiting elocution lessons. Most black students are gifted and well prepared, and they arrive unapologetically accustomed to and expecting special attention.

What impresses me from my current perspective is the complete reversal of racial figure and ground from the period covered in this volume's accounts to the present. A majority of Berkeley's African-American students have no interest in today's version of Senior Pilgrimage (there are versions of it). The students who might caution today's Ida Jackson would be more concerned about the authenticity of her blackness than about her being snubbed by white students.

Black and most other social groups that have been historically excluded from the main American story are currently determined to ensure that their parts of this history are told in, and help structure, the American future. Universities are where those stories are officially rendered. For many students, the goal is to ensure that those construing America are representative of its population mix. Thus the movement to diversify the faculty of this university in this state. Black students are in the front ranks of this effort.

There is support for the ambition of any American in the oral histories of this volume. We are mostly strangers in this baby nation. The struggle of black people to have their genius acknowledged and expressed is a particularly distilled and intense version of all American stories. We were slaves and America was a primitive enslaver. Thus the stories of this volume are part of the necessary sustenance for future black American success stories. The fact is that UC Berkeley has produced leaders. Many of the African-American leaders who pushed their way through this university became leaders largely in various black communities. Contemporary and future leaders, to achieve the promise of their predecessors, will be required to lead in an extraordinarily complex world where no group dominates and all groups must be attended.

The stories in this volume are stories of strength and resolve. Read them with resolve and be strengthened for the new world we face.

RUSS ELLIS
Vice Chancellor, Undergraduate Affairs,
University of California at Berkeley

Introduction

The Continuing Challenge

With ethnic and racial diversity an increasingly urgent social concern and public policy issue, there is growing need for information about the aspirations and achievements of the different segments of America's richly varied population. Because African Americans have played significant roles in the nation's history since its earliest days, their experiences are especially important as we seek to better understand and deal with an ever more complex society.

Like other groups who see themselves and are perceived as culturally different from the larger population, many black men and women have found education vital to their economic success and social progress in the wider community. School experiences and particularly higher education also have provided an important avenue for contacts between races, some contacts more cordial than others.

Previously untapped information has recently become available about the considerable number of African Americans who have completed a college or university education in the first half of the twentieth century. Much of this information is in collections of tape-recorded interviews in university and local history archives. Notable among these collections are the Black Women Oral History Project at Radcliffe College, the Black Leadership Project at the University of California at Los Angeles, the Negro Political Leaders and University of California Black Alumni projects at the University of California at Berkeley, and Gwendolyn Etter-Lewis's research for *My Soul Is My Own*.[1]

This book draws on such material to present a composite portrait of minority graduates of primarily white colleges from 1914 to 1955. The individual narrators comment on their family life, student days, and their considerable accomplishments in professional careers in business, education, government, science, and other fields into the late 1980s.

The immediate, conversational quality of these narratives offers a one-to-one experience, like an older friend or relative telling what it was like to be a black college student in the 1920s, 1930s, and 1940s. Despite 30 years of affirmative-action programs and increases in minority enrollment, many African-American teenagers do not think of college as an option. In many cases, no relatives or friends have gone to college, to set an example, offer encouragement, or lend a hand over inevitable stumbling blocks. Without mentors or role models, too many young potential scholars have just not considered going on to higher education.

Strong role models are provided by the narrators in this book. In addition to the example set by their own achievements, many of them speak of their interest in offering assistance to young people, reflecting the mission of racial uplift and service which has long been strong in African-American philosophy.[2] One goal of the volume is to pass on these stories and standards to future generations in the hope that they will inspire today's young people to go on to college. Equally important, the narratives provide a means for those who have had little or no contact with black men and women to become acquainted with some distinguished African Americans and gain a sense of another culture. As Stanford playwright and performance artist Anna Deveare Smith comments, "If I put myself in somebody else's language, then I understand something more about them."[3]

Although this material focuses on students at the University of California at Berkeley, a number of the narrators attended other schools in addition to Cal, including City College of New York, Antioch College, San Francisco State College, and the University of Manitoba. Recent publications such as *Blacks at Harvard* indicate that African-American students at colleges in other parts of the country have had similar experiences.[4] Undoubtedly, a search would reveal supporting information about the number and quality of minority graduates in the early years of this century.

Anecdotal evidence in the following chapters tells us that in the 1920s and 1930s there were perhaps 12 to 20 black students among 8,000 to 9,000 undergraduates at Berkeley each year, and maybe 100 or so at a time in the 1940s and 1950s when enrollment was 20,000 and rising—a nearly invisible 0.04 percent. In those years registrars did not record the ethnicity of students and, as Ida Jackson tells us, pictures of African-American student activities were not welcome in the yearbooks.[5]

As late as the mid-1950s, Charles Patterson comments, "You could look a long way without seeing another black like me."[6] Although these few might have been considered "token blacks," not very noticeable on campus, their determination to get an education led them to put aside or find a way around whatever obstacles they encountered. It was a period when there were few, if any, student assistance programs and no minority outreach efforts. They decided they wanted to go to college, and they went up to the registrar's office and enrolled.

The era described by these narrators ended with the sweeping social changes that occurred after World War II. With the boom in black enrollment resulting from affirmative-action policies created in the late 1960s, the number of black graduate and undergraduate students increased from 226 in 1966, 1.02 percent of the student body, to 1,944 African-American students in 1988, 6.12 percent of the total. This compares with a total of 6.8 percent blacks in the overall California population in 1990.[7]

University of California at Berkeley sociologists W. R. Ellis, Jr., and Troy Duster bring the picture of African-American student experiences up to the late 1980s and early 1990s in the Preface and Afterword they have, respectively, contributed to this book. They write about campus life and draw from extensive survey interviews from the 1960s to 1980s with African-American and other minority students that provide a view of the contrasts and continuity with previous years. These contemporary comments report on student perceptions of themselves and the complexities they face in increasingly multicultural college communities. To some it seems as if demographics, economics, and political change have conspired to block the expectations of minority men and women. In other cases, the concern is expressed that persistent racist attitudes mean continued lack of sensitivity to and awareness of minority viewpoints.

The distress and frustration expressed by young African Americans in the 1980s are reminders of the long history of the search for social justice in America. Many of the narrators in this volume were active in the struggles of the early twentieth century that brought about the major social and political changes of the 1960s. Their comments are evidence that today's students are not as isolated as they feel in their own struggles. From these roots perhaps the current generation will be strengthened as they prepare to deal with the world of the twenty-first century.

Historical Perspective

A few determined black men and women have made their way to the University of California since the early 1880s. Many of them have distinguished themselves academically and in a wide range of careers. The first reported African-American student was Alexander Dumas Jones of San Francisco, who enrolled in 1881.[8] Then as now, attitudes toward people of color in California were contradictory.

Among the heroes of the nineteenth century were James Beckwourth, one of the mountain men who led settlers through the treacherous passes of the

Sierra Nevada; William Leidesdorff, a ship's captain who became chairman of the first American school board in San Francisco and founded the city's first public school; and Mary Ellen Pleasants, who ran a boardinghouse and used her earnings to help runaway slaves. All of them were of African or mixed ancestry.

Delilah Beasley's valuable annotated bibliography of African-American historical publications refers to black persons among the military units that secured California from Mexico, the mining communities of the Gold Rush, and the crews of ships bringing the first businessmen and farmers to San Francisco.[9] They contributed to all the activities of settling the West. And yet, despite the frontier spirit of independence and individuality in which the West continues to take pride, the question of whether slavery would be legal marred the pursuit of statehood until California joined the union in 1850 as a free state.[10]

It took another 30 years of organized effort by California Colored Conventions and several court decisions before the legislature abolished segregated schools in 1880.[11] With little available to him in the way of high school education until that time, Alexander Jones must have been one of a very few young blacks who would have qualified for admission to the university the following year. Perhaps he did his preparatory work in another state or was self-educated. It is likely that he had a sense of adventure, as well as mission, and was just waiting for the ban on black enrollment to be lifted.

By 1900 the U.S. Census reported that the black population had risen to 11,045 from 6,018 in 1880, approximately 1 percent of all Californians and fewer than the Chinese, Mexican, or Native American populations then.[12] The University of California, which graduated its first class in 1873, was growing slowly too. By 1903 dignitaries such as Booker T. Washington appeared on campus, while making a tour to raise funds for Tuskegee Institute.[13] Among the audience may have been Charles Edward Carpenter, class of 1905, who was the first black man to graduate from the university. The first black woman graduate would be Vivian Rodgers, class of 1909.[14]

Although little is known about Jones, Carpenter, or Rogers and what it was like for them on campus, firsthand accounts by African Americans who were students between 1914 and the 1950s tell how they felt about their college days. They present a story of determination, hard work, and ability. Almost without exception, these men and women completed their college educations and went on to be successful in their chosen careers and to distinguish themselves in social and civic organizations.

Most of the following narrators graduated before federal government programs for World War II veterans and, in the 1960s, for affirmative action for minorities began to make it somewhat easier for black youth to go to college. Their comments therefore reflect the efforts of those who succeeded at the university without the benefit of special funding or tutorial programs.

Together their experiences are a rich part of the university's history and are the roots of a long tradition of African-American achievement in higher education that is shared by succeeding generations.

The narratives illuminate the ingredients for success of African Americans and the relationships between cultures in times past. They provide guideposts as well for other and more recently arrived groups seeking to cope with playing fields where the rules have been set by earlier immigrants. Such information is vital as we enter a period where no one group comprises a majority of the state's population. In the fall 1993 census, the total of 21,173 undergraduate students at Berkeley included 1,183 African Americans, 239 American Indian/Alaska natives, 7,656 Asians, 2,956 Hispanics, 7,219 Caucasians, 1,662 other, and 258 foreign students.[15]

In addition, the chapters in this book offer informal conversations with intelligent, articulate people who appear to have enjoyed the opportunity to say what they think about the university and other institutions, often in quite salty terms. The narratives convey a sense of the pervasive racism of these people's early years and their determination to succeed in college despite existing obstacles. Perhaps because of their success in later life, they are objective in relating experiences of rejection and discrimination that can make a listener cringe.

Accustomed to hard work in school and out, they all said that encouragement from relatives and other adults helped them reach their goal. "Get an education. It's the one thing the white man can't take away from you," is a common comment.[16] There are quite frequent references to a helping hand from white people, and invariably there are stories of enjoying the pranks and parties of student life. Several speak of the college campus as the place where for the first time they felt free of the pressures of being black.[17]

Chapters are arranged chronologically, with the earliest reporting university experiences from 1914 through 1922 and the final ones from 1944 to 1960. Within this span three separate though overlapping and interrelated phases of African-American student life can be seen. For purposes of discussion, these phases are identified as the pioneers, trailblazers, and bridge builders.

The pioneers were the lonely few who found their way to college on their own. Only a handful of black students were enrolled at any one time from 1914 to 1931, and so there were few peers to whom they could turn for advice and little in the way of organized counseling or support services for students black or white. It was a struggle for all of the African Americans just to find the money for fees, comparatively low as they were at the time, and a place to live.

There was encouragement from parents, relatives, and other black adults. Many elders took responsibility for providing jobs for students or finding them housing. A black steward at the Oakland Athletic Club hired successive generations of students as busboys in the gym, where they could study at night, for example,[18] and a chef in Monterey moved to Oakland to open a restaurant near the campus "where he might give employment and financial aid to minority students."[19]

Because there were so few of these pioneers, each became the first or second in Northern California in whatever field of work he or she chose after graduation: the law, teaching, social work, librarianship, pharmacy, elective politics. It is not surprising that all these careers were involved with helping other people. With his or her success, each accepted the sense of responsibility that is traditional in the African-American community to assist others as he or she had been helped.

Among those to whom they lent a helping hand were the men and women in the second group of interviewees, described as trailblazers. Several in this group refer to members of the pioneer group who intervened on their behalf—such as a teacher who introduced a schoolboy to music or a political figure who put in a word with the right people at a critical point in a student's career. Even though the trailblazers completed their educations during the economically depressed 1930s, they were strong enough to set their sights on futures in specialized, highly skilled professions to which African Americans had not previously been admitted.

Several found they had a gift for science and math early in their college years. Perturbed but undeterred by put-downs, they pursued their enthusiasms to succeed in optometry, chemistry, and aeronautics during exciting times in our nation's history. Chemist Lloyd Ferguson tells of assisting the superb group of Nobel laureates that worked at Cal during World War II.[20] Optometrist Marvin Poston braved white downtown Oakland to set up a practice that would serve all races and helped devise ways to broaden access to vision care.[21] Archie Williams's love of airplanes and running led him to dazzle the world by winning an Olympic medal in his sophomore year and to earn a pilot's license as an undergraduate before he went on to a career as a U.S. Air Force officer.[22]

Where the pioneers had developed organizational ability in the National Association for the Advancement of Colored People (NAACP) and pressing for the employment of African Americans in civil service and wartime defense plant jobs, the trailblazers escalated these skills to become advocates for issues that involved the entire community. Building coalitions across economic and social lines, they worked to establish pilot urban renewal programs, had a hand in shaping state and national equal opportunity programs, and began to elect members of the group to public office, eventually into the office of mayor of Oakland, California—a city of half a million and the first city of that size to have a minority mayor—and to Congress.

The third group among these notable alumni are categorized as bridge builders—African Americans who have had a much larger impact on their colleagues and communities than their numbers would indicate. These are individuals in business, government, and public service who, through choice or circumstance, live and work at the interface between cultures. Among them are a national banking official, a member of the state supreme court, and a vice president of a major corporation.

The corporate official, Charles Patterson, speaks of relating to two cultures in this way as being marginal, in the sociologist's sense.[23] Robert E. Park has described this situation as being "full of creative potential" and "the place where one can best study the processes of civilization and of progress."[24] W. E. B. Du Bois calls it "two souls, two thoughts, two unreconciled strivings; two warring ideals in one dark body, whose dogged strength alone keeps it from being torn asunder."[25]

The narrators in the trailblazer group have functioned at the upper levels of policy and decision making. As one interviewee notes, "I was the right man for the job at that time, regardless of color. There were not many people around who had the experience and qualifications needed. I would have been a good appointee even if I had not been black . . . even though it might have been politically convenient at the time."[26] They emphasize the importance of including members of all ethnic and racial groups in discussion; they urge variety in the search for solutions to society's increasingly urgent social problems.

Some say that when a bridge is built, it is stepped on; others that it joins opposite sides across a chasm. The bridge builders described here set an example for young black people and for ambitious men and women of other backgrounds as well. In following through on their education, the narrators have worked their way up the ladders of business, politics, and government to compete successfully at the highest levels.

What are the secrets of their success? Like the pioneers and trailblazers before them, the bridge builders came from hardworking though often humble backgrounds. Whether they grew up in farm communities or manufacturing towns in the eastern United States or the burgeoning sprawl of Los Angeles and the Bay Area, the narrators have some experiences in common. As children, they received encouragement from a parent, relative, minister, or teacher. And they were taught to expect to work hard and accept responsibility for family chores and for helping friends and neighbors.

As they learned to use their intellectual gifts, they also gained self-confidence and the ability to find their way around the system—in the college registrar's office, the business world, or the structure of political parties. Though each narrator comments on experiences of racial discrimination, he or she expresses little bitterness. Justice Allen Broussard, for one, says, "Growing up in Louisiana, I had a lot of personal conflict because of my race and because of my religion. It would have been easy for me to hate people who were different from me, but for some reason that did not happen. I have race and ethnic pride, but I don't have bitterness and animosity.

"If I were a hater, I would not have been able to be involved in the activities

I have been [that] contributed a lot to my developing a sense of responsibility to the community."[27] Among the activities he has put his energy into recently have been interracial, statewide committees to study means of lessening racism in the courts.

Among other instances where these men and women have been among the first African Americans in previously all-white situations, Charles Patterson, vice president for public affairs of World Airways, was delegated as World's contact person with cultural and civic organizations. This soon led to his appointment to numerous boards of directors, from museums to planning councils to charitable foundations. Of these experiences, he comments, "I got the feeling some of the members heaved a sigh of relief when someone like me appeared who came out of the corporate sector."[28] He goes on to note that in the 1970s there were only a few places where white and black leaders were able to talk on a continuing basis.[29] "To my thinking, on occasion some of [the white board members] wanted to do good, but didn't necessarily understand fully what the problem was that minority groups were trying to address,"[30] and, "I feel that if you have a different life experience than someone is used to, then you can develop the notion that there are other ways of doing things."[31]

These narrators are interesting people who have mastered complex skills and lead productive lives. They are self-possessed and competent and exhibit considerable personal charm. While such traits can be irritating to some people, these men and women have used their talents on behalf of the community in general. Their accomplishments are especially impressive in relation to the economic and social barriers that confronted African Americans in the 1940s and even later in many cases.

At the beginning of World War II, Assemblyman Byron Rumford recalls, "a black person couldn't get a job in a service station. . . . I mean just an ordinary manual labor job, no particular skill, no particular profession."[32] Even with their college degrees, Archie Williams and Lloyd Ferguson were advised that they were not likely to be hired as engineers or chemists;[33] Marvin Poston was faced with a faculty member who did everything he could to keep him out of the School of Optometry;[34] and as late as the 1950s, Emmett Rice knew when he was a young economics Ph.D. that he would not be hired by a corporation.[35]

The Black Community in Oakland, California

In addition to data about the personal characteristics and accomplishments evident among these early African-American college alumni, there is important information about the city of Oakland in these oral histories. Ten of the book's 13 narrators grew up or have made their adult careers there. From them, it is clear that the black community has long been a significant part of the history of the city and of the University of California.

The university campus is a mile from the city's northern boundary, and this proximity is likely to have been a factor in making higher education seem more accessible to young African Americans living in Oakland. Archie Williams recalls that he could see the Campanile, the university's landmark clock tower, from his home. "I wanted to go to that damned school," he says. "I made it and got my degree."[36]

San Francisco across the bay has been a more glamorous city, but Oakland has been a key player in the economic life of the region as the transportation hub of Northern California. The location there of the transcontinental railroad terminus in the late 1800s made Oakland especially important to African Americans. The luxurious passenger and dining cars of the great age of train travel were largely staffed by black men, as were accommodations on the many steamships plying the Pacific Coast from Seattle to San Diego.

Making their homes in Oakland, these black employees formed the nucleus of a substantial property-owning community that established numerous religious, social, and cultural organizations for the good of its members. Many of them were active in the Brotherhood of Sleeping Car Porters and other workers' associations. Lessons learned in the labor struggles for job security and decent wages transferred easily into creating educational, civic, and later political groups responsive to black interests. Union official C. L. Dellums describes the process in an oral history recorded in 1970.[37]

Although Oakland was not a focus of this book's research per se, cumulatively the narrators provide a vivid picture of the quality of life there for black individuals. Their accounts of civic and professional activities reflect the gradual growth of their acceptance into the city's governance, first in interracial projects in the 1930s and 1940s and in citywide politics in the 1960s and 1970s.

Greater numbers also added to the importance of black residents to the city in the years following World War II. From 8,462 in 1940, they increased to 47,562 in 1950, while the total population rose from 302,163 to 384,575.[38] The first 15,000 came in search of defense jobs in the great shipyards around San Francisco Bay, jobs for which they had to lobby and picket; the next 25,000 came because of continuing hard economic times in the South.

These wartime and postwar increases in the number of residents strained the city's ability to provide services and strained "the unwritten rules that had governed race relations since the turn of the century."[39] There was concern that Oakland, like other cities in the nation, would experience race riots. And yet, from the beginning of this period, there were efforts to bring blacks

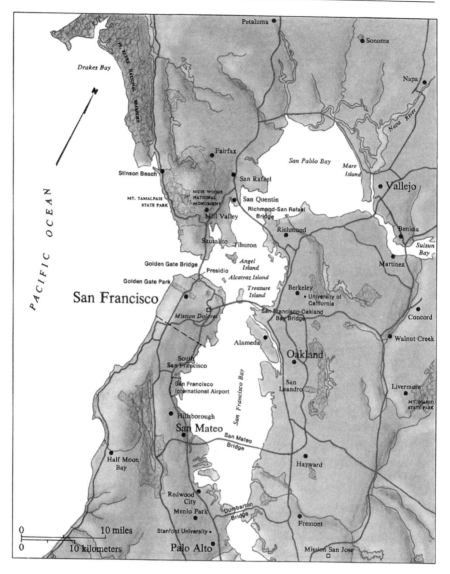

and whites, as well as Asian and Hispanic residents, together to work out ways and means for civic progress.

Black and white labor leaders, concerned with social equity in addition to economic action, joined forces as early as 1944 in Oakland to begin the long push for broader representation on city councils, school boards, and the courts. Oral histories by Byron Rumford, Lionel Wilson, and Allen Broussard tell of these campaigns.[40] They began by seeking appointments to various boards and commissions, for which an African-American business and professional association, Men of Tomorrow, proved to be a very effective base, along with the East Bay Democratic Club.

Various African-American candidates ran for elective office, gaining experience and testing acceptance for minority views under the guidance of Rumford himself and D. G. Gibson, a legendary purveyor of black publications who was a mentor for black political aspirants for 50 years.[41] In 1948 Rumford was elected to the state assembly for an Oakland-Berkeley district, but it was not until 1965 that Joshua Rose became the first black person to sit on the Oakland City Council. In 1960, however, the black community won a judgeship when Wilson was appointed to the municipal court. Elevated to superior court in 1964, he was promptly replaced by Broussard, who in 1981 was appointed to the California Supreme Court.

In the meantime, the Ford Foundation sent money for a multiyear community development demonstration project in the 1950s. The Alameda County United Crusade followed with a series of social planning ventures. Louder calls for more urgent action were added to the process in the 1960s as cultural awareness and black pride organizations developed. Among them were the Black Panthers, which also emerged from the social ferment of Oakland.

Although the Panthers' aggressive manner shocked many people, Broussard and Wilson found them a positive influence for a long time: "They were expressing their concern about the whole law-enforcement mechanism and, in the main, doing it peacefully."[42] The Panthers' school breakfast program won widespread approval.

That all this energy and dedication to a better life in Oakland has continued through 50 years of economic and political ups and downs, and that the city did not burn, is a tribute to the narrators in this book and others like them. Justice Broussard says, with pardonable pride, "People were saying that Oakland was a powder keg. But for some reason, there was always a cohesiveness in Oakland that just prevented trouble from ever happening. As members of Men of Tomorrow, we do think that because of what we and a lot of other people were doing in the community, it never did blow."[43]

With the establishment of the first federally funded War on Poverty program in the nation in 1965, the establishment of a large U.S. Department of Housing and Urban Development job-training and public works program in 1968, the election of labor leader C. L. Dellums's nephew Ronald to the House of Representatives in 1970, and Judge Lionel Wilson's election as mayor in 1977, the black community became dominant players in the leadership of Oakland.

"In a very real sense, Oakland has arrived," says Charles Patterson. "People talk about the slow pace of development and I say, 'If you had been here in 1968, you would realize that the city has strongly turned around. The notion that if you didn't get this or that project, you blew it, is all wrong. All the things that go into making this a better city take time, money, and effort.' "[44]

Taken together, these commentaries suggest that the city, in a sense, is a laboratory in the struggles with urban issues of our time. Narrators offer hope for future solutions in references to lessons learned in community organization and intergroup cooperation, as well as to such experiments as the Oakland Metropolitan Forum, that make university technical skills available to the city.

Cumulatively, these oral histories record the painstaking and exhilarating progress of African Americans in this century in higher education and the wider community. For some of them, as Troy Duster and W. R. Ellis, Jr., discuss in the Preface and Afterword, the achievement of increasing the numbers of black students enrolled in college in the 1960s and 1970s has been followed by an equally challenging period of changing expectations and redefining goals.

"We were naive," explains George Mason University historian Roger Wilkins. "We thought that segregation was the box we were in. We thought if we could get rid of that, there would be acceptance."[45] Men and women like these early African-American graduates of the University of California seem well equipped to show the way to resolving the issues and anxieties to be surmounted in the twenty-first century—the problems, as it were, waiting beyond the last one solved. Surely they are at the head of the class in ability, in education and experience, and in dedication to improving the quality of life. In a world critically short of adequate leadership, they are sorely needed to share in finding new directions. Finally, they are impresssive role models for aspiring young people of all ethnic backgrounds and stimulating reminders to older generations of the social strength that lies in diversity.

Ida Jackson's words from the 1920s perhaps may be equally hopeful for young people today. "I challenged myself to see if I could do this or that," she recalls. "I did enter the university. The attitude of the students didn't deter me.

"I do feel that it's a good philosophy to have a certain amount of confidence in yourself and be willing to tackle whatever interests you. You get something out of it whether you win all the way or not. It's a valuable experience to go into unknown territory to prepare yourself for anything that follows."[46]

Acknowledgments

For inspiration and guidance in the planning and design of the University of California, Berkeley, Black Alumni Project, from which most of the chapters in this book are drawn, special thanks are due to Fannie Jeffrey, former head of the campus Visitors Center, and Norvel Smith, a founder of the UC Black Alumni Club and former vice chancellor for student affairs. Their initial encouragement and Dr. Smith's unflagging interest have kept up the spirits of project staff for over 10 years. Series editor Don Ritchie's early suggestions were most helpful, as have been the light hand of Mark Zadrozny and other Twayne staff.

Professor W. R. Ellis, Jr.'s enthusiasm for oral history and for including in academic governance the full range of voices asking to be heard secured the support of then chancellor I. Michael Heyman for the project in 1984. Ellis's observations on the impact of African-American students on the Berkeley campus and Professor Troy Duster's essay on his work on racial and cultural diversity in higher education are valuable contributions to the book. Studies by the Institute of Social Change, which Duster heads, begun in the early 1960s and extending into the 1980s, continue to explore student concerns where the interviews in this volume conclude.

The early generosity of the van Loben Sels Foundation was particularly welcome in getting the interviews started, as was the gift of the Alexander Gerbode Foundation when it looked as if the project would not go forward. A timely grant from the Morris Stulsaft Foundation provided for publication of completed oral histories. Additional gifts from individuals testify to the wide-ranging recognition of the importance of African-American contributions to the history of our times.

Preparation of this volume was made much easier by the enthusiasm for the project of Peter Hanff, interim director of the Bancroft Library, and Willa Baum, head of the Regional Oral History Office. Numerous friends and colleagues provided welcome advice and/or assistance in reviewing the manuscript, including Sue Bender, Carole Hicke, Anne Smith, Bob and

Carolee Finney, Ed Gordon, Isabel Mather, Willy Morris, Pat and Jim Morse, Harriet Nathan, and a number of others, all greatly appreciated.

Eleven of the 13 interviews presented were recorded by staff members of the Regional Oral History Office of the Bancroft Library at the University of California, Berkeley. One was produced by the University of California, Los Angeles, Oral History Program and one by the Schlesinger Library at Radcliffe College; both institutions granted permission for use of their work, as did K. G. Saur, a Reed Reference Company, holder of publication rights for the Radcliffe oral history. All three programs have extensive experience in the field and work within the goals and guidelines of the national Oral History Association.

The Pioneers, 1914–1931

I

WALTER AND ELIZABETH GORDON

Social Progress in Law Enforcement and Public Administration

Walter Gordon was born in Georgia in 1894. When he was 10, he came to Southern California with his family. His wife's people came to Oakland from the Carolinas in 1872. Both were grandchildren of slaves. Gordon received a B.A. from the University of California at Berkeley in 1919 and a J.D. in 1922. He was an All-American football player, coach, Berkeley policeman, and later president of the county NAACP for many years. His wife, Elizabeth Fisher Gordon, trained as a teacher at San Francisco State College and became a leader in the YWCA and other community organizations.

Walter Gordon's dedication to legal and correctional reform led to his being appointed to the California Adult Authority in 1943, governor of the U.S. Virgin Islands in 1955, and a federal district judge in 1959. He retired to Berkeley, where he died in 1976.

Walter Gordon

My mother was named Georgia Bryant and my father was Henry Gordon. [His] father was owned by General John Brown Gordon; that is where we got our family name.

My father told me an interesting story about the two Gordon families. During the Civil War, my Grandfather Jim was at the front with the general as his personal servant. When they came back from the war, the general told

This chapter was adapted from Walter Gordon, "Athlete, Officer in Law Enforcement and Administration, Governor of the Virgin Islands," in *Walter Gordon Oral History Project,* vol. 1 (Berkeley: Regional Oral History Office, University of California, 1980). Interviews with Walter Gordon conducted by Amelia Fry in 1971. The volume includes an interview with Elizabeth Fisher Gordon, conducted by Ann Hus Brower in 1976, after Walter Gordon's death. A few details of family history were updated in 1993 with information provided by Edwin Gordon, Jr., the Gordons' grandson.

grandfather, "Jim, you're free now and you're privileged to leave. I don't believe in slavery anyway." The general said, "You can stay here and work the farm and we'll pay divide."

My grandfather stayed and worked on the farm, and they divided the income. Farming didn't bring in much money, so they went on to running a sawmill and railroading until the general went into politics. He became the governor of Georgia and later a senator in Washington, D.C.

Later on in the 1950s, when I was governor of the Virgin Islands, one Sunday the guard came up and told us there was a young man and his wife to see us. So I went down. He was General John B. Gordon's grandson, who was down there at a meeting and knew of the connection between our families. He brought about 15 people from his group to visit us. The man who was leading them was S. Ernest Vandiver, Jr., who later became governor of Georgia. They all talked, asked me questions. We were having a lot of fun.

Finally, one of the fellows said, "Say, we're getting along all right here together, aren't we?" And I said, "Well, why shouldn't we? We are all Georgia boys together," because they always call a Negro "boy." And they just laughed. Yet when Vandiver got to be governor, by gosh, he was a strict segregationist.

Going back to my family, my dad had only a second-grade education, but one of his brothers was a preacher and all three of his sisters finished from Spelman Seminary in Atlanta and became teachers. That was the Negro tradition in the South of girls teaching and men working, so men didn't need the same kind of education.

Aunt Nora was the oldest sister. I only saw her once, when I was about seven or eight years old. She was a tall, stately woman. She went to the Belgian Congo as a missionary for about 10 years. She married a man who was Jamaican, also named Gordon. I've been told he was the first Negro to preach in Westminster Abbey.

By the time I was born, my father was working in Atlanta. He was doing janitor work, and then he was a Pullman porter on the railroad. When I was about four or five years of age, Papa took me to Memphis, Tennessee, with him when he went there on a Pullman car. It was during the Spanish-American War, and many of the fellows I saw on the train were soldiers.

Papa got to be the head janitor at the English-American Building in Atlanta and had four or five Negroes under him; he got $30 a month as the head janitor. He and my Uncle Hugh also had a little neighborhood grocery store. Uncle Hugh ran it and the kids used to steal things because Uncle Hugh would fall asleep!

Papa delivered the groceries in a wagon pulled by a mule. Sometimes he would take me with him in the wagon. One time, my dad stopped and went to vote. The election official made me mad; he wanted to know, "Who's going to vote, you or the mule?"

My father was never anything but a Republican. My Uncle Dawson was a Garveyite for a while. He believed in Garvey's idea that Negroes should all go back to Africa. Uncle Dawson followed Garvey too for a while and collected money for him. When he wanted some salary and traveling expenses, Garvey told him, "If you didn't get your money out of what you collected, you're not going to get any from me."

Uncle Dawson quit the movement when he saw the way it was and went out to California and pastored a church in Riverside. He wrote my dad that it would be a good place to raise his boys (we didn't have any sisters). When I was 10 years old, we came to Riverside too. I went to school there from the fourth grade up through high school. I think I was the first colored kid to graduate from that high school.

I was a little slow in the fourth-grade work coming from a segregated school, particularly for math. I remember my school teachers in Atlanta were nice, but so many of them hadn't finished college. But I caught up, and when I graduated from high school, my credentials were accepted at the University of California without any trouble.

Did you encounter segregation in Riverside?

When I was a kid in grammar school in Riverside, it was all white. We had no connection really to any organizations like the YMCA. I used to go along there and just lean up against the fence and look at the kids play handball and tennis and all like that. Nobody ever said a word to us about it—we had nothing like that.

How did you decide to go to the University of California?

I had wanted to go to the University of Southern California because USC had a great football team and I was a football player in high school. But my dad didn't want me to go there because it was a Methodist school and he didn't want me to go to a particular religious school.

When I was about 16 years old, a colored fellow visited us who was president of a Negro college. My dad told him he was thinking about what school I'd go to. The fellow said. "Well, if I had a say, I'd send him to a state school—a racially mixed school—because on graduation he has the same diploma and the same education that the whites have."

I know that a lot of people do go to the colored schools; that's how Booker T. Washington got started, and I have a healthy respect for him. As a boy,

I heard him talk in Riverside. He said that the races can be as the palm of the hand in working, and socially they can be as separate as the fingers. As I grew older, I didn't agree that there should be that social difference. To put it simply, that is not the way I like to live.

When I was young, there were very few Mexicans in Riverside and they stayed to themselves. The Negroes, even though they had integrated schools, were just kind of separate socially. I held that against them. But the University YMCA had sent me a book called *The Freshman Bible,* so when I came up here as a freshman in 1914 I wandered into Stiles Hall [the campus YMCA]. Nobody paid any attention particularly, although I was the only Negro. Everybody spoke to me, and later on I used to go quite regularly. Harry Kingman, who was the director then, and I became good friends.

Did you experience any discrimination as a student?

The only place that I would feel it would have been in going out for football. Athletics was practically the only privilege. There was no Negro fraternity.

One time, I had left the gym and gone down to the shower and some tall white fellow whose name was Gildersleeve made a crack about, "Why do we have to have Negroes."

Another white fellow named Bell who was also out for football was under his shower and I said to him, "I bet I can lick the guy who said that." And he said, "If you can't, I'll help you." I never forgot that. Later on, Gildersleeve was just as nice as he could be. So those kind of things pass. I went out for football, and I didn't have any trouble with other members of the team.

How about housing?

I didn't know a soul when I came up. But my dad was an Odd Fellow, and he knew this man who knew a Fellow who was a printer in Oakland and told him I was coming up to Cal. I got off the boat and went to his shop, and he sent me to a rooming house a few blocks from campus. Later on, I got a room in a rooming house a colored woman had upstairs over a store. I was pretty lonely, didn't know anybody but myself.

The next year I met Ed Covington, who had been on the track team at Atlanta University. We got a place in another rooming house, run by a white woman. I got a job waiting tables at the faculty club to get a good meal.

Were you able to date white as well as Negro girls?

I wasn't dating *any* girls. [*chuckles*] The only girl I dated up here was the one I married, Elizabeth Fisher. She was going to State Normal, the teacher-training college that later became San Francisco State University.

I knew some white girls in Riverside, but then they opened up Polytechnic High School and made it an all-boys school. That was after two or three girls got pregnant in their senior year.

And then my dad was just as strict with my brother and me as though we were girls.

When my brother and I would go to a party, my dad would always be watching us, telling us what time to be home. He was a policeman then and rode his darn bicycle, so we could always see him. One night, my brother was going to get in a fight with somebody and started to throw off his coat. Papa showed up and said, "Don't be so crazy. That man could cut your stomach while you're getting your coat off." And that's true.

He was such a dandy fellow. He was about six foot two and he weighed 235, nice-looking guy. Bless his heart, he said to me when I was a freshman and went back home—it was the first time he talked to me like a man—"You'll pick up things for yourself and your dad don't need to tell you much. I was pretty strict on you boys and I know many times you felt mad. I thought you'd be mad at me after you were grown."

I said, "No. I thank you." No telling what would have happened [without his advice], because in a small town like Riverside there were not many colored people. Some of them didn't care, and Papa did.

What kind of courses did you take at the university?

Coming out of high school, I'd never had a lecture course until I had one at Cal in history with Henry Morse Stephens, who was a famous professor then. He was kind of short and fat and had a beard. I was just so enthralled listening to him talk that I forgot to take notes. I darned near flunked the course, but I caught myself in time. "What are some of the salient points changing world history," he said one day, and I had to look up what "salient" meant. I got better acquainted with Professor Stephens when I waited tables at the faculty club.

Then in law school I had another great professor, Max Radin. He could talk on any phase of the law. Years later when I was president of the NAACP in Oakland, I had him come and talk to the members. He and I and Henry Morse Stephens, too, talked a lot of times about the race question and why there should be segregation of the races and prejudice.

I pretty near got in a fight about this race thing when I was driving a truck up at Mare Island naval base while I was in law school. Ed and I went up there to see about getting a job. It was loaded with whites, all getting jobs. I had my hat on and so did everybody else, but the white guy at the desk told me to take off my hat and said, "I've got nothing for you but digging ditches." So I took the job.

Eventually the two of us did get hired to be swampers on a truck, to help load and unload. A colored fellow named Hansen was the driver of the truck, and we were moving these hundred-pound cement sacks around to different buildings from eight o'clock in the morning to about four o'clock. After two or three days, this Hansen said, "Gee, I've never done anything as hard as hauling this cement."

I said, "Don't you know the picture? That guy in the office is giving us the works. He wants us to quit. You're the only Negro truck driver on the base and they put us with you and we've been doing nothing but move cement." We agreed that we'd move every damn sack of cement on the base and never let out a squawk. I wouldn't quit. Besides, it was more money than I'd made in a long time—$4 a day.

Another time, a white truck driver cursed a colored fellow and the colored fellow pulled a knife and slashed out at the white guy. It didn't hurt him; he knocked the knife out of the colored guy's hand and started chasing him away.

The colored guy started hollering to us, "Aren't you going to help me?" We said, "Help, nothing. You had no business starting it. He hadn't done a thing to you."

Those are the kinds of things that happen. Some of them are so petty, but you fight over them anyway. They make you mad, but I don't condemn everybody because some people act like that. And I don't like to be condemned just because another Negro does something wrong.

What made you decide to go to law school?

I never wanted to do anything else but be a lawyer. I remember when I was a boy, I went with my dad a lot when he drove the grocery wagon with the mule in Atlanta; I'd be sleeping up on the shelf behind him. One day, a streetcar hit the mule and the wagon turned over and over and I was injured. A woman took me home in her arms, my head all wrapped up. Later on, my dad had to go to court; I went with him, and somehow I liked it.

My dad wanted me to be a doctor. That is probably due to the tradition in the South that Negro women who go to college are going to be teachers and men who go to college become doctors. Lawyers—you wouldn't even have any Negro lawyers down there. Negroes weren't represented in court hardly ever then.

I told my dad, "I don't have any inclination in that direction. I'll take a medical course if you insist on it, but I don't think I'd be much of a doctor." And he said, "You go ahead and become a lawyer."

We used to talk football and he'd say, to tease me, "You learned how to run from me." He could run like a jackrabbit, and he'd chase me to make me run my heart out. And he'd say, "Don't go out there and play football. We've got enough muscle men in our race. We need some men with brains."

You entered law school in your senior year at that time. It took me three years. Being on the police force and going to law school, I didn't sleep very much. See, all the law school classes were in the morning. Just as soon as I got off work at the police department, I'd leave my gun and badge and uniform and go up to law school. After classes, I'd go home and sleep. Then during football season, I'd be on the field at four o'clock. At night, I would study. I'd have a day off a week and my vacation and spend all my time studying law.

Some of us would sit together and share our notes. If there was something I didn't have, somebody else would help with it and I helped them with criminal law.

How did you get to be a Berkeley police officer?

On July 4, 1919, I remember, I left the Berkeley YMCA where I was living and was going over to see my girl. Gus Vollmer, who was chief of police and taught criminology at UC, came out of the Elks Club across the street and said, "Walt, I want to talk to you. How'd you like to be on the police force?"

I jumped and said, "Are you kidding me? If you think I can make a policeman, I'll try it."

He said, "When the next vacancy comes up, it's yours." About the same time, Andy Smith talked to me about coaching at Cal. I told him I was going on the police force. And he said, "Well, you can do both." And that's the way it came out.

Do you think Vollmer offered you a job because he wanted to have a black man on the police force?

I don't think he thought of that. Some people wrote him that they were glad he had appointed a Negro, and he wrote back, "I appointed him because I thought he would be a good policeman."

Vollmer was a lot like Earl Warren later on. I used to tell people who were against Warren, "He was the best policeman we had in Alameda County when he was district attorney." Our police department in Berkeley did everything as the law required. When you arrest me, you tell me that I don't have to talk.

We always used to do that. The law didn't want anybody to brutalize any prisoner.

I never hit a man with a nightstick and I only had to use a gun twice. There were some tough customers to deal with though. One guy who turned out to be a regular barroom fighter and some others tried to get me to lose my temper by saying things like "you black sonofabitch."

One guy reported me to Chief Vollmer and I said some pretty strong things in response. What he said made me feel like breaking every chair in the office. The next day, I was waiting for the chief when he walked into his office. I said, "I'm ashamed the way I talked yesterday." All Vollmer said was, "I just want to know how you kept from hitting him, 'cause I felt like hitting him myself." We became very close, you know.

Vollmer used to tell us, "You represent the public, all the people in Berkeley from the mayor on down. You should always be above reproach. You know, you have to be the boss; if people feel you are afraid, you'll get the worst of it. I want you to take care of yourselves, but I don't believe in beating people up. He wanted his officers to be college graduates so that you would be capable of going on higher.

Did you go in the military during World War I?

I signed up for the Student Army Training Corps [SATC] down in Riverside, but when I came back up here they turned me down because of my trigger finger. Well, I'd never shot a gun in my life, but the guy at the draft board said, "That's what I said."

So I went to Dr. Legge at the campus hospital and said, "Gee, I want to get in the army. I feel funny not being in the service." So he examined me and said, "You're in."

I was to go to officers' training camp in Texas, but the coach said I was scheduled to play football on the day I was supposed to leave. I said, "What do you mean!" He didn't want to tell me, but finally he said, "They're not taking colored down in Texas."

That's what we were up against. They had a camp in Missouri some place for colored. A lot of fellows I knew went there. Then the war ended on November 11, 1918, and that was the end of the SATC. So I finished that football season. I won a silver cup for Most Valuable Player.

Weren't you All-American in 1917 too? The first African American to be named?

The first Californian. I was the first colored person to make the football team at UC.

That's how I got to know Earl Warren, playing football. When he was district attorney in the thirties, we talked about how he wanted to reorganize our prisons. I was practicing law in Oakland then, and I was president of the NAACP in Alameda County. (In those days it was whites and Negroes together, and we had a lot of cases like segregation in housing.)

There was a case where this Negro had held up somebody in Los Angeles and had shot him and killed him. He was sentenced to death. After papers had been put on file appealing the decision to the supreme court of California, the fellow was executed. I happened to read it in the newspaper, and I was shocked. It was the law that if a man appealed his case, it was an automatic stay until the court heard it.

So I called up George Hatfield, a white fellow who was a state senator, whom I'd met when he was U.S. attorney over in San Francisco. I said this execution ought to be investigated. He called me back and said he'd formed a committee and, "We'd like to have you act as attorney and go with us when we hold hearings in different places around the state. We'll take the attorney general too," which by then was Warren. So this would have been after 1939.

One of the things we found out was that when a man was sentenced to die, they would send the death warrant along with him to the prison where he was to be executed. They put the death warrant in the safe and the appeal papers were just put in the files. That's what had happened in this boy's case: the public defender never did push the appeal.

After the hearings, the committee all agreed that we ought to have a better appeal process in murder cases. After talking it over with the commmittee, I wrote the law. I spent hours with Professor Kidd, who I'd studied criminal law with at Cal, finding precedents for some of the details we wanted to include.

That became the law of California around 1940, as I recall. In substance it meant that no death warrant accompanied a person when he was sent to San Quentin Prison and that they should keep a man alive until every other suspect in the whole picture is cleared one way or the other, or until guilt is determined one way or the other.

When Earl Warren got in there as governor in 1943, one of the first things he did was start improving matters in the prisons. He appointed me to the Board of Prison Terms and Paroles. I was also on the commission to review how prison sentences were decided and how the prisons were run. We changed the name of the board to the Adult Authority. I became head of that in 1944 and served as chairman until I became governor of the Virgin Islands in 1955.

You can understand when they talk about the death penalty, it involves an awful lot. I have talked with men who were on death row, and I have mixed feelings. I have a basic feeling that we may not be justified in taking human life, even though there are a few instances where we say it is all right

11

to execute a person who has killed another person. Even though we go to war and kill, we don't necessarily feel that wars have settled very many human problems.

I think it is so obvious that the death penalty does not deter anybody from committing murder. If a man is a gibbering idiot, our human instincts and feelings make us feel that we shouldn't execute him, and we don't. I've always stuck to the idea that the act that we call "crime" is the result of the emotions of a person which cause him or her to commit a crime, rather than intellect. A lot of crimes are done under the stress of giving in to emotions that are like a madness.

I remember one young fellow who was in solitary up in Folsom Prison, big husky guy. He walked into the Adult Authority hearing, and we asked him why he tore up the plumbing in his cell.

He said, "They wouldn't let me listen to the radio and hear my brother play football (this was before television). So I asked him if tearing up his cell had let him hear the ball game, and he said no.

I said, "Your judgment wasn't very good, was it? I know you're a lot brighter than that, but you don't use your head for anything but a hat rack. We're here to help you, but you've got to help yourself first."

He said, "Nobody has talked to me like that before. Do you think I'll ever be able to get a job?" And that guy straightened himself out. The warden said he couldn't do this and that, but he did find him a job in the prison hospital.

We're so mixed up about color too. It makes me mad when these Negroes get to talking about "blacks"! It is not descriptive of the American Negro. I tried many cases in the 1950s on this question of segregation in housing for white people who sign a lease and then want to get out of it. I've reminded the judge that in the South, if you've got a drop of Negro blood, you are considered a Negro. In Illinois, if you've got a little more than 50 percent, you are a Negro. Texas held that a white man was a Negro because he associated with Negroes.

Many individuals have a lot of white ancestors. My wife's father's mother was Irish, born in Ireland. I've got Negro, white, and Indian blood. What am I?

Elizabeth Gordon

What was it like growing up in San Francisco?

My grandparents, Elizabeth and John Andrew Wilds, had both been slaves, but they were brave enough to leave the South and come to California with their young children.

My grandfather used to say, "I carried a boy under one arm and a girl under the other." They lived in Oakland at Tenth Avenue and Tenth Street. He owned a team of horses and was in the hauling business. He and my grandmother also owned cows and sold milk.

My mother and father lived in San Francisco after they were married in April 1895. I had gone to stay with my grandparents during Easter vacation the year of the 1906 earthquake. I was sleeping on the third floor in my grandmother's room. It was cold that night, so instead of saying my prayers on my knees, I got into bed and pulled the covers over my head and said my prayers there. When that earthquake hit at dawn, I knew I was the cause!

When I was in grammar school in San Francisco, I was the only minority in the class. Then I went to Cogswell High School and was on the tennis team and was captain of the basketball team for three years. I enjoyed my classes, especially chemistry and physics. I wanted to make my grades as good as possible so I could get into college.

Was it difficult at all to have so few minority students?

. . . I just felt you were there and that was that. There was always somebody that you could depend upon that liked you, so you didn't have to go with your fists up. You never even thought about color. It is hard for some to believe, but that's how it was.

For Walter, it was different because he had grown up in Georgia until he was nine years old. He came into Riverside with southern segregation exposure and he had to grow out of it. Sometimes I would notice, if we were going into a restaurant or into an ice-cream parlor, there would be a hesitancy on his part. He and I met either in 1914 or 1915. I met him through Lee Purnell, who was a little older and was also at Cal. We didn't start to go out together until after peace was declared.

And you did go on to San Francisco State College?

Yes. It was called the normal school then, and they mostly trained teachers. There was an elementary school attached where you did your practice teaching, named for the president of the college, Dr. Frederick Burk. When I registered, Frederick Burk called me in and asked me why I was there.

I said, "Because I want to be a teacher." "Well, where do you expect to do your practice teaching or to teach? We had a Chinese girl, and she had to go back to China to teach."

Of course I said, "I thought I would be teaching in San Francisco." "Well," he said, "I worked 11 years to build this school and I'm not going to have it torn down by one person."

I was about to cry when I left, and I held in my tears all the way out on the cable car until I got home. The next day, my father went down to see Dr. Burk. He told him, "My name is Fisher."

"Oh," said Dr. Burk. "Margaret's father?" "No," my father said. "Elizabeth's father." Margaret Fisher had blue eyes and red hair. Then my father said, "I pay taxes, and as long as I do, Elizabeth will get her training where the other girls do."

Dr. Burk said, "No principal will take her in the city schools." My father said, "We'll see about that."

So my father and I went to see Miss Saunders, the principal at the school where I had gone. He told her what Dr. Burk had said, and Miss Saunders said, "When she finishes, I'd be happy to have her." And that's where I went when it was time for my student teaching.

I didn't go into teaching because Walter did not believe in a wife working. What happened was, while I was waiting to take the examination for regular teaching, I went down and applied for a job in the insurance office where my father worked. They accepted me and I went to work as a file clerk. Instead of making $50 a month, which was the starting salary for teachers, I made $85 a month. So I kept that job until we got married.

Even after we were married, I wanted to be independent. This is probably what made me go outside and give time to the YWCA after we were married, on the local and the state boards.

Walter's schedule was not easy, although I can never remember him complaining about it. He'd go to law school straight from police duty, and in the fall he'd be coaching. After the babies came, he'd always be there to heat the bottle for the 2 A.M. feeding. Friday was his day off, and as a rule we went to the Fulton Theater to see the plays they put on.

One time when he was on patrol duty on campus, he saw these boys rolling a barrel of beer along. So Walter went to President [Benjamin Ide] Wheeler and said, "I don't like to see them doing that on campus, and I don't like to make an arrest on that." And Wheeler told him, "Just leave them alone, Gordon. By the time they get to the other side, there will be no beer."

He never let law school interfere with his football. He would scout the other teams too. Sometimes I went with him and he'd have me take down how many steps the kicker takes before kicking, things like that. He would make notes and draw plays.

After he graduated from law school, Vollmer pushed him to leave the police department. "It's time for you to give full time to your law," he'd say, because Walter was curtailed about the kind of practice he could do as long as he was on the police force.

When did you hear that President Eisenhower wanted to appoint him governor of the Virgin Islands?

The first thing I knew about his being offered the governorship, he called me from San Luis Obispo where the Adult Authority was meeting and told me, "I've had a call from [Richard] McGee," who was director of the Department of Corrections. "Someone called him looking for me. He wants to know if I want to be governor of the Virgin Islands. McGee said if I didn't want it, he'd take it."

Most of the people we met there were lovely to us, and we enjoyed entertaining people who came through. The house came with a butler and a cook to see that everything went smoothly. Walter's first priority was that they should be allowed to elect their own governor. His second was to take care of the water problem. They had no water supply except the rain; eventually they installed desalting plants and the problem was ended.

We would go to governors' conferences, and later on to judicial conferences. One was in St. Louis where we had an unfortunate experience with a hotel and didn't stay for the conference. Another one was in Williamsburg, Virginia. Nelson Rockefeller [who was then governor of New York] wrote to Walter telling him that he would have a place for him to stay and not to worry.

We expected that we would stay in the Virgin Islands until President Eisenhower left office in 1959 and then we would automatically move out too. But, instead, they appointed Walter to be judge of the U.S. District Court for the Virgin Islands. Walt was surprised because he was thinking that we would be coming on home. But there was a vacancy and they asked Walt to take it because they thought he would make a good judge.

The only thing I wished was that it had been here instead of in the Virgin Islands. We would have had a chance to see the grandchildren grow. We missed that. But we did come back to Berkeley in 1968.

I always felt it's hard for a man to give up his work, so I encouraged Walter to go into Rotary (he hadn't been a member before), and he became a member of the Berkeley City Commons Club, where he also saw friends that he hadn't seen for some time. And he would go over to the Commonwealth Club in San Francisco with a friend for their luncheons and lectures; Walter had belonged to that since 1938.

Then he was appointed to the city redevelopment agency. I called that his workshop. He enjoyed working with people. I think this is what kept him going as he got older.

2

IDA LOUISE JACKSON

Overcoming Barriers in Education

Born in Mississippi in 1902, Ida Jackson came with her mother to California in 1917. Two of her brothers were employed by the railroad in Oakland, and she won a civil service position at the post office in San Francisco. Although Jackson had received a teaching certificate at Dillard College (later New Orleans University) in Louisiana, she enrolled in the University of California, Berkeley, completing her B.A. in 1922 and M.A. in 1923.

A member of the NAACP board of directors while still a student, she also founded chapters of the black women's sorority, Alpha Kappa Alpha, at Berkeley (1921) and other western colleges. She became the first African American to teach in the Oakland public schools and continued efforts to improve education for minority children for nearly 30 years.

From 1934 to 1938, Jackson was national president of Alpha Kappa Alpha and organized a summer school for teachers and later a health clinic in Mississippi. She began doctoral studies at Columbia Teachers College in New York, leaving to spend a year as dean of women at Tuskegee Institute.

With her brother Emmett, she became joint owner and manager of a thousand-acre sheep ranch in Northern California. She continues to encourage black youth to pursue higher education through endowed scholarships.

I grew up with five brothers in Vicksburg, Mississippi. I'm the youngest and the only girl. Emmett, the youngest [brother], was my best friend and pal. He and my mother helped me through the University of California. Also he was with me in every move I made until he passed on.

My brother William came out to California first. He decided that things were better for blacks in California. He got a job on the train and came out

This chapter was adapted from Ida Louise Jackson, *Overcoming Barriers in Education*, 1984 and 1985 interviews with Gabrielle Morris (Berkeley: Regional Oral History Office, University of California, 1990).

here in 1917. He sent for my mother in 1918. She came out and brought me. I was in boarding school at Rust College at the time.

You see, my father passed on when I was 10. He and my mother wanted us all to put education ahead of everything. They wanted all of us to have an education. My father used to say, "Education is the one thing the white man can't take from you." He had suffered losses through the system that existed at that time, racism, in the southern states. A man had to be pretty strong to hold onto anything he had that was of value that a white person wanted.

My father was a farmer, carpenter, and a minister, so when he wasn't working at one job he was working at another. Maybe two at a time. He had seven families that lived on the plantation that he owned south of Vicksburg that he was able to keep after he was forced to leave all he owned in Louisiana in order to save his life.

My mother always said I could go to school as long as I wanted to get an education, but if I wanted to court—to use the expression then—her help for my education would end, because "boys and books don't mix."

I'm ahead of my story. I stayed two years at Rust College. Then I transferred to Dillard College, which is now New Orleans University, and graduated from the normal department with a certificate in teaching and a certificate in domestic science and art. On the basis of that I was offered the chance to teach two beginning classes in sewing in Peck Home, which was part of the university. I was teaching there when my mother decided to come to California and came and got me.

Was teaching sewing the kind of thing you wanted to do?

Not especially. But everybody had said I was supppposed to teach; there was nothing else to do to earn a living. I was interested in law as a career, but a black man didn't have a chance as a lawyer in the courts during that day, even in California. And it was out of the question for a woman as a way of making a living. There weren't too many opportunities [even when we got here] because good old California proved not to be as liberal as my brother had thought because people are people [wherever you go].

We were taught that no man was our superior unless he was more honest, had a better education, or a better character. Those are the guidelines by which we were brought up. We were taught to protect ourselves and rather die than be humiliated by being a coward and not stand up for our rights. They were trying to give my brothers courage to fight for their rights. They felt I would be all right because a woman had a better chance in the South at that time.

Then, too, we lived in a neighborhood that was predominantly white in Vicksburg. When my father bought the land, it was country. It came to be suburbia when wealthy whites moved into the neighborhood as I was grow-ing up. It was a desirable tract. It was a beautiful hilly area. Our white neighbors were very friendly. When my father died, they were very kind to my mother.

When Mama was getting ready to leave to come to California, and it was known throughout the town, we were surprised at the number of whites who would stop by and talk and try to discourage her from leaving. She continued packing while they talked. So we arrived in California with four barrels of dishes and two trunks of silver. Mama said she had worked too hard to acquire the silver that I had polished when I was a child. Mama said she was not leaving it behind.

My brother told her not to bring any quilts, that it was warm out here, that she didn't need them. They used to have these quilting parties where the neighbors would come. If a neighbor was making quilts, all her friends would find time to come to the house and help do the quilting. They would have food and socialize together.

My brother William worked on the Southern Pacific Railroad. Emmett had come to California, too, by then and also was working on the railroad. William told a friend of his who was in business, "You know, I have a feeling my mother and sister might come while I'm away. I have given them your address, so you look out for them if they come."

As we were getting off the train in Oakland, William looked up and saw me [just as he was leaving on another train]. This fellow took us to a place in West Oakland where we got a room.

Did you know anyone else in Oakland when you arrived?

We knew a member of one black family here, Hazel Shelton Leonard. Through that family we met another family that was from Vicksburg. I remember being at one of their homes, and a friend of my brother's said, "Well, what are you going to do?"

I said, "Oh, I'm going to teach."

They burst into laughter and said, "The day you apply for a job, the paper will carry the news 'Burly Negress Applies for Job in Oakland Schools.' "

After a week my mother said, "I have never lived in anybody's house but my own." She had brought a letter from the church to which we belonged, which was Methodist Episcopal then; now it's United Methodist. That first Sunday we went to church and were introduced to several of the leading people in the community. Among them was one black real estate dealer, E. B. Gray. He had his office downtown in Oakland and was very successful. He found us a place to live on Fifty-eighth Street, which my mother bought. We moved the same day. I remember Mrs. Ridgeway found a cot for my brothers to sleep on, and a bed for Mama and me to use.

Did you apply to the university right away?

No. I took a civil service examination for the post office and passed, number 13. Lo and behold, I got a letter saying that I could have an interview with the superintendent of mails at such-and-such a time. When I went for the interview, they told me that the only opening they had I might not want, because it was in San Francisco and the job required working from four in the afternoon to eleven at night.

He said, "You live in Oakland, so you'd have to get the ferry back and forth. Getting off at 11:30, you'd have to get the last ferry," which left at 11:45. "You might not make it." I said, "That's fine, I'll take the job." So hurray, I didn't have to be home at night! I think he was pretty sure I wouldn't take it. But I said that's just what I want. And my brother Emmett met me at the train every night when I came home from work.

I was laid off from the post office job, and so were all the other women. They said they needed the jobs for men coming back from World War I.

Then one day when I was in downtown Oakland, I met Alvin Nourse, a young man I'd known in New Orleans who was attending the University of California. There were so few Negroes in town then that you would be noticed. I happened to have a transcript [of the classes I'd taken] at Dillard because my professors there had been very interested when they found I was coming to California. They suggested that I take my records with me.

Alvin said, "Well, come on to the university and look it over." He had a Model A Ford that was sort of dilapidated. I rode out with him and he said, "Let's go over to the administration building and see if you can register."

The registrar said, "I don't think you can enroll. Classes have already begun." I was so disappointed that he said, "On the other hand, I'll give you this registration card. If you can find professors who will let you sign up for 10 units of classes, I will let you enroll." We went from place to place and I registered for 13 units of work.

How many other black women were there on campus in 1920?

I think in all there were about eight.[1] I am responsible for bringing Alpha Kappa Alpha sorority to Cal, which is the first black sorority in the nation and first at the University of California. You see, at southern colleges there were clubs of different sorts, often named for blacks who had achieved, so we organized the Brathwaite Club on the Cal campus.

Then I got the women students together and we decided to apply to Alpha Kappa Alpha to start a chapter at the University of California. Some of the famous black women of that period—Dean Lucy Slowe, Dr. Maudelle Bousfield—and several outstanding women of the nation at that time in the field of education were members of Alpha Kappa Alpha.

This sorority required us to get the dean's approval before they would accept our application. I made an appointment to see Dean Lucy Stebbins. The day Dean Stebbins was to sign our application, the *Daily Californian* had an article that another sorority had been formed, with Vivian Marsh as president, Louise Thompson as secretary, and Elizabeth Fisher as treasurer.[2] Dean Stebbins said, "Why don't you girls all join one sorority? There are so few of you."

Had you and Vivian had disagreements?

No, we were very good friends until that time. Vivian's home and mine were the only places that black young people had to go. The others attending the university were renting rooms, so the social gatherings were at her home or mine.

The charter members of Alpha Kappa Alpha were Ruby Jefferson, Coral Johnson, Myrtle Price, Virginia Stephens, and Oreathial Richardson [Tatum]. Virginia Stephens became the first black woman to pass the bar examination for the state of California. She graduated from the law school at the University of California and later coached prospective lawyers for the bar exam.

Did you have any favorite professors at the university?

Dr. J. B. Breitweiser was very much interested in my career. He gave me a lot of encouragement. And Dr. Lee, who was in vocational education, and William Kemp, dean of the school of education. Several years later, it was through Dean Kemp that I went to Tuskegee Institute as dean of women. The president of Tuskegee got in touch with him and asked him if he knew of a black woman graduate of Cal who would be qualified to be dean of women at Tuskegee. Dr. Kemp called me in and interviewed me and then recommended me to President Fred Patterson.

Dean Kemp said, "I think you'd make a marvelous dean of women, but I don't think the South is the place for you." He said, "I'd hesitate to recommend your going to any place below the Mason-Dixon line." I think he said that because I was so outspoken on my views of race. I often wondered about Dean Kemp's recommending me for the position at Tuskegee but, you see, there weren't many blacks on campus for him to suggest.

As I see it now, I must have been pretty militant. I'm pretty sure that if I'd been a man living in the South, I would not have survived. My mother had always wanted to come to California, so I probably would have come here. As a child, I do know I rebelled at almost anything that seemed unfair. So much so that my brother William nicknamed me Emma Goldman, after the woman who wrote the poem about the Statue of Liberty—"Give me your huddled masses, yearning to be free."

This gets me into another category: soon after we organized as a chapter of the sorority, we decided we wanted our picture in the yearbook. So we each put in an amount and got the $45 together. Again, my brother William helped us get the money together. So we went up and paid it at the student office and they sent us to the photographer. We went and had our picture made as a group. Then, when the yearbook came out, we weren't in there. It was just a terrible thing.

We went to Dean Stebbins and she couldn't tell us anything about it, so we went to President David Barrows. I was the spokesman for the group, and he told us "we weren't representative of the student body."

Did you think of going to law school?

I abandoned the idea because I knew I had to make a living, and there was no opportunity [for me to practice law if I did pass the bar exam]. It was many years before I could take some courses just for the sake of knowing. I remember how happy I was when I went to Columbia and could study for the sake of studying.

Were you involved in the National Association for the Advancement of Colored People?

Yes. I was on the board of directors when I was 19. I was going to Cal then. The board members created an education committee, and they asked me to come on the board and be the chair.

When I applied for a teaching position and was not employed, [I went to the NAACP]. Walter Butler was president in the Bay Area then. He had attended high school with some members of the board of education here in Oakland. He interviewed those men on my behalf. Miss Anita Whitney, who was one of the influential whites who were members of the NAACP, also intervened for me.

At the time I applied, it was an unheard-of thing. Apparently it was a deep-seated feeling that no blacks should become teachers in the Oakland public schools. There were very few black children in the Oakland schools, and those that were there were not being trained to further their education. When I was teaching, I encouraged some of my more brilliant students to go on to college.

When they would go to the counselor, she would tell them, "Now, don't think you can go into the teaching profession. Don't think because Miss Jackson is teaching that there will be other black teachers." That was in 1925 and '26 and '30. Up until recent years, black children in high school were not directed into high school classes that would prepare them for college.

I received the state secondary [school teaching] certificate shortly after I got my master's degree in 1923. That's when I went to the Imperial Valley to teach. Mr. Will Wood was state superintendent of schools. It was he who sent me a telegram offering me the position.

The black people in El Centro had decided that since their children could not attend Central Union High School there, they didn't want white teachers in the black Eastside High School. The state superintendent got involved with the issue and contacted the placement office at the University of California, asking if they had a black graduate—a colored woman was the term then—who was qualified to teach English and foods and clothing, what we now call home economics, and I was recommended.

When you did come back to Oakland to teach, you also ran a youth drama group. How did that get started?

I was director of the junior choir at First AME Church. Until I came along, black children rarely had an opportunity to get on the stage. If they were in a singing group, they were far back on the stage. Of course, those of us who fool with music know you put your best voices there, so we tried to make ourselves believe they put blacks back there because of their voices, but that wasn't entirely true.

I decided that I had profited so much by the experience I had had as a child doing things before people in the neighborhood that it would be valuable for other children. Very shortly after I got in the school department, I started the drama group.

Each year I would have an operetta or a play. I gathered all of the black children from the various high schools into the group. They looked forward to it. The rehearsals were a social gathering; all of us got a lot of fun out of it.

I've always worked for more opportunities for black people. I helped organize the National Council of Negro Women with Mary McLeod Bethune and Lucy Slowe, who was the dean at Howard University. Lucy Slowe and I drew up the constitution for the council and helped divide it into regions.

Like the NAACP, the council wanted to encourage more blacks to get higher education and to fight the prejudice that was in the schools. The average white man at that time just didn't think of blacks ever being part of the mainstream of things. When I say the white man, I mean the masses; they've never thought in terms of a black being able to teach them anything. Maybe cooking, since blacks like seasoning. Maybe they thought we could teach them something there.

For a long time, most people didn't know that I was teaching. [When I mentioned it to people I'd meet], they would say, "I didn't know we had any colored"—that's that we were called then—"teachers in the schools."

In addition to teaching classes, I had a couple of periods for counseling. I was given certain students to counsel, and of course they were predominantly blacks. At the time, there weren't that many blacks in the Oakland schools, but I have never fostered segregation.

How did you find time to be national president of your sorority and to organize a teacher training institute in the South?

I don't know. Since I've gotten old, I have wondered how I did all the things that I did then. I was responsible for Alpha Kappa Alpha coming to the West and forming the chapter in California. The national body had my name and address. When they divided the organization into regions, I was the person they remembered out here, so they appointed me regional director of the Far West. I organized a chapter at UCLA, a chapter in Arizona, the chapter in Spokane, and in Seattle.

I guess the idea of a teachers institute originated with me.[3] Who else would be crazy enough to go to all that trouble! Starting the Summer School for Rural Teachers was still based on my opinion that they needed to have the education to help the race. The masses of black people then lived in rural areas. If their teachers were better prepared, they could inspire the youth to go ahead and get an education.

I had heard Dr. Arenia Mallory talk about blacks in the rural South. She said it was almost as bad as it was during slavery days. She presented such a gloomy picture that I made an appointment to talk with her at her campus in Mississippi in 1933, on my Christmas vacation. I saw enough that it made me feel that we should try to do something about it.

As soon as I was elected national president, I sent out a call for volunteer teachers to go south and teach at the summer school. It was a plan of my own. I didn't dare take it up with the national because the directors did not all see things as I saw them. I guess I got about 30 responses, but I could only take eight women. I did it this way: I chose three people from St. Louis. One of them had a car so, you see, I only had to pay for their gas and oil. The music teacher and the math teacher came together from Cincinatti. [The other two came in my car with me.]

Dr. Mallory housed the summer school at her Saints Industrial and Literary School campus in Lexington [Mississippi]. The teachers that were attending the summer school taught children in the morning. Then in the afternoon, my staff taught the teachers. Some of the teachers who came to us had to work on plantations so they couldn't give too much time to our school.

We only conducted the summer school for two years. For six more years, we concentrated entirely on health and health education. We started the health project in Lexington, Mississippi, and later moved it to Mound Bayou. Dr. Dorothy Boulding Ferebee came from Washington to head the clinic.[4] She filled her car with a nurse and a nutritionist who came with her to work in the clinic.

We visited the homes and saw that children were emaciated. They had routine diets, you know. I'm saying you know, and yet you may not know. We found that in some instances the cotton was grown right up to the door. They didn't have space for a garden if they wanted to plant [vegetables for their family]. We added the nutrition class because people needed to learn how to use what was available, that they could grow.

Mrs. Eleanor Roosevelt heard about the health project and invited Dr. Ferebee and me to Washington. There we met that great and gracious lady. She was very interested. While I was there, some members of the Washington, D.C., board of education sent my name in, and I was invited to be a guest at that White House Christmas tree lighting. There I was on the platform with Franklin Roosevelt, the president of the United States.

The interesting thing about telling the things I actually experienced is that we had people envy us the experiences we had going down to serve in Mississippi. They thought we were having such a wonderful time! Then they found out that we had to go the distance from here across the street to the outhouse, that there was no toilet. And that we got hot water for baths by putting a large container on a stand, filled with water. The heat from the sun heated the water.

At the clinic, we started out by having the children immunized against smallpox and diphtheria, but Dr. Ferebee would help whatever parents came. Most of them needed help. Later we added a dental clinic. Dr. Mary Wright from Boston was our dentist.

I did a lot of public speaking about the clinic. I probably appeared often in Oakland telling about it. Anybody that needed a speaker and had no money to pay, they thought of me. I'm a firm believer in prayer; the only way I can account for some of the things I did is just that God was helping me. We closed the clinic in 1943 because we couldn't get the money to run it.

By then, we found that chapters of Alpha Kappa Alpha sorority in other cities had become interested in promoting better health among blacks [and started different kinds of health services]. Here in Oakland they operated a dental health clinic. It was named for me, but it was the idea of Cornelia Logan, who was a teacher in the public schools.

We conducted dental health clinics for a period of years. They started the project in the schools to do regular dental examinatons for poorer people. We got certain black dentists to agree to take whatever children we sent to them who could not pay. So many days a week they would give these children free dental care.

We [also] worked with the city health director and the school health director [on starting a] tuberculosis clinic. I worked with them in the clinic, which we operated at night.

How did things go in the Oakland schools? You took some time out to do graduate work at Columbia too.

One year I took a sabbatical to go to Columbia Teachers College and study for my doctorate. I got to the point of writing my dissertation at Columbia, as I had done at Cal, but it was during the depression days.

As I advanced, the professors I knew would say, "Of course, when you write your dissertation, you're going to write something about your own people." I had a friend in the law school who had the same experience. We didn't realize that we might be helping blacks by doing a profound study about blacks. We believed that the white man thought we weren't prepared to do in-depth research. I don't think I ever expressed that opinion to any professor that I had. We either develop more courage as we grow older, or lose it.

I would have liked to study vocational education and vocational guidance, in terms of helping blacks to get out of the routine and into other fields that weren't open to us. The theory when I was coming along was "blacks don't do this." "We don't have any blacks in that field." But I would have had to take time out from work to do the research, and I couldn't afford to do that.

While I was in New York, the president of Tuskegee wrote Dean Kemp at Cal, as I told you, asking him if he knew of any black woman who was prepared to come serve as dean of women. My name was recommended. Dr. Patterson, the president, contacted me in New York and sold me on the idea of going to Tuskegee.

I guess it was an honor, but there was a lot of work to do. You've got to search for the honor. It was a very challenging job because, although Tuskegee is a great institution, it was geared toward men until comparatively recent years. During the period that I was at Tuskegee, the situation was such that a black woman could do more, in my opinion, socially. The American pattern has always been to subdue the black man. If any graciousness was shown, it was more to the black woman.

Of course, I tried to build up the women's department and organized activities among the women. I believe I was the first trained dean of women they had. I wanted the women students to develop themselves to the highest ability, so consequently I organized activities among the women students.

I took the job for the experience in administration. I had applied for an administrative job in Oakland because I had credentials from UC Berkeley and Columbia that prepared me for administrative work. But the superintendent here said they "weren't ready for a black principal." He said I needed experience, so that's why I went to Tuskegee. At the end of my year there, the superintendent wrote me saying that since I had done so well at Tuskegee, he felt I would want to stay there and work among my own people. He sent me a resignation blank.

I replied by asking him what my assignment would be the next year in Oakland. They sent me to McClymonds High School. It has always been known as a troubled school. [Like Prescott School where I had taught before,] it was in an area where a great many foreign-born and the few blacks that were then in Oakland lived. It seemed as though Prescott was set apart as the sort of place where, if some principal wanted to get a teacher out, he would send her to the West Oakland schools.

There were some dedicated teachers there who realized they were molding children. Some very fine teachers were at Prescott; some of the finest in the system. Some chose to teach there. When I began teaching at Prescott, a protest group was formed. They called on the superintendent to question him about having hired a black teacher.

I was interested primarily in teaching children, so whatever efforts were made to make my life uncomfortable didn't register. It was a challenge. I was determined to make good on the job, and I like children. There were some splendid teachers who did not openly revolt [even] when they had more blacks teaching in the schools.

I never had problems from the standpoint of race with my students, ever. The first children that welcomed me were whites. I remember two little Italian girls with an armful of geranium blossoms coming to my door and saying, "Teacher, we brought you these flowers. We like you." It did something for me.

I was an unpopular person, so I tried not to call attention to myself. [As an example of what happened,] after a few days I was not allowed to keep the class I was hired to teach, a sixth-grade class. Instead, they gathered the retarded and the problem cases and gave me that group. Among the other things I remember, they gave me for music a class of seventh- and eighth-grade boys whose voices were changing.

There were a few teachers who were friendly. One of them volunteered to help me. She said, "Would you like to teach my English class and I'll take your music class?" She told the principal she was going to take the class, and she took it over. That was Albertine DuBois Smith, who was highly respected and had a lovely voice. We became good friends.

During World War II, a great many people came in from the South, both white and black. Many of them came from rural communities, and their children had only gone to school three or four months a year. That's why so many of them were considered retarded. They weren't retarded mentally, but they hadn't been exposed to much of an education.

How did you and your brother decide to buy a ranch in Northern California?

For months, I had noticed Emmett carrying with him the want ads section of the newspapers and wondered why. Eventually he said, "Are you going to be busy this weekend?" So I went with him to this little town a hundred miles away and we went to the recorder's office.

He had bought this ranch in Mendocino County, and now he was going to record the change of ownership. The recorder asked how he wanted the deed made out. He said, "Emmett Lee Jackson, a single man, and Ida Louise Jackson, a single woman."

I said to him, "Emmett, you know I don't have any money!" He said, "You don't manage to have any money, but you do keep a good car. All I require of you as joint owner is to provide the transportation that we can go back and forth in." That's how I became half-owner of a 1,280-acre sheep ranch.

It was called Lookout Ranch, at the summit of a range of hills 11 miles from the Pacific Ocean. We had a view of the surrounding country and fir trees and redwoods. There were areas of the ranch where we could see the ocean. There was a grove of fir trees and redwoods that started at the gate and went all the way back almost to the house. It was a beautiful place.

I think we were the first black landowners up there. They were not necessarily more open to black people, but I had all the social life I could handle with black people here.

I still hoped to some day become a principal or school administrator of some sort. But Emmett said, "Sister, you will never be anything but a teacher in Oakland. Why waste your time there? You can make more money managing the ranch. Why don't you leave?" They continued to give me the problem students and eventually I realized Emmett was right.

You didn't see any changes even in the 1950s, after the Supreme Court said that education for blacks should be equal to that for whites?

How can I put it without making a sweeping general statement. That didn't affect the white majority and their idea of the Negro's education. Very much like when freedom was declared, so many slave owners didn't feel that it applied to them, and they didn't release their slaves. Throughout the South, there were very few places where it made any difference. But this latest

28

decision, I found that in the South, when they found that they had to admit black students, they did a complete turnaround.

Most of the people who were qualified to teach here, up to and including the period that I came in, those who did go to teacher's college at San Francisco State or the University of California, went South to get teaching positions because they couldn't get them here. I asked a native daughter why she was going south to teach and she said, "I couldn't endure what you did as a teacher in Oakland."

Have you stayed in touch with university alumni activities?

I've been a life member of the alumni association for years; it had no program into which a black person would fit. You see, California hasn't proved to be the Mecca that most blacks thought it was. To put it roughly, the black could go to the shows and sit anywhere he wanted; he was paying the money for that. But when it came to equality of opportunity in employment, things above average, the racial factor entered. It has never disappeared.

Fair employment legislation has been a help in many places, but it's limited in itself. When the law was passed about equal opportunity hiring, Asians and Mexicans got the jobs. We are still the last hired and the first fired.

But I do continue to love the university. I remember I visited the campus when I first got to California. I looked around at all the marvelous buildings and the size of the campus. The schools that I attended, the black colleges that I had seen, however beautiful, didn't come up to anything like the University of California.

I said, "I wonder if I can handle this?" I had a conversation with myself and I said, "I dare you to try this," that sort of thing. I guess I wouldn't have been too disappointed if I hadn't made it. I used to challenge myself to see if I could do this or that. I did enter the university. The attitude of the students didn't deter me. As I may have said, I grew up with courage, or something that made me accept a challenge. My mother was a courageous woman.

I do feel that it's a good philosophy to have a certain amount of confidence in yourself and to be willing to tackle whatever interests you. You get something out of it whether you win all the way or not. It's a valuable experience to go into unknown territory to prepare you for anything that follows.

Of course, I did some foolish things. I remember when it came to Senior Week activities on campus, Oreathial Richardson, one of my sorority sisters, graduated at the time time I did. And two or three black men graduated the same day. Senior women were supposed to wear white and carry a white umbrella for the traditional Senior Pilgrimage, where they visited certain sites on campus.

I told Oreathial we should go. She said, "I'm not going. They'll snub you."

I said, "We'll be together." She didn't go, but I went. My friends laughed at me for going.

I said, "I'm not concerned about what other people think. I want to know what they know. I want to see those places. I want to participate in graduation time and see what it's like."

I marched in the procession. Somewhere I have the picture my friends made of me walking along alone. I turned around because I didn't want them to make my picture. I recognized myself by the back.

3

TAREA HALL PITTMAN

NAACP Official and Civil Rights Worker

Tarea Hall Pittman, known as "Ty," was born in 1903 and raised in Bakersfield, California. Her father came from Alabama in 1895, and her mother arrived in 1880. Her father owned and operated a farm and established the local branch of the National Association for the Advancement of Colored People; her mother was the organist at Mt. Zion Baptist Church. Pittman entered the University of California at Berkeley in 1923, completing her undergraduate degree in social service at San Francisco State College after her marriage to Bill Pittman, a pioneering black dentist. In 1940 she received a master's degree at Berkeley.

For 40 years, she was commentator of a radio program called "Negroes in the News." She was president of the California State Association of Colored Women's Clubs in 1936–38 and later of the California Council of Negro Women. During World War II, she worked with the Travelers Aid Society in Richmond to help newcomers find housing and jobs. Active in the NAACP since her student years, she became a full-time staff member and eventually director of the West Coast Region, guiding lobbying activities in the 1950s that led to passage of the California Fair Employment Practices legislation. She continued volunteer civil rights work until her death in 1991.

My parents knew all of the people in town. They grew up with the town. When my dad went into the bank, the bankers and tellers would say, "Why, hello, Will. How are you?" By the time my mother and father were married, they were able to build a home. We had a nice house, and we had things that everybody else had. So we were not depressed in any way.

This chapter was adapted from Tarea Hall Pittman, *NAACP Official and Civil Rights Worker,* 1971 and 1972 interviews with Joyce Henderson (Berkeley: Regional Oral History Office, University of California, 1974).

Was there much discrimination against African Americans in Bakersfield?

It was a very, very prejudiced place. It was terrible. There was no problem in going to school. There was no problem in getting jobs in certain areas. But you couldn't get a job as a clerk in a store or a secretary in an office. None of these jobs were open to Negroes. Domestic work was open to women. The men could get work with the railroads because Bakersfield was a division headquarters for the big railroads. Santa Fe and Southern Pacific had big shops there.

When I hear people talking about busing, this is very interesting to me because busing was the thing that brought about the excellent educational opportunity that we had. All [the families in the] area got together and formed the Kern County Union High School at Bakersfield. Because of this we had one of the biggest high schools in the state of California, and we were able to have every opportunity—all of the languages, and all of the departments were advanced because of the school being a union high school. And all of us who lived in the outlying areas rode a bus to the high school.

Was there prejudice against blacks at your high school?

Yes, we had some problems. But we all had friends. You see, we already had our place. Many of the parents of those students that were there had been classmates of our mother and father.

After my father's mother and father came to California, their 13 sons and daughters lived with them until they married and left. My father's mother lived to be a very elderly woman, and she was the matriarch of that family. They had a terrible time trying to get her to come off that ranch after she was in her eighties. At 85, my grandmother was a phenomenal woman—she could just get out and walk to downtown Bakersfield and back better than I could ever think about doing now.

I come from a family of great talkers. My uncle, Mansion Hall, would make very fiery speeches about anything he talked on. My father also; all of them were.

My mother was quieter than the rest of them. She believed in very strict discipline. We had things that we were supposed to do. We knew exactly what we were to do and we did it! My father would be out on the ranch. My mother was a very capable woman and did a lot of things in running the household.

What was your motivation in coming to Berkeley? Was it hard to persuade your parents?

I took a college preparatory course in high school. From the first day I went to high school, I was intent on going to college, and I wanted to come to Berkeley.

I just kept at it. I just kept worrying them about wanting to come here. Then we had three Negro students from Kern County Union High School who were a little ahead of me who came to Berkeley.

Did you have any problems finding housing when you came to Berkeley in 1923?

The only housing that was available for Negro students was in private homes. There were not very many of them, nor were they close to campus, which created a problem. Some male students got food and lodging at the frat houses where they worked.

What about white sorority houses?

White sorority houses didn't have Negro girls working in them. A lot of them had Negro cooks.

But we made friends very easily. The YWCA cottage right outside the university campus was a meeting place for students at noon. There were parties and social events given there. It really was a sort of a Mecca for students, and Negro students were welcome to a certain degree. I never remember feeling foreign there, like I wasn't wanted.

The other place where we felt very much at home and had dances was Stephens Union, the student center on campus. It was a very pleasant building, right there on Faculty Glade. We could go out and sit under the beautiful trees. I was entranced with the campus. It was so beautiful!

During my freshman year, we founded the Delta Sigma Theta sorority. The university had an intrafraternal council, but something arose that we couldn't be represented on this council. We were just a poor group because there were so few of us.

Why didn't the council allow you a spot?

Well, it was just plain prejudice! Most times the people who discriminate do not wish to be identified as discriminating against you because of your race.

Even back then they didn't want to say it was because of your race. They did it under the guise that we shouldn't be allowed to belong because we didn't have a house.

We didn't have a fraternity house or a sorority house. We all lived out in the city, with the exception of the men that lived adjacent to campus. But they were working in the frat houses. My husband-to-be, William Pittman, happened to be one who was working at the post office—one of not too many. My husband had untold stamina! Even as an older man, he worked extremely hard, and he didn't want to quit practicing dentistry.

Dean Lucy Stebbins was very, very active during this controversy about the council. She was the dean of students and she maintained that we were college women and that as long as our scholastic average was what it was supposed to be that we would have to be admitted. Dean Stebbins was very outspoken in her espousal of the Negro women on campus.

How did you meet your husband?

I was in undergraduate school at the University of California, Berkeley, and he was over in San Francisco at the University of California Dental School. There were just a handful of Negro students on campus. At the beginning of the semester, Alpha Phi Alpha fraternity had a party for all of us. It was at one of these first-of-school social events that I met my husband.

I didn't think he was that handsome, but a lot of the girls thought he was very handsome. He was well dressed and he had access to a car. Very few people had a car at that time.

I've asked Bill a lot of times, "How, at that time, when you didn't see any Negro dentists in Oakland, did you decide that you were going to become a dentist?" He can't really explain why he chose dentistry. One just didn't pick that up in college. You know, sometimes you're doing your undergrad work and still don't know what you want to be. But that was always his goal.

My husband was very tall, even as a teenager. He put his age up during World War I and got in the army. At that time, you could enlist and say, "I'm 21 years old." He had just begun his freshman year when he went into the service. This was 1917! The recruiters didn't care. They had been accused of being biased and not letting any Negroes enlist. I guess they thought, "We'll take one or two to prove that we aren't prejudiced." So they took Bill, and the next thing you know they had sent him overseas. He got some mustard gas that gave him quite a time, because the sickness it gave him would recur.

I met him in 1923, and we were married in 1927.

Had you graduated?

No. You see, the university had told me that I was too underweight. Looking back now, I guess maybe they thought I was susceptible to tuberculosis or something. They ended up making me stay out a couple of semesters. When I came back, I decided to change majors. I liked teaching, and I had no problem, but I felt a prisoner in that classroom. The thing I was very much interested in was doing fieldwork with people.

I stayed out quite a long time, because I had married and Bill had to finish dental school. When I went back to college, I built up a completely new major in social service. When I graduated from San Francisco State, I decided that I would go to the school of social service at Cal and get my master's degree. So this is what I did. It was quite a circuitous route that I took.

I think I made a good choice. But if I had had more insight into what I really might have been capable of doing, maybe I would have gone into law. But I entered the social-work field, and I was intensely interested in it. During World War II, I had a placement at the Richmond Travelers Aid Society and the USO [United Services Organization].

From 1936 to 1938, you were president of the California Association of Colored Women's Clubs. What were their goals?

We were very anxious to see that Negro families, and particularly Negro women, participated in political activity. Some of them, when women finally got the vote, never bothered about voting at all!

The Fannie Wall Children's Home in Oakland was another thing that made me want to be able to speak authoritatively as a social worker. It was a project of the association, and I knew it was being run like somebody's private home and not according to standards. The reason the authorities let it go on for so long was because they couldn't open up any foster homes with Negro parents, and they didn't have any place to put all these Negro children; so they were glad to have a Fannie Wall Children's Home to absorb some of these children who ordinarily would have been in a foster home.

Some of them were delinquents, some of them came over to us from the probation home, some were just orphans, and some of them were abandoned. So we were working hard to see if we couldn't bring the home up to standard.

We were also interested in working with the juvenile court. It came to us that if a group of children were accused of something, they'd take the children to the detention home. Then, somehow or other, all of the little white children and all of the rest of them who were not Negro got bailed out. But the little Negro children were held to answer. So we were very interested in the juvenile court for this reason, and we did a number of very outstanding things.

Even back then there was a lot of agitation in connection with the prisons, and we were very anxious to get a separate prison for women. Finally, we got Tehachapi, which had formerly been an all-purpose and a male prison, turned over as a women's maximum-security prison.

Then you were president of the California Council of Negro Women. What were their concerns?

That was from from 1948 to 1951. The general concerns of this group, which was made up of clubs located throughout the state of California, was to raise the standards of black homes, particularly as it referred to the well-being of women and children. The council is made up of various departments, such as legislation, arts and crafts, music, homemaking, health and housing.

The council is a group of women who are not all alike along a social line or in the upper economic bracket, although there are some professional women in it. But the rank-and-file person is interested in the poor, in the disadvantaged, in trying to upgrade women in their jobs and to see that they get additional skills, and to see that their housing is better, their families are better fed, their children are taken care of while they're working. It is a grassroots women's organization.

I understand that in 1947 you served on the Alameda County Grand Jury.

I was on several grand jury committees. I was particularly interested at that time in the condition of the jail and the detention home, which is really the juvenile hall. We visited these places and made recommendations based on our visits and we asked, even at that time, about reforms in that whole juvenile hall setup.

Every year the grand jury makes recommendations and eventually some of the things do get done. Year after year, the board of supervisors is apprised of the situation and that you are trying to get them to do something about the reforms that you want to see carried out.

Were you active in the NAACP, too, while you were in these other groups?

I was very, very active in the NAACP. All of their work is done through committees. This means they set up an education committee, a membership committee, finance, labor, and industry committee, a youth work committee, a veterans' committee.

The NAACP is an organization set up to serve people, and we would get many complaints that people had applied for positions, taken examinations, and were never called. We would then go to the civil-service commission and try to find out why these particular Negroes didn't pass or why they couldn't get placed on the list to be appointed. We would go to the board of education, to the city manager or the city council or the county board of supervisors, or whoever was in charge of that particular institution, and try to find out why this discrimination existed and what could be done about it.

Of course, the chief offenders were the police department and the fire department. We really went after that. We finally got a few black men on the police force and a few in the sheriff's department. We finally got several Negro women in the sheriff's department. All in all, we broke down much of the discrimination that had to do with housing the prisoners and tried to do away with police brutality.

This was very much talked about at that time and we worked very hard on it, *very hard*. I don't know any program, outside of trying to place Negro school teachers, that we worked any harder on than we worked on trying to do away with discrimination in the county and city facilities.

We even did some boycotting at that time. We asked people not to patronize a certain place. We were instrumental in getting the civil rights law put on the books where people could be fined. It is true that it was only a hundred-dollar fine and court costs, but this was a step forward. We got that passed in the legislature sometime in the fifties, I think.

Public accommodations such as restaurants, hotels, and motels were very high on the agenda then. It was a long time before we could get restaurants, hotels, and motels (motels were the worst) opened to Negroes because they would say that they were full. Today there are very few places that will discriminate against people.

We absolutely opened up public accommodations in this country. We have opened them up even in the Deep South, so you know we have opened them up here. It was very hard to get that passed, as many of the men in the legislature were so conservative and reactionary.

I was working with the schools trying to get black teachers in the schools, and on the labor and industry committee trying to do something about other jobs. We worked very hard during the war years because the cry went out that there would be no black people working in Kaiser Shipyards, and Kaiser Shipyards was the big employer. There was war housing, but they weren't going to let any Negroes live in the war housing. So this became one of our very, very big fights.

We'd meet no less than once a week, and we'd generally meet at night because most of our people worked. Our open public meetings were always on Sunday afternoon. We would meet in one church or another.

The education committee was set up to try to do something about the schools generally. We were working with the schools, trying to get them not to discriminate against the Negro students. The committee was very instrumental in breaking up blackface minstrel shows. The Elks Club had at one time a yearly minstrel show. Finally, the attorney general wrote an opinion that no school could house an entertainment where any race was ridiculed.

For years, we were trying to get "Negroes" spelled with a capital "N." We were going to the papers and trying to keep them from playing up cuttings, scrapes, and rapes and writing, "This was a black." This made the public feel that we were sort of a subculture, because the papers didn't play up anything that was good.

You'd think that no Negro ever married or died or anything else because, unless it was someone very, very important, it never got in the news. Death notices have to come out and be published, but other than that, there would be no notices. It was unheard of to have a Negro wedding picture in the paper!

Finally, we got Miss Delilah Beasley hired by the *Oakland Tribune,* and we had a Negro page in the paper. She was given the position to write a Sunday page of news about Negroes. This began in the 1930s, maybe the late 1920s.

Then in 1935, the Negro Education Council of the East Bay banded themselves together to put on a weekly radio program, "Negroes in the News." Now, the whole intent behind that was that if we could get on the air, we would be able to offset this lack of news about Negroes by having a regular program that people could listen to and actually hear something other than that someone had cut someone or been arrested in a crap game or something like that. This was the way the radio program began and it has never ceased to exist. I was the commentator, and I did it just as a hobby. I had had several courses in radio in my college work and I was anxious to do this because this was sort of like a laboratory to see what we could do with this sort of program.

How did you get a fair-employment bill passed in California?

There were various attempts to get legislation. In 1953 we began a cooperative effort with church, labor, social, and civic groups coming together to get the bill passed. NAACP had a commitment for a strong civil rights bill, one that had sanctions and enforcement provisions. We had meetings in the northern area and the southern area of the state. Then we worked out of the capitol in Sacramento.

For the first time, we had a lobbyist that stayed in Sacramento full time. I was the lobbyist, and we had other people. I was in the capitol working with the author of the bill, with the heads of the two houses, to find out when the bill was before the legislative committees.

I also gave testimony at all the hearings. We had other spokesmen too. It wasn't just Negroes who testified. We had many, many other people in labor and the churches. The Friends [American Friends Service Committee] had a lobby; labor had a lobby. Lobbying was a very hard job. We were running up and down the halls and trying to find out where the legislators were. If you were a certified legislative advocate, you could go to the floor of the assembly or senate in those days. I was the legislative advocate for the Committee for Fair Employment Practices, and that was this cross section of organizations.

I put full time into this in Sacramento. I would come home to the Bay Area on occasion or perhaps weekends because most of the legislators went home then. But mostly I stayed in Sacramento because we were so busy and were trying to do so many things.

One of the techniques that we voted to use in March of 1953 was a mobilization. It was the first meeting of that kind that had ever been held, where we would call in the main membership of the sponsoring organizations and we would have them to come into the capitol itself in Sacramento. We had a mobilization for two days. When they came in, we had workshops on how to go and see their legislators.

On Sunday afternoon we called a big mass meeting at one of the largest churches in Sacramento and had Assemblymen Byron Rumford and Gus Hawkins and a number of others who were co-authoring the bill to attend. We tried to let people know why we had to have the bill, what abuses there were in employment and this kind of thing.

There were those who felt that we should include housing. We knew that there was gross discrimination in housing, but we realized that it would just add to our difficulty in trying to get the employment legislation on the books.

What groups were testifying against the fair-employment bill?

There were many, many individuals. I think we had strong opposition from the state Chamber of Commerce and the California Apartment House Owners organization. We had conspicuous opposition from many of the clergy, even though we did have the support of organizations like the Conference for Christians and Jews. The main push and input into the passage of the FEPC [Fair Employment Practices Commission law] came from the minority-group community, joined by the widest cross section of people and support that we had ever garnered before or since in this state for a piece of legislation.

We attempted to get statements in support from outstanding legislators and all the way up to the governor's office. We were not successful during the governorship of Earl Warren and, after that, Goodwin Knight. Warren would not put himself on record. Governor Warren did not make the statement that he would not sign it, but he would not take any leadership in getting it passed. He simply turned his back on the legislative conferences we had, and we could not confront him with anything publicly. Goodwin Knight said that if it was passed he would not sign it, that he would veto it.

Governor Edmund G. Brown, Sr., stepped up front and center and said that he would fight for its passage and he would certainly do everything he could to get it passed and he would sign it into law. And this is what he did. So we got the FEPC law passed in 1959. Governor Brown named the first members of the commission, and they were confirmed the same year.

How many Negroes were named to the commission?

Only one, and that was C. L. Dellums.

Do you think your job was harder because you were a woman?

I think I got the same treatment that a man would get.

When did you become acting director of the western region of NAACP?

I became acting director in 1959. One of our problems in the regional office of the NAACP was that we didn't ever have a researcher, and we lost so much because we had no one who could feed us the information when we came in. This is why I don't have some of the documentation that I should have.

NAACP is a crisis organization, and we were just coming and going. We'd come in and think we were going to go one place, and we'd find out something had broken out, and we had to go someplace else. So it was a thrilling thing.

After you retired as regional director, you didn't stay retired very long. What was your next job?

With the Opportunity Industrialization Centers [OIC], raising funds for their western region, working directly with Reverend Leon Sullivan in Philadelphia. I was housed in the West Coast Regional Office of the NAACP, and I worked in the same nine western states that I was acquainted with and traveled in for 20 years for the NAACP.

The OIC is funded by the U.S. Department of Labor, but they also have to raise funds in the private sector. This is an organization that seeks to weld together the interest of industries and corporations with skills-training programs and interest in the unemployed and unemployable in developing those skills, with a view to having them absorbed by industry.

So I have been working directly with heads of corporations and industries, asking for support of OIC. I want to make it very clear that I still consider myself a retiree. I told Reverend Sullivan that I could not look forward to staying on for more than six months or a year.

4

MIRIAM MATTHEWS

Library Advocate for Negro History and Advancement

A woman of exceptional energy and determination, Miriam Matthews was the first African-American librarian in the Los Angeles Public Library system, where she worked from 1927 to 1960. She assembled an extensive collection of materials on blacks in California and, in 1929, helped to organize Negro History Week.

Born in Pensacola, Florida, in 1905, she came to Los Angeles with her parents in 1907. After enrolling at the University of California, Southern Branch (now UCLA), where she was a founding member of Delta Sigma Theta sorority, Matthews graduated from the University of California at Berkeley in 1926. She completed library training at Berkeley in 1927, and in 1945 received a master's degree from the University of Chicago Graduate Library School.

Despite efforts to overlook her talents, Matthews rose to be a head librarian and in the 1940s was appointed regional librarian for the south-central area. In addition to organizing book clubs and lectures for library patrons she became well known for encouraging local black artists and in 1950 became a co-founder of the Associated Artists Gallery.

I was the second of three children of Reuben Hearde and Fannie Elijah Matthews. When I was two years old, my parents decided they did not wish their children to be brought up in a segregated atmosphere, so they moved our family to California. We came on the Santa Fe Railway. Our trip to Los Angeles took eight days.

Although there was segregation on the trains at that time, there were no separate cars for Negroes. White and Negro passengers were separated by a

This chapter was adapted from Miriam Matthews, *An Oral History Interview*, recorded in March 1977 by Eleanor Roberts for the Black Women Oral History Project (Boston: Schlesinger Library, Radcliffe College, 1981), 369–71, 373–88, 390, 392, 394–95, 397–402, 404–405, 411, 416–20, 422–23, 432–37, 449. © 1981 by Radcliffe College. Reprinted by permission of K. G. Saur Verlag, a Reed Reference Publishing Company, and the Arthur and Elizabeth Schlesinger Library, Radcliffe College.

curtain which could be moved easily to expand either section. When the Negro section was getting too crowded in our car, my father, who appeared to be white, asked the conductor to move the curtain. When he discovered my father wanted him to give the Negroes more space, he cursed him and did not move the curtain.

There were comparatively few Negroes in the city then. My mother said when she went downtown when she first arrived, she never saw another black face. By 1910 there were 7,600 Negroes in Los Angeles, only slightly higher than 2 percent of the city's population.

My father was a painter and a good one. He received his training at the Tuskegee Institute in Alabama. The day after our arrival in Los Angeles, he went out to look for a job and found work right away. For a while, he was employed by a firm of building contractors. Later, my father built a successful business by himself, and my mother kept the business records. Most of his customers were wealthy white people who always recommended him to their friends. He kept a large crew of painters busy except during the depression years until a short time before his death in 1949.

My mother had planned to be a teacher, but gave up a normal school teacher's course to get married. An excellent dressmaker, she made all of her children's clothes and most of her own. In good times and bad, my mother always managed to save something from every paycheck.

We were always well fed, well dressed, and comfortable. We had a piano, and all of us took music lessons. We attended dancing school to learn social dancing. Our first automobile was purchased in 1917. It was a 1914 Model T Ford, purchased secondhand for $250. For that period, I'm certain one would consider our family "middle class."

Our family physician, Dr. John Outlaw, had a large automobile in the days when very few people owned any kind of a car. As small children, we were delighted when he had to make a house call, because we knew when he was ready to leave he would let all of the children on the block crowd into his car for the thrilling ride to the corner! Dr. Outlaw had arrived in Los Angeles from Washington, D.C., in 1901. He may have been the first Negro doctor to settle in the area. My parents received good advice from Dr. Outlaw on subjects other than medicine, which proved helpful to them as new arrivals in the city.

What do you recall about your school experience?

The elementary school was right around the corner. My mother always heard our lessons. While she was helping my sister with her first grade reader, I listened, and since I was interested, my mother taught me to read it from cover to cover. We had a very pleasant time throughout our elementary school days, studying and playing happily with both black and white class-mates, although there were only a few of the former.

I attended 14th Street Intermediate School. I was in the honor society every semester except one. That was the winter of 1918–19 when a severe epidemic of influenza forced them to close all the schools. Then I had taken Spanish in intermediate school, so when I got to high school this gave me a chance to take two extra subjects, and so I graduated high school at 16.

The small groups of Negroes who were at the high school in those days encountered some prejudice. For example, one student had filed to run as a candidate for the senior board, and the faculty advisers forced her to withdraw her name. Mr. Goddard, our twelfth-grade teacher, gave my sister an F on her midterm report card without giving her the customary unsatisfactory notice beforehand. My father went to see the principal, who took him to Mr. Goddard's room.

After my father stated his case, Mr. Goddard said, "Miriam is quite smart, I'm sure she can help Ella bring up her grade." The next time we had an essay to write, I wrote both my sister's essay and mine. I received a B + and my sister a C. Most of the teachers were kind and unbiased and I have many pleasant memories of my association with them.

Mr. Goddard was responsible for all the graduation arrangements, includ-ing senior honors. When I learned that he had notified all those who were eligible for senior honors except me, I secured my transcript from my home-room teacher and showed it to him, asking why he had not called me.

After making a pretense of looking over my grades, he said, "Oh, yes, you are all right." In addition to other privileges, those with senior honors were supposed to be seated right behind the faculty and speakers on the night of graduation. Mr. Goddard had already arranged the seating and refused to change it to put me near the front. My sister Ella, Lois Towns, and I were seated in the third row from the top. Italians and other dark Europeans were placed in the top rows also. So they discriminated against them too.

I was a rather shy and retiring person all through high school and most of college, yet I did go to see about this without even consulting my parents. And later on, in work, even though I wasn't what I'd call a brash, forward-type person, I always quietly said my piece when I thought something was not right.

Were there any minority teachers at Los Angeles High School?

Not while I was there. The first two were Charles Thomas and Josephine Blodgett Smith, who started teaching at Los Angeles High in the physical education and home economics departments in 1952. Earlier, Hazel Gottschalk Whitaker was assigned to Jefferson Junior High School in 1936, and Clarissa Lovingood Matthews, my sister-in-law, to Carver Junior High School in 1937.

Historically, when the teachers' examination was given for the Los Angeles City School District in 1911, Bessie Bruington Burke, a Negro, placed seventh in a field of 800. Despite this fact, it took a lot of community pressure to secure her appointment as a teacher at the Holmes Avenue School that year. She became the first Negro principal in Los Angeles seven years later and served as principal of three other schools before her retirement in 1955.

In the twenties, it was customary to mark "c" for "colored" behind the names on Negroes on the eligible teachers list. Nothing is said about the days when the Los Angeles city schools paid the carfare of both black and white students to hasten segregation.

Fay Allen was the first Negro elected to the Los Angeles City Board of Education, back in 1939. Most of the teachers, black and white, sang her praises, because she was the first school board member to make regular visits to the schools to find out firsthand what their problems were. Her efforts to make other needed reforms did not make her popular with certain groups. They managed to defeat her, when she ran for reelection in 1943, by placing a white housewife named Allen first on the ballot, confusing voters who wished to vote for Fay Allen.

What about the social side of high school?

Most of the high schools held their senior proms in hotels where Negroes were not welcome. However, when there were programs in the auditorium for the entire student body, Negro students were included. Naida McCullough, an excellent pianist, played a very difficult classical piece one day. Several Negroes contributed their musical talents to other programs.

Our social life was simple but fun. On Friday evenings we would go to the homes of different friends, roll back the carpets, and dance. All those who knew how to play the piano would take turns providing the music for us to dance by. The host mother would provide the refreshments, which would be fruit punch and cookies usually. Larger parties or dances would be at the St. Philip's Episcopal Church parish hall, the Masonic Hall, and a few other places.

Mothers were on hand everywhere to act as chaperones. Most of the girls danced only with other girls until they were 16 years old. In most cases they did not go on dates alone with young men until they were 18. After my brother got his first pair of long trousers, my mother did permit the three of us to go to house parties without her in the family automobile. We used a little rice powder and a pale pink pomade lipstick. Unless you were very forward, you did not use real lipstick or rouge on your cheeks.

I went to the University of California, Southern Branch, for my first two years of college. Attending college in my hometown seemed like a continuation of high school, so I transferred to UC Berkeley in 1924. Being on my own away from home was a valuable experience for me. It developed my character and made me more independent.

What was UC Berkeley like when you went to school there?

Berkeley was calm and peaceful then, a typical conservative college town. The same atmosphere prevailed on campus, where a bonfire rally or a football game produced the greatest excitement among the students.

There were no dormitories in Berkeley in those days for black or white students. I roomed in the home of Mr. and Mrs. Leon F. Marsh, about a 25-minute walk from the campus. My brother, Erskine Ragland, and Charles Diggs lived around the corner. I first met Mrs. Marsh, who was Vivian Osborne before she married, when she came to Los Angeles in the spring of 1923 while she was still a student at Berkeley to establish Pi chapter of Delta Sigma Theta sorority on the campus of the University of California, Southern Branch.

I was one of the five charter members of Pi chapter and its first vice president. Mrs. Marsh established most of the chapters of the sorority in the western states. Vivian and I have remained friends through the years, and I was her houseguest in 1976 when I attended my fiftieth college reunion in Berkeley!

Were there many minority students going to Berkeley when you were in college there?

Not too many, and a number of them came from the Los Angeles area. When I went to Berkeley, it was *the* place to go. When I went to the Southern Branch, the campus was small. I enjoyed the intimacy of the campus there and the personal contact with my professors and classmates. At Berkeley, my classes were very large (with a few exceptions) and were held in huge study halls. The rolls were taken by the seats that were vacant. If you were absent and someone sat in your seat, you were marked present.

Being a Spanish major was lucky for me because those classes mostly had eight to twelve students. I was elected to Sigma Delta Pi, the Spanish honorary society in my senior year. Most of my Negro girlfriends were planning to be teachers, but that was the one profession I decided I did not wish to follow.

When I was a sophomore, I studied most of the time with Charlotte Cavell, a white friend. One day when we were walking across campus, Charlotte happened to mention that she planned to be either a physical education teacher or a librarian.

Somehow the profession of librarian struck a responsive chord and I said, "That's a good idea!" A few weeks before graduation I filed an application with the School of Librarianship at Berkeley. The director of the library school told me they would accept the 30 highest in scholarship for the next class. Naturally, I was delighted when I received my letter of acceptance.

My family and a number of friends tried to discourage me from taking the course in library science, because they said I would not get a job. Just before Christmas vacation I asked one of my professors to request permission for me to do practice work in the Los Angeles Public Library. For some reason, she felt it was necessary to tell the administrators that I was a Negro, so they assigned me to a small branch in a mixed Negro-Jewish neighborhood. Mrs. Hortense Mitchell, the branch librarian, proved to be a real friend. Her generous assistance made all my subjects more interesting and meaningful during my second semester in Berkeley.

At that time, there were no black professional librarians. However, there were two black clerk typists in the Los Angeles Public Library, Olive B. Minter and Etheline Clark. The latter had a flair for telling stories to children, and they were attracted to her. Even though she had no professional training, Mrs. Clark was permitted to act as a children's librarian for a short time.

When I received a certificate in librarianship in May, my brother, Charles, received his A.B. degree at the same commencement exercises. He later graduated from the Boalt Hall School of Law and was the only Negro in his class.

Within a few days of graduation, I went downtown to see the assistant city librarian, whom I had met when I was doing practice work. She was very cordial and spent almost an hour with me. Just as I was leaving she gave me a postcard to address, so they could notify me as soon as the announcements for the library examination were issued. She told me that this examination was given every year in the month of June.

A day or two later, Dr. John Outlaw, our family physician, phoned and asked my mother if I was planning to take the civil-service examination for librarian. She told him I was, but the examination would not be given until June.

He replied, "I'm reading my morning paper and today is the last day to file for the examination." I hurried down and secured an application blank and filled it out there in the civil-service office. The examination was always given in May, so they lied to me.

Some parts of the examination were easy for me, while others were not. When I received a notice to report for my oral examination, I knew I had passed the written. After the oral examination, I didn't hear from the civil service for several months. In the meantime, Mrs. Mitchell told me to talk to Miss Kennedy, the second assistant city librarian, about summer work as a substitute.

The minute I walked into Miss Kennedy's office, she said, "We see you have taken the civil-service examination," and told me that they had to appoint the 26 graduates of their library school first.

I replied, "I understood this was a city civil-service examination and I expect to be appointed where I appear on the list." She countered by asking me why I did not go South to do some pioneer work for my people. I answered, "If I wanted to do some pioneer work for my people, I would need some experience first. I can think of no better place to get it than right here at home."

Then she asked me what I would do in the event my grade was not high enough for one of the available 18 vacancies. When I indicated that I would return to Berkeley to earn my master of arts degree in library science, she immediately sent me out to do substitute work. No one in the entire public library, including the city librarian, had a master's degree at that time.

On October 1 I received a permanent appointment as assistant to the branch librarian at the Robert Louis Stevenson branch. It served a largely middle-class white "Anglo" population and a small pocket of Mexicans in a section near the city limits. Among our best patrons were a retired physician and his wife and a young Episcopal priest. These three and several others would not let anyone but me wait on them.

After only two years at the Stevenson branch, I was transferred to the Helen Hunt Jackson branch as librarian in charge. Before I actually moved there, a committee of Negroes visited the city librarian to criticize me, saying I was too "high hat" and would not be a good person for the position. Nevertheless, I had a good relationship with my library patrons, both black and white, and that branch had the largest circulation in its history during my five years of service there.

I organized a library book club, and at the first meeting the crowd was so large it overflowed from the auditorium into the children's room. The two prominent citizens who reviewed books that evening were vigorously applauded. Mr. Perry, the city librarian, heard about it and wrote me a letter complimenting me on its success and asked for an invitation to the next meeting.

Late in 1933 the Vernon branch librarian became seriously ill and died. Dr. John Diaz, a Negro doctor, went to the assistant city librarian and told her I should be appointed branch librarian there. The Board of Library Commissioners approved my appointment, and several others, effective October 1, 1934.

My first day as a branch librarian, I received many flowers and telegrams from friends and former colleagues, even though others who were members of my sorority and supposedly friends didn't even congratulate me. I plunged into my work with great enthusiasm.

Monthly meetings of the Vernon Library Book Club began in October. In May 1935 a little-theater group was organized for young people. African masks made by Beulah Woodard, one of our patrons, were exhibited. During the years that followed, both black and white artists exhibited their work at the Vernon branch.

Due to growing interest in the Negro and race relations, I made a special effort to build up the library's collection on Negro history and literature from my personal file of newspaper and magazine clippings along with materials solicited from others. Former staff members told me they were proud of the knowledge they had acquired on Negro history at Vernon. This experience taught me that many right-thinking white people who have had no contact with Negroes are not aware of the immensity of their problems with our democracy.

Wishing a change of scenery, in 1940 I arranged for a six-month leave of absence to work in the New York Public Library. It was an exciting and rewarding six months. What a letdown to learn when I returned home that the 1940–41 budget for the Los Angeles Public Library had been cut drastically, cutting schedules to three days a week at certain branches and involving wholesale transfers and some layoffs. Due to a misunderstanding about my leave of absence, I was on the layoff list. Only because of advice from our library representative on the Los Angeles Employee Association and persistence on my part was I able to preserve my civil-service status and my job.

In the spring of 1944 the library administrators decided that all branch librarians who had been in one branch ten years or more had to be transferred to prevent them from getting into a rut. When I asked the assistant city librarian why I had not been contacted about a transfer, she replied, "I guess you'll just have to face it, Miss Matthews."

"Face what?" "Color," she responded. I told her I did not think there was anything to face, since I had the same education, spoke the same language, and therefore could work in one part of the city as well as another.

She repeated our conversation to the city librarian, who came out to the Vernon branch a few days later to see me. She wanted me to know that she was not planning to promote me, no matter how many degrees I acquired. This incident convinced me that the only thing to do was file an official request for a year's leave of absence. My mind was fully made up to specialize in another library field and not return to the Los Angeles Public Library.

Was that when you went to the University of Chicago and studied for a master's degree?

Yes, in 1944. Again, it was suggested that I should prepare to teach in Georgia, "to help bring up the level of the Negro education in the South so they will be ready for integration." I answered, "What about the Kentucky hillbillies? Are they ready? You begin integrating people at the level where they are."

During my oral comprehensive examination in Chicago, conducted by the entire Library School faculty, one of the professors asked me if I objected to *Little Black Sambo,* since he heard it had been criticized by a number of Negroes. I said, "I would not object to it printed in its original form as an East Indian folktale, but certain American publishers have made it look like a caricature of the American Negro." An Irish professor reminded them that the Irish had been a despised minority group, too, when the potato famine in the mid-nineteenth century drove them to our shores. They were the poorest of the poor and had a hard time finding a decent job.

"Library Activities in the Field of Race Relations" was the title of my thesis.[1] It included Negroes, Mexican Americans, Jews, Indians, and all types of Orientals. I sent a questionnaire to 50 libraries throughout the country to secure information on their activities to promote racial and cultural understanding, which included a suggested list of library activities conducive to this end. "Employment of minorities" was one of the items on this list, and my faculty counselor asked me to omit it because it had to do with administration. I told him any type of library program had to do with administration.

"Moreover," I said, "if they can't practice it, they shouldn't preach it."

Before I completed my year at the University of Chicago, I heard from the city librarian in Los Angeles [saying] they would save a branch for me. She had the nerve to make some comments about my work at the old branch and the new neighborhood I would be working in, I suppose thinking it would make me apprehensive.

When I got back I had no problem with the public, as in all the other branches where I had worked. In fact, a number of the patrons said they were glad my predecessor was gone because she was too tired to get off her seat to serve them.

What happened when Harold Hamill became the city librarian in 1947?

Since Mr. Hamill was born and raised in Washington, D.C., where there was segregation, and worked in Baltimore and Kansas City, where there was segregation, I was doubtful about my prospects for promotion under his administration. Shortly after he took over the reins, he held a general staff assembly to get acquainted and announce some of his plans for the library. He said he believed in democracy, but that can mean almost anything.

I started making arrangements [to go to] law school. The day before I was to pay my tuition, I was called for an interview with Mr. Hamill. He told me they had divided the city into six regions [and] said, "Miss Matthews, would you be interested in one of the regional librarian positions?"

I replied, "Yes, indeed," and immediately gave up my plans to attend law school.

A committee of white citizens called on him to say they did not want me to be the new regional librarian because I was a Negro. Mr. Hamill told them I had been appointed because I was qualified. Also that he was not reconsidering my appointment.

You became a librarian at a time when your chances of succeeding were practically nil. What made you go on and how did you handle it?

With rare exceptions, I did not mention to anyone outside the familty circle the discrimination I had suffered until after I retired. Strangely enough, it didn't bother me at all, even though I was not a very aggressive person.

My parents and friends all said, "You won't get a job." Friends who graduated about the same time I did, who planned to teach, waited until the thirties to get a permanent appointment; yet by an odd twist of fate I secured mine just a few months after graduation. This might prove it pays to take a chance.

How were race relations really during World War II?

The war industries brought thousands of people to Los Angeles, particularly from the South. Southern blacks were ready to enjoy the lack of legal segregation in California, while the southern whites resisted conforming to our laws. Although salespeople continued to treat the longtime Negro residents with courtesy and respect, they were often rude to the new arrivals. Some stores did not wish to wait on them at all, until they learned that they could pay cash for fur coats and other luxury items.

It was a long time before Negroes broke into the sales field, unless they were fair enough to pass for white. There was a fair amount of passing, judging by those I knew personally. Some Negroes resented them, and actually exposed them to their employers. Others thought if they had a good job they couldn't get any other way, well, the more power to them.

Your entire family, from photographs I've seen, are very fair-skinned.

Well, you can't always tell by pictures. My mother's and father's family trees are almost identical in terms of the number of Negro, Indian, and white ancestors. They both had a great-grandfather who was full-blooded Indian, they both had a certain amount of either English or Scotch-Irish blood. My mother was brown-skinned, while my father was fair enough to pass for white.

There was a tendency, in certain Negro social circles years ago, to favor those with a light or light-brown skin. Personally, I have not felt my color· was any special advantage or disadvantage. By and large, if you are known to be a Negro, you feel the sting of prejudice no matter what your color. When the library instituted staff ratings, what they were really rating me on was my attitude, you know, in terms of speaking up about race. I could run circles around most of them in terms of the amount of work I put in, and I knew it was of good quality.

How would you characterize your overall experience as a member of the library staff?

It was a very happy experience for me, and I had a whole circle of friends. Many have been guests in my home and I in theirs, even as overnight guests. Miss Helen E. Haines probably influenced my success in the library world more than any other individual. It was in her class on book selection at Berkeley where we first met. Her course was stimulating but difficult.

In 1946, when many people thought Communists were infiltrating government, Miss Haines urged my appointment as chairman of the California Library Association Committee on Intellectual Freedom. The following year, the county board of supervisors ordered all employees to sign a loyalty oath, and next they voted to appoint a committee to approve the books purchased for the county library. Our committee went to work opposing this censorship effort. Representing the California Library Association, I told the supervisors that we believed it was the responsibility of librarians to provide books presenting all points of view. The supervisors suspended their motion.

You are credited with starting the first observance of Negro History Week in Los Angeles. What did that involve?

As a member of the Association for the Study of Negro Life and History, I was impressed with Dr. Carter G. Woodson's campaign, initiated in 1926, for such a celebration. In 1929 I decided to try to stir up some interest here. First I wrote articles for the Negro press. I published reviews of books on the subject and organized library exhibitions of African-American books and pamphlets and also art produced by Negro artists. I gave talks on Negro history and race relations to school classes and community organizations, both black and white, in various parts of the city. Eventually the mayor issued an official proclamation for a citywide observance of Negro History Week. I'm a firm believer that Negro history is not just for blacks but for everyone.

I have been collecting books on the Negro in America for a number of years. After my retirement in 1960, I concentrated on collecting photographs and copies of original documents from pioneer black families.[2] This collecting hobby of mine might be compared to a treasure hunt. I'm delighted when I make a rich find and frustrated when I arrive just a little too late.

Will you tell us about your collection of works by local black artists?

Although I started helping artists in the mid-1930s, the bulk of my art collection has been built up since I retired.

When the Los Angeles Negro Art Association was organized in 1937 to promote local Negro artists, I served on its executive board. The first important function was an exhibition that fall at the Stendahl Art Gallery on Wilshire Boulevard.

Since the work of Negro artists was rarely hung in white galleries, and they had no galleries of their own, 11 black artists banded together in 1950 to open the Associated Artists Gallery. Artists of every race and creed could submit their work. During its short existence, it set an example and left its mark on the artistic community of Los Angeles.

Beulah Woodward, a black sculptor, was the first artist I helped, back in 1935. An exhibition of her work, which I arranged at the Vernon branch library, led to a one-woman show at the Los Angeles County Museum, a first for a black artist. Not only was Beulah Woodward an excellent artist, she was a born leader who gave unselfishly of her time to help Negro artists. She was the director of our interracial gallery, and I was a member of her lay board.

Alice Taylor Gafford was another founder of the gallery and also helped found several art associations. She put away her paintbrushes for the last time shortly after her eighty-ninth birthday in 1975. Her art career began at age 49, after working more than 25 years as a professional nurse. As her sponsor and unpaid agent, I arranged Alice Gafford's first one-woman show in 1941, also many other group and one-woman exhibitions.

I learned a great deal about art from both of these women artists. Today I help black artists primarily by purchasing their art and displaying it in my home, including the hall, kitchen, and service porch. The extras are stored in boxes in the closets and under the beds.

Out of all the things you've done, what do you consider your most important achievement?

I would have to list first of all my leadership in opposing censorship and promoting the cause of intellectual freedom locally and nationally. Secondly, I would mention the research I've done on the history of the Negro in California, which has proven useful to a number of individuals and institutions. And last, I would cite my fight against race prejudice in the Los Angeles Public Library system (and elsewhere), finally achieving recognition as a librarian, not as a black librarian.

I feel this helped make it easier for those who followed. There have been at least a half-dozen black librarians appointed as principal librarians, the grade I held. One, Loyce Pleasants, has been appointed as a division librarian, supervising all the central library departments.

What do you consider the significant influences on your life?

At the top of the list, I would place my parents' training, aid, and support at all levels, particularly my mother's encouragement, which gave me confidence in myself. The church and my religion definitely were stabilizing influences in my life. Going away to college, having to make my own decisions and handle my own finances, helped me to build character and become more independent and resourceful. My choice of a profession probably changed my life a great deal, and without a doubt my travels were a definite broadening influence. I greatly appreciate having learned early in life to stand on my own two feet, to form my own opinions, to stick by my principles, and to speak up for what I thought was right.

5

BYRON RUMFORD

Legislator in the Public Interest

William Byron Rumford (1908–1986), called Byron by his many friends and colleagues, was born in Arizona and sold papers and shined shoes as a boy to help out the family. Later he boxed for the Arizona Athletic Club using the name Young Joe Gans. "I don't give up easily," was the lesson learned in the ring that he carried into a long, successful career as a pharmacist and legislator during years of significant political change.

At a high school teacher's urging, he attended the University of California, becoming, in 1931, possibly the first black person to complete pharmacy training and later the first minority pharmacist at the county hospital. In 1942 he purchased his own pharmacy in Berkeley, which soon became a crucible for his growing interest in public affairs.

During World War II, Rumford worked on committees to ease tensions between local residents and the many defense workers coming in from the South and helped to build black political organizations. In 1948 he was the first black assemblyman elected in Northern California, serving until 1966.

He was a leader in epic struggles for legislation in civil rights and environmental protection and in encouraging young African Americans to become active in politics. While in the legislature, he continued his own studies, receiving a bachelor's degree in political science in 1949 and a master's degree in public administration in 1959. In the 1970s he was appointed assistant director of education for the Federal Trade Commission Bureau of Consumer Protection.

Mine was a broken home, you know. My mother's maiden name was Margaret Lee Johnson; my father was Chauncey G. Rumford. My mother was married again, to Elmer J. Williams.

This chapter was adapted from William Byron Rumford, *Legislator for Fair Employment, Fair Housing, and Public Health,* 1970 and 1971 interviews with Joyce A. Henderson and Amelia Fry (Berkeley: Regional Oral History Office, University of California, 1973).

My father's family moved to Los Angeles from Colorado Springs around 1910. They were originally from Iowa. My father's aunt, Eva Carter Bruckner, wrote a lot of poetry and did a lot of painting. She was a close friend of Delilah Beasley, who wrote *Negro Trail Blazers of California*[1] in 1916.

I was born in the little mining town of Courtland, Arizona, on February 2, 1908. My mother and grandmother, Louise Alice Johnson, came up through Texas and New Mexico up to Arizona in 1907 when it wasn't even a state and you had to be tough to survive. They tell me Grandmother ran a boardinghouse in Tombstone and later moved to Tucson. Then there began an influx of Negroes, and the whites established segregated schools. My grandmother said she was not going to bring those kids up in a segregated environment, and she moved to Los Angeles. My mother and brother and I stayed because my mother had a job doing housework and didn't want to go to Los Angeles.

But then my dad and mother were separated, and my dad [went] to live with his mother in Los Angeles. My older brother, Chauncey, went to live with them. Later on, my mother and I moved to Phoenix, where she married Elmer J. Williams, who was a barber. In the early days the barbers were an exclusive group of people. They were the only professionals we had outside of preachers and a few doctors. We had five or six barbershops in Phoenix with 10 or 12 Negro barbers catering to whites. They were all making money. In 1915 we came over and established residence in Los Angeles.

My stepdad didn't like the barber business as it was practiced in Los Angeles because here he had to work on Negroes and they didn't tip. So he said, "We're going back to Phoenix." And we did, and, of course, they developed a family of their own. At 10 and 12 years old, my brother and I were selling papers, delivering papers, doing everything under the sun to make extra money, because we were an extremely poor family.

I finished high school in Phoenix in 1926. We had a segregated high school with four teachers who were very influential on our lives; they were very close to us. One of them was Ellis Knox, who later got his Ph.D. from the University of Southern California and became a professor of history at Howard University. He had graduated from the University of California and he was one of the main reasons I went to Cal. I had no idea of ever going to college before I met him.

I was 18 years old, and I arrived in San Francisco with nothing but a suitcase and a desire to go to school. I got a room in a crummy old hotel near the railroad station to save money. I worked a year on the railroads in Oakland, and then the guys I worked with said, "Why don't you go to Sacramento Junior College with us; you'll save money." I did that for a year and then came to Cal. Dr. Kimbrough, who became a dentist in San Diego, and Joe T. Gier, who later taught electrical engineering at UCLA, and John

Coleman, now a doctor in Los Angeles, and I all attended Sacramento JC and Cal.

My last year in high school, I'd gotten a job, $5 a week, filling bottles and working in a drugstore in Phoenix, so I was thinking of going into pharmacy. I was accepted into the UC School of Pharmacy in San Francisco, and one of the fellows in Sacramento was going there, too, and got me a job parking cars at night at a club in North Beach. I made good money working on the door and parking cars and paid my way through school. I didn't get all A's in my classes, but I was satisfied to get through.

I graduated in 1931 and took any number of examinations for state employment and passed. Not too many blacks worked for the state at the time; you were lucky to get a job as a janitor. I think I frightened everybody when I went for my oral examinations. They were asking silly questions about Joe Louis that had nothing to do with the position, and I flunked. They were really trying to get rid of blacks, and we had no recourse.

Eventually I took an examination with the county and went to work at Highland Hospital in Oakland. They just sent me a notice to go out to Highland as an assistant pharmacist. Dr. Benjamin Black, who was director of the hospital, was an old army physician and was supposedly a very prejudiced person. He looked at me and said, "You'd cause trouble." I told him, "I've never caused trouble with anybody in my life." He said, "Well, we'll give you a chance."

I said, "Well, thank you." I needed the job, you know; it was during the depression. I stayed at Highland approximately eight years and then I quit and started back to school. I was unhappy with the job; it was routine.

How did you happen to get hired by the hospital when no black person had been hired before you?

I guess I've always been a barrier breaker, in a sense. I've been a very persistent kind of a guy all my life. I just carried through on things that I had to overcome. It was like getting accustomed to going down the track or hurdling; it's just another hurdle. In this case all I wanted was a chance to go to work and do a job. Dr. Black did give me a chance and we never had any trouble. As far as I know, nobody else who was black was hired in a professional capacity while I was there.[2]

Frankly, I had friends on the county board of supervisors, too, but I didn't ask them for help until after I began working there. The salary was very low and I attempted to get it raised. One of them was Tom Caldecott, whose father had a drugstore at Ashby and Adeline streets [Tom was later an assemblyman and a judge], and we were good friends. Harry Bartell, who was chairman of the board of supervisors, was also a friend of mine, and he went to bat for me to get a raise a couple of times.

They finally raised the salary during the war. People were making more money in the shipyards than I was making! So I left. The odd thing was that when I told Dr. Black I was leaving, he didn't want me to leave.

About a year after I left Highland I had a chance to buy this drugstore in Berkeley, where I had worked when I first graduated from pharmacy school. The man who ran it was drafted, and his mother took over the business, but she didn't want it. So I was at the pharmacy from 1942 on.

What kind of service did you do in World War II?

About 1944 Governor Earl Warren appointed me to the rent-control board for the East Bay. That was part of a federal program to keep rents and prices from going sky-high when things were scarce during wartime. We heard appeals from people who thought they weren't getting enough return on their property and people who thought their rents were too high.

I was also an inspector for the state venereal disease control program, assigned to the Oakland Health Department. We had to deal with army camps and persons who were carriers. I worked with the military and with the city clinics. We'd go out and bring in people who were scheduled for treatment, if they didn't show up for an appointment. We did a good job of cleaning it up; I have to pat myself on the back.

Were you able to do anything then about improving housing opportunities for black people?

Frankly, during that period, because of the influx of people from the South, we had an exaggerated social problem. We organized the Berkeley Interracial Committee, which had 400 or 500 members. They did a lot of good work to welcome people and to ameliorate some of the problems. Signs appeared saying "No Negro Trade Solicited," and we urged that they be taken down. Whatever the problems that arose, we'd try to iron them out.

There also began to develop statewide organizations with which we were affiliated, like the Committee for Fair Play, which tried to do something about the Japanese evacuation during the war. They were very effective, too, in trying to bring about a smoother acclimation, I guess you'd call it, for those from the South who were moving to the West during the war. This was quite a transition, you know. Many people had opted to make money from wartime conditions, and many of them weren't particular about how they did it. Some people lived two to a room with a sort of "hot bed" arrangement; one worked in the night and one worked in the day.

Some of the "more stable citizens" were a little unhappy with the newcomers. People were just fearful of this great influx of blacks. We had incidents on the bus and on the trains going back and forth to the shipyards in Richmond—shoving, pushing, fighting, and things of that nature. You see, not only did you have the blacks, you had white southerners moving out here—the Okies. There was always some kind of incident in line to get your paycheck, that type of thing. It would spill over into the bars and restaurants in Berkeley. The Interracial Committee functioned wherever they [were] needed to make things easier for the newcomers. The real basic problem was finding places for these people to live and making them feel welcome. As an offshoot, they had the interracial church, the South Berkeley Community Church.

Why did you decide to run for the state assembly in 1948?

I had always been interested in politics, even as a young adolescent when I was delivering newspapers. In Berkeley I got involved in the Appomattox Club, perhaps one of the first Negro political organizations in the Bay Area. At that time it was not considered possible to get a black candidate elected, so we supported candidates we thought were right on our particular issues. We worked for Franklin Roosevelt.

Out of that grew an effort to elect a black city councilman in Berkeley. I think it was Tom Berkley who ran first early in the forties, then Mrs. Frances Albrier ran. Out of these efforts grew a desire to elect somebody to the state legislature. So, in 1948, I sponsored Berkley as the person to run for the assembly. A general meeting was called. The CIO [Congress of Industrial Organizations] left-wing labor unions were very strong then in politics in this area, and they were attempting to say who would run in the black area—as they do now. So we met with them and we met with the ministers to talk about selecting candidates for the 17th Assembly District.

Mr. Berkley decided that he didn't want to run, but several other people were anxious to run. So they asked me if I wanted to run. They told me the CIO wouldn't support me, so I said, "Well, maybe I am interested in running." I'd always felt our problems related to the established government, and I just was not concerned with their interest in fighting world problems.

So the leadership scheduled a caucus to be held by the Negro community to select a candidate. The rules were whoever wanted to run would let the chairman know and have two people there to speak for him. Then the candidates were to speak for so many minutes. Well, it was just a question of getting your friends out there at the caucus.

I can't ever forget—there were about four people who expressed their desire to have people speak for them, and here was Tom Berkley, who I had taken down for the purpose of having him endorsed, and that night he spoke for someone else! It didn't go over too well with people who knew about it. So we had a vote, and I won. I was selected to be the candidate.

Some people were very upset about the results, but we went on and won the community support and, by and large, the backing of the Ministerial Alliance, which gave us the real support. The ministers have been a powerful group in the community life of blacks since slavery and still are.

The primary election was so close that we went to court because of some precincts where the votes didn't show up. We had a recount in Judge Hoyt's court. The recount showed that we were pulling up in areas that the other side hadn't suspected, so they gave up. I won the general election by some 30,000 votes.

At that time we were striving for fair employment, and we were fighting for abolition of discrimination in the National Guard and in the hiring of teachers. Taxes were always an issue; they always will be. You see, the black people had little representation in Sacramento prior to Gus Hawkins of Los Angeles, who'd already been in the assembly some years when I got elected. He was carrying these bills before I arrived and suffered just one defeat after another.

Of course, coming from Alameda County, Governor Earl Warren knew something about me, even though he was a Republican and I was a Democrat, and when I went to Sacramento he knew the things I was interested in. In the legislature we took a position on Warren's health bills, and he was a help to me too. He was a great guy—there's so much difference in that courthouse now than when he was there. I just don't have any confidence in that outfit at all!

One of the first things I did was the bill to abolish discrimination in the National Guard. Warren encouraged me to press for this, and he assured me that if it got to his desk he'd sign it. That was a great thing for a freshman assemblyman, because they had been trying for years to get it through. A couple of years later, he personally suggested to me that he wanted to see the fair-employment practices bill passed.

In 1953 I invited him to address the national meeting of my fraternity, Alpha Phi Alpha, which was meeting in Berkeley. It rained every day—I'm telling you, it rained in sheets—and Warren had had an operation, and he got up out of that sickbed and came to that convention in all that rain.

How did you muster support for the National Guard antidiscrimination bill?

Well, it was quite an experience that first time. I went to the committee meeting, it was at night, and I sat and sat and nobody showed. Then I went around and talked to fellows on the committee and explained how important this was. I finally got them to meet and got the bill out of the assembly. They thought the senate was going to kill it anyway.

There wasn't one person at the senate committee meeting and I thought, what kind of government is this? I had to convince this [chairman] who was from an old Sacramento family and ran things as if he owned the place. I told him I thought it was time we changed our attitudes if we were asking people to give their lives.

"I don't know," he said in this gravelly voice. "You can't get people together ummm (he meant in the army). But I'll talk to some of the fellows; maybe we can get somewhere." And he told me to come see him in his office. So I went to see him.

"Aaah," he said. "I think we can help you. Send your bill up on such-and-such a day. No discussion. We're going to vote it out." So I did and went up to the meeting. And that gravelly voice said, "Here's bill such-and-such and so-and-so-and-so-on, and you have it. The bill is out." Just like that.

A fair-employment practices bill was introduced for the first time in 1945. Gus Hawkins handled it first, and later we took turns. It finally got through in 1959, after the Democratic party had it in their state platform. Before then a lot of legislators, particularly senators in the rural areas, didn't have any black constituents. I talked to labor leaders asking for their support for an FEPC bill, and they had a weak-kneed approach. They'd get up and say they were for it, you know, but some of them in the background, I think, were working against it. Particularly when there is a scarcity of jobs, you're likely to find labor shying away from supporting anything that dilutes jobs for their membership.

Who did help you get fair-employment legislation passed?

We had some help from the statewide committee for fair-employment practices, the NAACP, and the Jewish Labor League. We probably had a minister or two, a Mexican American, a Japanese American. Bill Becker gave a lot of time to it and also helped me with other legislation. I think he was with the Council for Civic Unity; later he was with Pat Brown in the governor's office. They'd send people in to talk to legislators in their offices, and a change in opinion began to take place. The party was putting pressure on some Democrats to vote for it even though it wasn't a popular issue in their districts. And in some other districts Republicans voted for it because they thought it was basically and morally right. We had a lot of good men who were white in the legislature helping us.

When we got the Fair Employment Practices Act passed, the whole job picture changed completely! You would see clerks in stores, clerks filling prescriptions. Before then, we couldn't get a black person hired as clerk in a department store. And there was a time a black person couldn't get a job in a service station. Now nobody thinks anything of their color. The question is, have they had the training?

It's hard to say whether fair employment or fair housing was more important. What comes first, a job or a house? If a man can't get a job, he can't get a house. There had been a legislative study that indicated there was widespread discrimination in housing throughout California. And housing acts had been passed in a dozen or so states. So there was a need for legislation to prevent discrimination in housing here.

In 1959 there was a bill covering public-assisted housing by Gus Hawkins, and there was some fight about that, and another bill by Jess Unruh to broaden the existing civil rights law to include all business, including real estate. Then in 1963 we in effect combined Hawkins's bill and Unruh's into AB 1240 and gave it administrative enforcement procedures. Originally, we had included single-family homes, but those provisions were removed in order to meet some people's objections.

Senator Luther Gibson held AB 1240 in committee for three months while we sent amendments back and forth. Finally, on the last day of the session, Senator Joe Rattigan moved that the bill be set as a special order of business for eleven o'clock, which meant the bill had to be voted on then, even though it upset the agenda and some of the legislators. The vote was finally taken around 11:30, and we got 24 votes to 16 against.

The bill then had to go back to the assembly for concurrence with the senate amendments. Unruh, who by then was speaker of the assembly, indicated there would be no legislation passed until that bill was dealt with. So we did take it up, and there was little debate, except that the opposition said that an initiative would follow if this bill was passed, and the initiative, of course, did follow. But then the final vote was taken, and there was tremendous applause from the assemblymen.

The California Real Estate Association, the Apartment House Owners Association, the [state] Chamber of Commerce, and other business organizations made California the battleground for a national showdown on housing legislation. In that initiative they were trying to establish in the constitution a basic concept that would give them the right to discriminate—the right to sell or to deal with whomever they desired as far as the use or sale of property is concerned. That was Proposition 14 in the November 1964 election, and it became a highly inflammatory issue dealing with blacks and whites.

Some say that housing is one commodity that doesn't obey the law of supply and demand. What had happened is that more and more in the West and in the North, you had segregated patterns—persons of minority and other cultural groups have been isolated and separated. Largely in the black areas it is by design, and it has created an intolerable situation where there is a limited amount of space, congested areas, highly conducive to crime and all the things that reduce the effectiveness of society. The consequence is a natural tendency to break out of these areas, on the American principle that an individual can go as far as his ability and economic condition will allow him. That's been the basis of much of our housing fight. It isn't that we want to live next door to a Caucasian; it's that we're interested in the neighborhood and, of course, the neighborhood is composed of people, who may be black or white.

Now the proposition was fought in every corner, every little nook in California. Some outstanding newspapers were in opposition to it; the state labor federation came out against it; churches and prominent citizens came out against it. And yet when the vote was taken, Proposition 14 passed almost 2 to 1. It was a sad day in California, but the propaganda that was used was, in effect, that the blacks were coming from all over the nation to occupy homes in California. The whole campaign was built on fear and racism. There were even those who expressed themselves as being liberals who felt this proposition was necessary in order to protect their homes. And because of the confusing way the proposition was written, many people voted "yes" thinking they were voting for fair housing.

Numerous cases were filed in opposition to the vote, and in May 1967 the U.S. Supreme Court upheld the California Supreme Court in declaring Proposition 14 unconstitutional. Therefore, the Rumford Fair Housing Act is still on the books.

You were also chairman of the assembly's Public Health Committee from 1953 through 1966. That involved you in some of the first air pollution control legislation.

Actually, I wrote my master's thesis at Cal on air pollution. We developed the first regional air pollution control law in 1955. The irony of the whole approach to the solution of smog was that we were trying to legislate against the forces of nature. You couldn't pass a law to prevent pollution without passing laws to eliminate the source, but at the time nobody knew what was causing it.

There were several theories. The petroleum industry was so sensitive to the charge that they set about trying to recapture the sulfur that was thrown off in the air. A Los Angeles county supervisor came to Sacramento and demanded that we pass a law to get rid of smog. That was ridiculous! We made trips to Detroit to talk to the automotive industry and they were very reluctant to accept the theory developed at Cal Tech about unsaturated hydrocarbons until they'd done some research of their own.

At first we couldn't get to first base with legislation. It was too technical, and it wasn't affecting people anywhere but Los Angeles. The federal government wouldn't even talk to us about smog. The people in California paid a tremendous price in taxes for the research that is now accepted throughout the world that the source of smog is the exhaust of the automobile. We were able to convince the automobile industry that the problem was of such a serious nature that they should send their technicians to appear before the California legislature, and they did.

65

Tom Rees, who was in the assembly and later in Congress, had the most drastic solution—he said he'd introduce a bill to abolish the use of automobiles if something wasn't done by the manufacturers! There was also talk of improving public transportation to get people out of their cars. We made a trip to Germany to look at systems there.

And we did studies on radiation control because there was growing interest in the consequences of the use and misuse of X-ray machines. We put in a lot of control measures and standards, which were important. Aside from that, we were in a period when the federal government said the states could now take over peacetime uses of atomic energy.

This meant that we had to set standards for the uses of isotopes, disposal of wastes, and that type of thing.

Later on, our investigations found that there was a large contamination of DDT pesticide in milk supplies. We were so far ahead of other parts of the country that it was unbelievable! When I got to Washington, I found people were talking about things we'd studied 10 years ago!

I'd like to ask about your 1966 campaign for the state senate.

I'll try not to be biased on this one. I might say that I had always a deep respect for the law. I believe strongly that there was wrongdoing at the courthouse, and officials shaded their eyes to it. I've never felt that one should stay in office forever; you must change with the time.

When the legislature was reapportioned [in 1966], Alameda was given another seat in the senate. Rather than divide the county into two seats, those doing the reapportioning saw fit to have two seats at large—largely, I believe, because they were fearful that some black might be elected from a portion of the county.

I filed in the Democratic primary for one of the seats, and so did several other people. I defeated all of the candidates by more than 30,000 votes. There was very little campaigning on the part of the Republican opposition in the general election, and we were feeling that we had an excellent chance of winning the race.

On the night of the election the county registrar of voters office was using for the first time a new computerized vote reporting system. We were down at the courthouse where we always went to get the returns, and a reporter came to me and said, "There are some 10,000 votes in the back that have not been counted."

I was incredulous, and I went to the registrar and said, "What is the reason?" He said they wouldn't go through the machine for some reason; they'd probably count them the next day. Then they announced that all the returns were in and I was behind by 600 votes. The next morning a group of us went back to the courthouse to see what we could find out. We only

Elizabeth and Walter Gordon in 1955. *Photo by E. F. Joseph.*

Ida Louise Jackson as
a student at Columbia
University Teachers
College in 1935.

Tarea Hall Pittman in May 1973.

Miriam Matthews in 1984.
Photo by Judith Sedwick.
Reproduced with permission
from Women of Courage,
Black Women Oral History
Project *(Boston: Schlesinger*
Library, Radcliffe College, 1984).

Byron Rumford
in June 1966.

Archie Williams, holding his Olympic medal, in 1993.

Lionel Wilson in 1975.

Marvin Poston in 1982. *Photo by Janet Fries; courtesy* California Monthly.

Lloyd Ferguson
in 1984.

Ivan Houston in 1989.

Emmett Rice in
June 1984.

Allen Broussard in 1990.
Photo by Paul Latoures.

Charles Patterson in 1992.

saw a few damaged ballots, never anything like the 10,000 that the registrar had agreed were missing. We did do a sampling of ballots as the law allows. We pulled out 10 precincts at random and counted the votes to compare with the statistics he had. In each precinct we picked up from 20 to 50 votes—we'd increased our tally by over 300 votes in the 10 precincts.

Since we were supposedly only 600 votes behind we said we had no choice but to have a recount. In that process we came across a lot of strange things. The girls counting the ballots noticed that some of the ballots had never been folded as they're supposed to be when they're put in the ballot box, and there were write-in votes for Bob Scheer against Jeff Cohelan for Congress that looked as if they were done in the same handwriting.

The figures of the number of ballots returned and the vote tally didn't correlate at all; they were off by several thousand. One person I talked to who worked on a computer that night told us that five precincts did not report in the night of the election. No matter who I talked to about it, no one wanted to follow it up. I brought this to the attention of the grand jury, too, and they wouldn't take it up.

I did go on the grand jury myself in 1970, and we began to make inquiries as to the election practices. Our study showed a very inefficient system and no attempt to correct it. The irony of the whole thing is that the people who let this kind of election irregularity continue are doing more to destroy our political system than the kids who were out in the streets demonstrating at that same period, who the officials were very upset about. I believe that for better government in Alameda County they should all resign.

The Trailblazers, 1932–1948

6

ARCHIE WILLIAMS

The Joy of Flying: Olympic Runner and Air Force Colonel

Born in Oakland, California, in 1915, Archie Williams began setting track records in high school. He starred in meets at the University of California at Berkeley and won a gold medal in the 1936 Olympics. He graduated with a degree in engineering and a pilot's license. He was a career officer in the U.S. Air Force from 1943 to 1966 and went on to a second career as a high school math teacher and coach in Marin County, California, where he died in 1993. He and his wife, Vesta, operated a private flying service for many years. He was one of the first athletes named to the California Sports Hall of Fame.

My grandfather was in the Spanish-American War, so my mother was an army brat. He was stationed at the Presidio of San Francisco, and when he got out of the army they moved to Oakland. That's where my mom met my dad. He'd come from Chicago and had a grocery store downtown and also was in real estate.

My grandmother had a day nursery in Oakland, the Fannie Wall Children's Home, like a child-care center. Some of the kids were orphans or from broken homes. The women's clubs all helped run it, and Fannie would go around to these different organizations and ask for money to run the home. They'd give services, too, and help fix the place up.

They got a lot of good help from the community. For instance, the Athens Athletic Club, which was an upper-class businessmen's sports club, would donate a lot of food. A lot of guys I knew worked there as waiters. My grandmother liked to rattle the cages of some of the politicians to get them to help out.

She knew what was right and wrong, and she let you know. So did my grandfather and, in those days, any older person. If you got a spanking in

This chapter was adapted from Archie F. Williams, *The Joy of Flying, Olympic Gold, Air Force Colonel, and Teacher,* 1992 interview with Gabrielle Morris (Berkeley: Regional Oral History Office, University of California, 1993).

school, they heard about it at home, and you got another spanking there. Your mom spanked you, your aunties spanked you. They didn't have much trouble from the kids at all.

Family values meant a lot. If we kids got any jobs—I cut lawns, shined shoes, sold papers—"Here, Mom. Here's the money." If we needed shoes or show money or candy money, we got what we needed. Everybody pitched in and helped. That was during the depression in the late twenties, early thirties. Nobody had anything. You ate a lot of beans, but I never missed a meal, and I never went to school with holes in my shoes.

In north Oakland where I lived there weren't too many black families. There were no black kids in my class in school. All of my friends were white, except for a Japanese kid who lived near us. Most of the Japanese kids I went to high school with went to relocation camps during World War II. They were as American as I was; that was a dirty deal.

I knew I was black but I was never reminded of it. We were friends, we would go to each other's house, eat supper at each other's house. I had a few fights—all the kids had fights. Once, some of my friends took me down to a Boy Scout troop, and the guy told me I couldn't be one.

"OK," I said. "It doesn't matter." I knew there were things like that going on. I didn't like it, but that was the way it was.

When did you get interested in sports?

As a kid, we all played sandlot ball. Sometimes there would be a little track meet. I lived about two blocks from Bushrod Park. We would go there and race around the track just for fun. Sometimes we would go there and watch the big guys at a track meet. You'd see it and say, "I want to try that."

Later on, in junior high, sometimes we went against different schools. But we didn't have uniforms. We would just go out and have fun. Then I went to University High, and that's where I got interested in track. I didn't do too well on the relay team, but I ran the quarter mile—this was in 1933— and for that date, I had the best time.

I kind of fooled around in high school. I didn't have very good grades. A year or so out of high school, a friend of mine named Harry Osborne and I were caddying at a golf course, not making any money, just goofing off. He said, "Let's go back to school. Let's go down to San Mateo Junior College and check it out. It won't cost anything."

I decided it was something I wanted to do. In other words I'm bettering myself, not sitting around the house getting into trouble. So we signed up and found a lady down there who would let us stay in this little building in her backyard. For $5 a week, she gave us a place to sleep and breakfast.

I said to Harry, "What the heck are you going to be?" He said, "I'm going to be a dentist." I said, "I'm going to be an engineer." I started taking courses

I hadn't taken in high school, trigonometry and analytical gometry, and got A's. I took physics, surveying, stuff I never even heard of.

I said, "This little stuff is nothing." I told the counselor I wanted to go to Cal, and he said these were the courses you would take as a freshman there. What I was doing was getting the same credit as I would get at Cal, and the classes were smaller.

I decided I was going to get my butt into gear and started getting the grades. You were supposed to do two years at junior college and then go to the university as a junior. But I wanted to get in as a sophomore, so I did enough courses and was able to transfer.

I knew some guys who had gone there, so I knew all about the athletics. I used to sneak up there and climb under the fence and watch the guys run. Brutus Hamilton, the track coach who influenced my whole life, didn't even know I was there. I was just another guy who wanted to go to Cal. Later on, I went out for track, but I didn't go there for that. I wanted to get that degree. Nobody recruited me, and I didn't care because I was going to play in the physics lab. I did OK in my courses. I was satisfied with my progress. You have to keep your grades up to be in sports, and I was never in jeopardy. Brutus as a coach knew every guy on the team, and he knew everybody's grades.

When I signed up, the counselor said, "What do you want to be?" I said, "I want to be a mechanical engineer." "Why don't you be a preacher or real estate man. You ain't going to get a job as an engineer." "Sign me up for that, will you please," I said. When I was a senior, I went back to the same counselor, and he said, "I'll get you interviews with General Motors, Lockheed, and companies like that, and they'll tell you the same thing."

But that was what I wanted to do because I was fascinated with airplanes. I was an airplane nut. Another thing in the back of my mind—one summer I worked for the water company cutting weeds. I liked working there where the water came in from the Sierra Nevada. I thought, they hire engineers; this would be a nice company to work with. I talked to the personnel guy, but he gave me the same arguments the counselor had. In those days there weren't any Negro engineers, except for one black guy who was a year ahead of me at Cal.

The main thing I can say about Cal is that there wasn't any big push to help you find a job. They didn't have any placement program to help, not blacks, not anybody.

But you didn't have any trouble getting into Cal or taking the courses you wanted?

Oh, no. There were probably 30 or 40 black kids going to Cal in 1936. Maybe more. I knew them all. I knew some who weren't black. They passed.

In fact, the whole time I was in college there were certain sports that didn't play black athletes. You never heard of a black player in the Pacific Coast Conference. The first one was Jackie Robinson, who played football for UCLA in the late thirties. USC would recruit black athletes, and they wouldn't play them. I was told they did that so the guy wouldn't go to UCLA or Cal, where they would have to play against them.

I have heard that the Cal baseball coach then was not happy about having black players on his team.

Probably not. The basketball coach was probably the same way. Brutus Hamilton was an exception. The rest of them had a gentlemen's agreement: "We won't play no jungle bunnies."

In fact, the basketball coach had a black player he didn't know about, a guy named Thurston Davis, a star player on the team. He was a real light-skinned guy, with kinky yellow hair. All of us knew about it, and we never said anything. "We don't care. Let him get away with it. We've got a good joke going." He didn't know we knew.

That's the way it was. I'm not bitter, because the main thing was I got in. I saw that Campanile tower on the campus from my house and I wanted to go to that damned school. I made it, and I got my degree.

I never would have gotten into Cal if I hadn't taken those courses in junior college. If I had taken them at Cal, I would be competing against a bunch of high school hotshots and I would have been out of my league scholastically. And junior college is where I got a chance to run. We would compete against the Cal and Stanford freshmen. You had an idea how to rate yourself. How well you would do against those guys would tell you how well you would do later on.

When you transferred to Cal, somebody decided pretty quickly that you were good enough to run in the Olympics.

That's what they call the baptism of fire. I started Cal in the fall of 1935, and in the spring of 1936 I started competing with the tough guys in the regular meets every week.

The first real big racing I did was at the Long Beach Relays before the season started. We got in there and kicked their butt. I was the anchorman, and we beat USC and Stanford. That was the first thing that convinced me I could do it. Then at the biggest meet of the college season, what's now called the PAC 10, I won the 440 [yard race]. Then we went back to Chicago for the nationals, and I made the record.

In those days anybody who was doing pretty good: "Hey, man, this guy is Olympic material." But Brutus never kidded you about what you were doing. He never even bragged about you. He was the take-it-easy kind of guy. He was an Olympic athlete himself, second in the decathalon in 1920.

After the NCAA, there was a qualifying meet in Milwaukee. Then the Olympic finals were in New York City in July. It was hot, and it poured; I lost 10 pounds working out. I didn't get too excited like some of the guys. I was nervous like I always was, but it was just something I had to do. So I got in the race and ran.

Brutus used to tell me, "Every race you run is a final. If you don't win, then it is the final for you." The main thing is you run faster than they do, don't fall down, and don't run out of gas. A lot of my friends didn't make it. I really felt sorry for the ones who pulled a muscle or tripped or didn't do as well as they had before the trials. What I'm saying is that I beat everybody who showed up for the race.

In those days we didn't have very much money—no corporate sponsors and stuff like that. But they put us up in hotels and handed out the uniform. We had a blue coat with a shield on it and a straw hat and a pair of powder-white shoes. We looked like some school glee club.

The Olympic Committee put all the black athletes together in the same stateroom on the boat to Europe, all together in the Olympic village once we got to Berlin, as if they wanted to make sure we didn't mix with the other guys. In fact, I didn't have as much in common with some of these kids as with the white kids I went to college with. It didn't mean anything to me one way or another, but I did feel there was a lot of racial prejudice, a feeling that they looked at us as different.

Were any of you concerned about the fact that Hitler and the Nazis were in control of the government and reportedly didn't want black people there?

No. That was something that makes for good newspaper copy.

Speaking for the black athletes, the Germans treated us probably better than anybody else. They all wanted to talk to us. They wanted autographs. They wanted to take you to their homes, take you for a ride in their car. Their athletes were the same way. They were just a bunch of young college guys. That's what the Olympics were all about. We were all friends.

There were nine black guys that year on the American team. And we won more medals than the rest of the team. Jesse Owens won four, and there was only one guy who didn't get a medal.

We only got there five days before our races. There was not much you could do to work out on the boat, so we had to start training all over again. It was kind of tough because for my particular race, we had just one preliminary, say ten o'clock in the morning. The next preliminary, two o'clock in the afternoon the same day. Then the next day you run the semis at 3:30 and the final at five o'clock, with just an hour and a half between. So within a 24-hour period we ran four helluva races.

Sometimes after workout we would go down and watch the rest of the events. I wanted to see it all. Being there was like dreaming you were in something you'd thought about doing. Is this me? When it was over, and I came back here, I'd think, Did I really do that?

One year I was nothing; the next year I was in the Olympics. I didn't start thinking about the Olympics seriously until the year before. You're working up from the local meets and then the regional meets, the PAC 10, this kind of stuff. The Olympics is at the end of it. Every time you compete, you say, "If I do good this time, maybe I have a chance for the next step."

I admired and knew the history of the Olympics and all the guys who were in it in 1932. I knew who the best runners were and I'd say, "You'll have to beat this guy; you'll have to beat that guy."

The day of the race, Brutus said, "Just go in and do it like you've always been doing it." You could make up this big yarn about what goes through your mind. You're scared as hell. Running the 440, it's over with just like that. You don't have time to think, and you're trying not to get left behind.

Being up on the winners' platform is kind of weird. You've seen everybody else going through it. Now, here I am, that kind of stuff. You see your name up on the board; it was a great feeling. The head of the Olympic Committee hands you the medal—some French guy who wanted to kiss you. Get out of here! [*laughs*] They give you the medal and a scroll. It's sort of like graduating.

Afterwards we went on an exhibition tour around Europe, running against local kids for almost a month. When I got back to California, they took my picture at the university. In Oakland there was a parade, and I got a ride on a fire engine, got the keys to the city from the mayor and a gold watch.

While you were at Cal, you were on the board of the campus YMCA.

That was nice. It was the only thing they had going at Cal as far as interracial stuff. I never felt real heavy pressure about race there, but I did resent being excluded from jobs. For instance, they had a student branch of the mechanical engineering society. I wasn't eligible for that. I was discouraged because I felt that as an engineering student I should be entitled to belong.

I wanted to go into aeronautical engineering. In fact, I learned how to fly while I was at Cal. The federal government had started the student Civilian Pilot Training Program, I guess in 1939. I was told that I wasn't eligible, but Brutus went to bat for me to get in.

I was in the army ROTC, too, but it was a joke. It was something you had to do. We were just marching up and down in a field. You would just get a pair of khaki pants and an old, beat-up M-1 rifle.

How about social life as a student?

I joined the Alphas [Alpha Pi Alpha fraternity]. Actually, they were guys who had graduated from Cal; we didn't have a student chapter at that time. I was initiated by Bill Pittman [Tarea's husband] and George Johnson—he was an assistant law professor at Boalt Hall—and some other guys. Myself and Harry Osborne, the guy I went to junior college with, and Ted Smith were initiated at the same time.

There wasn't much social life for blacks in those days. Well, you were just going to college. It didn't matter to me. I was just there to get my degree. There were a couple of white guys on the track team that we were friends with. We would drink a few beers together once in a while. I knew a lot of guys in the white fraternities. They would probably have been glad to have me at their parties. They may have thought about it. But it didn't matter to me. We went out with black girls that were going to Cal.

As I said, there weren't too many black kids going to college. You've heard of Walt Gordon? He was a judge and a black football star. In fact, he was the first black policeman in Berkeley. When he was on the police force, he used to drive around in one of those big old touring cars, you know, with the side curtains. He was something to see. He really kept order; everyone knew who he was, and no one messed with him.

When he went into law practice, his partner was George Johnson. My father used to rent rooms up on our third floor to college students, and George Johnson stayed with us for a while when I was a kid. He would give us younger kids a whack on the rear if we got to be a nuisance when he was trying to study.

Flying training was conducted by a civilian outfit called the Oakland Flying Service. About the time I graduated in 1939 this guy named Harry Sham hired me to work for him as a kind of flunky to work on the airplanes. We were called ramp rats, grease monkeys.

He let me fly the planes. In fact, he staked me to a lot of flying time. I told him I'd pay him back later when I got hired as a pilot, an instructor. At that time the Oakland airport was really country flying. I think Trans-World Airways landed there, but it was mostly a bunch of flying schools and charter outfits.

I put in my time and finally got my instructor's license. Harry couldn't hire me because of the power structure in those days. But I had bootleg students who needed somebody to sign the logbooks.

Then I went down to Alabama to Tuskegee Institute in 1943. They had started training black pilots. They called it the Spookwaffe.[1] I went down there as an instructor. Tuskegee was training civilian pilots like Cal was. Mrs. Eleanor Roosevelt, the president's wife, went down there and saw that we were making it. She beat on the desk and got them to set up a program for military pilots.

So they set up a military program there equipped with five airplanes. They had two white instructors, and most of the supervisory personnel were white. They used our dinky little field at Tuskegee just for their primary training. They kept the airplanes there and flew over to Moton Field where they had enough room to practice their landings and all. While I was there, I taught as a civilian instructor. I took check rides with the military pilots to teach them to take off and land, do snap rolls and moves and whatnot. It was fun. I loved flying.

I applied for a commission in the air corps while I was still down there and they, get this, sent me to the meteorology school at UCLA. In other words I was too old to be a flying cadet, but I qualified to be a weather cadet. Tell me about the bureaucracy.

They didn't sign me up as an officer, I enlisted with the aviation cadets. The guy who signed me up knew I was teaching flying. He looked at my record and said, "You're qualified to be a meteorologist." I said, "Great, I'll take it." So they sent me to UCLA for a year, and I got a commission there.

Guess where they sent me? Right back to Tuskegee to be a weather officer. After I was weather officer for about a year, they said, "Hey, you know how to fly? See that damned DC-13? Get in the backseat and check that guy out." Made me an instructor. I was a lieutenant then in the army air corps. While I was there, I had three jobs. I was drawing weather maps, making weather forecasts, and teaching intro to flying.

We would get up in the morning and jump in that plane and check the weather. I would go up and fly around and see how the weather was, call back and say, "It's OK to fly." A couple of times the weather was so bad, we had to fly the planes away to Birmingham and spend the night. It was great because I was doing what I liked to do.

How many fellows were in that Tuskegee air corps unit?

They were training about 20 at a time. The first class only had five guys. B. O. [Benjamin] Davis, who ended up as a lieutenant general, was the commanding officer. The other guys were Lemuel Custis, Spanky Roberts—we all had nicknames—Mack Ross, and Jimmy Moore, [who] finally washed out. That was in 1942.

Tuskegee was still just an agricultural school then. When they started talking this flying stuff, they said that the jump from the plow to the plane was too much for black people. The word about training black pilots was,

78

"Let's give these coons these airplanes, let them go out and kill themselves." They figured we were going to screw up. But there was no problem. These guys were real good pilots.

Then they started recruiting black instructors. The only place we could get jobs was Tuskegee. We were getting $200 a month. That ain't much money. We went around to the other fields and found that white guys we knew who were teaching flying in some of the other schools were making maybe $400 or $500 a month.

The civilian guy who was running the program was the Simon Legree of the air corps. He found out what we were doing, so to keep us quiet he said. "If any of you guys get any ideas of quitting us, we've got your draft board telephone number. The next thing you know, you'll be getting a call from your draft board."

Have you heard of General Chappie James?[2] He died recently. He was the only black guy who made four-star general. He was a flying general, a really good pilot. Chappie and I were good friends. Vesta and I stood up with them when they got married.

Once we started putting out pilots and got enough of them together, they went to Selfridge Field in Michigan and satellite fields around there where they got their combat training in P-40s. First they were made up as the 99th Squadron. Then they were turning them out pretty fast, and when they got a bunch of them they formed the 332d Fighter Group.

They went into combat as a unit. I was too old to go with them. They sent them overseas to North Africa. They sent them to Sicily and Italy. That's when they got going good. They started shooting down planes. C. Buster Hall got the first one. His name was Charlie Hall, but his nickname was C. Buster.

Were some of the 332d officers West Point graduates?

B.O. was the only one I knew. He got the silent treatment there. He went through the whole four years at the military academy, and nobody spoke to him. He got the treatment that they give anybody they want to be hard on. Just because he was black, they didn't want him to make it. He stuck it out, and we're proud of him.

His father was one of the first black generals. His father worked his way up through the ranks. B.O. said [that] when he ate supper with his dad, he had to sit at attention, eat a square meal. That kind of stuff, and it rubbed off on him. He wasn't one of these slap-on-the-back type of guys. You better not. He would kick you out the door. He was a good guy, a straight arrow.

A lot of white guys didn't want to fly with black pilots, but they found out that these guys could shoot good and protect the bombers. That was what their job was, flying top cover for the bombers. They were criticized a lot at first, badmouthed and not given real jobs because some people didn't want them to make it. Later on, they were known as the Tuskegee Airmen and had a big fuss made over them.[3]

After the war, I was stationed at Columbus, Ohio, for training at the Wright Institute of Technology. I was there in 1948 when they integrated the air force. President Harry Truman said, "No more of this segregation B.S."

While I was flying, I would land at air bases, run my plane in, and go look around. They said, "This is the black rest room, the black mess hall." This would be in 1946, 1947. Even if you were an officer, they didn't want you to go to this officers' club and stuff like that.

They tried to court-martial a whole squadron up at some place in Indiana one time. These guys landed their B-25s at the field, and the base commander said, "You guys stay in this area. You've got your own officers' club." Some of the guys said, "Hell, I wonder what their officers' club is like? Let's go up and try it out." So the base commander put out an order to court-martial the whole squadron. That's like arresting the whole town. They laughed at him. That was about the time they integrated the air force.

Let's see. Later I had a real good job doing weather forecasting for the Fifth Air Force. Then I was stationed in New York at the command post for all the air defense on the East Coast. From there, I went up to Alaska. All these places, the wife and kids went along with me. I ended up as a major and a lieutenant colonel in the reserves. That meant that I retired as a lieutenant colonel. It don't mean anything.

How did you happen to come back to California when you finished your air force service?

I had almost 22 years in, and I said it's time to retire. I started thinking about what I could do. I enjoy teaching, so I checked out what it took to get a teaching credential. I was stationed in Riverside then, so I went to the University of California at Riverside and got all the education courses you need to get a credential. With my engineering degree, I had enough background to teach math or to teach science. This was while I was still in the service.

I like it in Northern California, so I came up to see my brother who was living in Hayward. He said, "What about over in Marin County? Do you remember Chet Carlisle? He's a school superintendent over there." We used to train together at Cal. He was a basketball player and a really good friend.

I came over to see him. "Hey, Chet. How are you doing?" "Fine. Do you want a job?" I said, "Yes." "OK. Keep in touch." Just like that.

A couple of months later he called, "OK, I've got you a job." He got me teaching math at Drake High School right down the hill here. He came down and interviewed me. They were hiring teachers in those days, back in 1965, so I got a job. So here I am.

It was beautiful teaching high school kids after teaching pilots. I loved it. In fact, I taught for 22 years. I even got into computers so I could teach that. I helped out coaching the track team and the golf team. And I kept my hand in with a flying service that my wife, Vesta, and I ran for a while up north of here.

Did you find some black kids who liked your classes in math and science?

We don't have many over here. Maybe three or four black kids in a class. Their parents were friends of ours. Most of the black kids live down near Marin City and go to Tamalpais High School. It's kind of a benign ghetto [right next to the pretty, well-to-do town of Sausalito]. These kids with problems live right above there, looking at yachts and things like that.

One time, I tried to get transferred there. We had an evening program there called Project Breakthrough. I worked with the kids there and got to know the bright ones. In fact, I still go down there and talk to those kids. I told the superintendent I would like to be transferred to Tam, but the principal said, "We need you here; you're doing a good job," and all this stuff. "We're short of teachers and can't do it now. Maybe later."

I felt I could do some good there. But I didn't make an issue of it. I was still learning myself.

Do you have any tips for the younger generation?

Take long steps and save your shoe leather. [*chuckles*] Actually, this: do the best you can.

7

LIONEL WILSON

Hero of the Playing Field and the Mayor's Office

Lionel Wilson was born in New Orleans in 1915 and grew up in Oakland, California. A talented athlete, he played and coached basketball and baseball, later playing competitive tennis into the 1980s. He graduated from the University of California at Berkeley in 1938 and Hastings College of Law in 1949. Active in the NAACP, the Democratic party, and other civic organizations as a student and young lawyer, he was appointed to the Alameda County municipal and superior courts. In 1977 he was elected the first black mayor of Oakland, a city of over 350,000, and served until 1990.

I was just under four when we moved to Oakland in 1919. The black community was much smaller than it is now. I don't think there were 10,000 African Americans in the Bay Area then.

My mother's brother, Ponce Barrios, had come out from New Orleans to work in the shipyards in World War I. He convinced my mother and father that their children would have better opportunities here. Three of us, two younger brothers and myself, came out with them.

We moved in with my uncle in his big old two-story Victorian house; then we moved to a house on 30th between Chestnut and Linden. A couple of years later, my father bought a little house around the corner. My father started out as a carpenter's apprentice, and later learned plastering, and a little of this and a little of that in the way of building. He just did the house all over himself. Then the other five children were born in that house.

We were pretty much on our own as children. Even from a little bit of a fellow, I was wrapped up in sports. When I was 10, I had a paper route, but I whipped through that paper route to get back to the playground. During

This chapter was adapted from Lionel Wilson, *Lawyer, Judge, and Oakland Mayor*, 1976 and 1990 interviews with Gabrielle Morris (Berkeley: Regional Oral History Office, University of California, 1992).

the summer, McClymonds High School opened the grounds as a playground and the coach, Doc Hess, was the recreation director.

He was a little bit of a man, about five feet four at the most, but he was a great leader of young people and a strong disciplinarian.

What was the mix of black and white children?

Very few blacks. A mixture of Portuguese and Italians and Irish. No more than 10 or 15 percent of the students were African American. The athletic teams were integrated.

At the age of about 12 I began to work in my uncle's barbershop after school and on Saturdays, shining shoes and keeping [the place] clean. I did that through high school. That's when I got to know D. G. Gibson, who later encouraged me and other young black people to get interested in politics.[1] He was already active in the Democratic party. I believe he had come to California by working his way on the railroads.

It was mainly my uncle who encouraged me to go on to college. He was a strong believer in education. My father was like many Creoles who felt that high school was enough, and it was time to go to work. But my uncle and my mother were the motivators that encouraged us to prepare for college. They made it clear to us that we should make the grades so that we could get into the University of California.

I don't remember anyone in my class going directly into Cal but me. Some of them went to the state colleges. There was a small group of friends whose parents were pushing them, and we formed a little social club.

To what extent was there racial discrimination when you were growing up here?

While there was far more discrimination and far more segregation in the South, there was an awful lot of it here. I remember when I got out of law school, after I came out of service in World War II, there were many places that wouldn't serve you food. You could only stay in a hotel if you could find one that was run by a Japanese. When my wife and I wanted to buy a home in Berkeley, we had to make the purchase through a white person.

There was one Negro teacher in the whole of the East Bay, Ida Jackson. There was one Negro teacher in the whole of the West Bay, Josephine Foreman, who taught in the parochial schools in San Francisco. There were no Negro teachers in the public schools of San Francisco. Now, there may have been people who were passing for white, because as a result of the discrimination, you found many people who were fair-complexioned passed for white to get better jobs. Some of them moved back and forth between being black and being white. Some of them just lived out their lives as white.

Employment opportunities were few and far between, except in some phases of the building trades—plastering, a few carpenters. Electrical or plumbing had little or no opportunities for Negroes. I remember during the 1930s depression the North Oakland YMCA, which catered to Negroes primarily, used to have classes preparing people to take civil-service exams.

I took the post office exam and was something like 52 on the list. I learned that they passed me up when I ran into someone who was a lot lower on the list who had been working for six months. At that time the federal government didn't ask for race, but they asked for a picture. One of my brothers, who's now a dentist, took the exam, too, and was lower on the list than I was. I was the darkest in the family; and when they looked at my brother's picture, they thought he was white, so they offered him a job.

After I graduated from Cal, I took the exam again and this time I was fifth out of 3,500. I was called for an interview, but I was told by the assistant superintendent of mails, "The fact that you're called doesn't mean that you are going to get the job," as well I knew.

When I entered Cal in 1932, there was a great deal of discrimination also; some of the professional schools you simply couldn't get into. Because of the Cal coach, Nibs Price, Negroes couldn't play basketball in the Pacific Coast Conference. There was one here and there who played football— Walter Gordon and Smoke Francis and later Tom Tryon, who was in the Oakland school department.

There weren't more than a handful of black men at Cal when I enrolled and several black women. I just filled out an application and sent it in.

What was your major?

When I was in my last year in high school, my family wondered what I was going to do after graduation. I said, "I'm going to study law."

By then the depression had set in, and they said, "If all you're going to be is another starving lawyer, boy, you had better go to work." Well, that was a fiction because there weren't any jobs anyway.

So I said, "Wait a minute, I'm going to college." "Well, what are you going to study?" So they decided I was going to be a dentist, so I entered in pre-dental. After about a year and a half, I realized my family didn't know what I was doing at college, and so I changed my major. My brother Kermit by then was at the university, and that gave me nerve enough to switch because he did want to go into dentistry and was good working with his hands.

I majored in languages for a while, then I realized it wasn't realistic in terms of getting a job, so I switched over to economics with a minor in political science. Just before I thought I was going to graduate, I learned that I was short three units in my major. I was so disgusted that I dropped out of school and stayed out a year and a half. But I did go back to pick up those three units, and that's how I graduated in the class of 1939.

By the time I graduated another brother, Barry, was at Cal. He was the navigator on a B-17 lost over Europe in World War II. Therein lies a story also, because there were no Negro navigators in World War II. He became interested in flying on a Thanksgiving Day: Ed Toppins, who was my doubles partner in tennis, was at our home. He was one of the first blacks in the Civil Aeronautics Administration program.

He took us out to the airport to see the Piper Cubs the students were flying. And from that day, Barry wanted to fly. After he graduated from Cal, Barry applied to the air corps and went before the boards they had which traveled around the country that would sit on different college campuses.

The major who was chairman of the board called him aside and said, "Look, son, I see from your college papers you're a Negro." He said, "Forget that, you're an American. If you go in as a Negro, you're going to get inferior equipment and inferior training. That's a lot of nonsense anyway." So Barry went in the air corps as white. He looked very much like my father, who was very fair and had grayish blue eyes, and he wound up as a navigator. Toppins, my doubles partner, was one of the first blacks in the original 99th Fighter Squadron. It was a segregated unit; all of our forces were segregated, you see.

They drafted me into the army; I went kicking and screaming. [*laughs*] After I had been in camp a couple of days, I went to the headquarters to ask about something. This corporal brought my service record out and put it on the desk. On the cover there was a small circle stamped in blue with a "w" inside of it.

After he answered my question, I asked him, "What does that stamp on my service record with a 'w' inside it mean?" He said, "That just means you're white."

"Somebody's made a mistake," I said. "I'm Negro." The poor guy was embarrassed. He scratched it out and reached under the counter and came up with another stamp which had a "c" in the middle of it for "colored."

After I came out of the service, I went to Hastings Law School over in San Francisco. Thirteen blacks started out in that class. One fellow had moved into Oakland after the war; that was Terry Francois, who became one of the first black supervisors in San Francisco; we became very close. Joe Kennedy, who became a superior court judge in San Francisco, was in the class too. Terry and Joe and I studied together.

I was working three part-time jobs because I had a nonworking wife and three children to support. The classes at Hastings then were in the morning, so you could work in the afternoons. I worked as a city recreation director, I worked as a janitor for my brother, and I worked in the Oakland YMCA for Josh Rose, who was later one of the first black councilmen here in Oakland. In fact, I came close to making a career in Y work, but they didn't pay very well.

When it came time for the bar exam, there was a black lawyer named John Bussey who had quite a reputation as a teacher for getting people through the bar exam. Actually, he was the first black judge in Northern California. Governor Goodie Knight appointed him to the municipal bench in San Francisco.

Before the results of the bar came out, in November '49, I went to work for George Vaughns, who was the senior black lawyer in the area. He knew me from the YMCA Negro branch. He had been on the board for many years, and I came up through it as a child and then started coaching and playing with its senior men's basketball team at the age of 18. (I didn't retire from that team until I was 44.) After about 15 months, I left and opened my own office in south Berkeley. I wanted to strike out on my own.

I jumped right into activities like the NAACP and the East Bay Democratic Club, which was built around Byron Rumford and D. G. Gibson. I brought in a lot of new, young people [including] Evelio Grillo. He was responsible for getting several black Republicans to change their registration and become active—Clint White, Don McCullum, and Charles Furlough. We had some outstanding people in the organization, and it built fast.

In the NAACP I was chairman of the Legal Redress Committee. We were fighting battles against school and job discrimination. And in my law practice I often provided legal aid for people who couldn't afford services. I guess it was because of the discrimination I had experienced through the years. I remember being here in the mayor's office in the 1950s with Byron Rumford, arguing with the mayor, the city manager, and the fire chief over the segregrated fire department.

There was only one firehouse where Negroes could serve, which meant that the number of firemen it took to serve that one house was the maximum number of Negroes who could work in the Oakland Fire Department. When we finished, the fire chief was the only one who spoke. He said, "If I were in your place, I would be saying the same things you're saying. But as long as I'm here, there will not be an integrated fire department in this city." A couple of years later, the council did pass an ordinance that abolished the black-only firehouse.

In 1953 you ran for a seat on the Berkeley City Council. What made you decide to run?

I don't remember who euchred me into running that race. [*laughs*] I suppose it was suggested that, "This will give your law practice more exposure."

John Mickle, the pastor of the South Berkeley Community Church, which was integrated, was urging a black candidate. He organized a mass meeting in my support. Another black man, Ura Harvey, ran for the school board in the same election. He was a storekeeper, a little older than our group. A very nice man, but he hadn't been politically active before.

I ran again in 1955. Vivian Osborne Marsh also ran for the council that year. She had been president of the state Association for Colored Women and was on the city's planning commission. Pretty much the same people worked on the campaign, and our base of support broadened. That time, on a budget of $600, I only missed election by around 700 votes!

About then I began to talk to various people about opening a law partnership. I got talking with Carl Metoyer, who was a few years behind me in law school, a very good lawyer. Carl and I were both Catholics, and our families knew each other; we're both out of Louisiana. Carl said how about bringing in Bill Sweeney? So the three of us bought a piece of property in Berkeley and put up a building for four lawyers. We were doing pretty well, and then we invited Allen Broussard to join us.

When I left in 1960 to go on the bench, Broussard was made a partner. Then in 1964, when I went from the muni court to the superior court, we got Allen appointed to my spot on the municipal court. About the same time Sweeney became the first African American elected to the Berkeley City Council.

The way my appointment came about was when Pat [Edmund G., Sr.] Brown was elected governor in 1958, he offered to appoint me to what was then the Adult Authority. I said, no, thanks. Then he leaked to the press that he was going to appoint a black person as his legal-affairs officer. There'd never been a person serving at that cabinet-type level in California. Pat asked two or three people to take that job and they said no; Pat's panicking, he's got to find a black to appoint. He asked me and I said, "No. I'm happy here in a new law practice." Finally, Cecil Poole, who'd worked with Pat in the San Francisco District Attorney's office, took the job.

Then Pat said, "There ought to be a Negro judge in Alameda County. Would you take it?" I said, "I certainly agree with you, but I hadn't thought about myself in that respect." "You'd have to move back to Oakland," he said, "because it's going to be Oakland Municipal Court." He ignored the people I suggested and said, "You let me know when you've made a decision." Once a month for 11 months he had a lawyer who was close to him call me and ask, "Have you moved into Oakland?"

That was the clue. If I'd moved into Oakland, then I had decided to take the appointment. Then one morning I went down to the courthouse on some simple matter, and the judge, the late James Agee, asked me into his chambers, and for 30 or 40 minutes he talked to me about all the reasons why I should accept the appointment.

He argued about the good I could do the community and what it would mean to blacks in the community and those coming before the court to know that there was a black judge there. That it would give them a greater feeling of security. Also that there was a future for me in the judiciary, and he was satisfied that it wouldn't be too long before I moved up to the superior court. When I walked out of Judge Agee's office, I had changed my mind.

From your work with the NAACP, were there things you wanted to see happen with the courts?

Oh, yes, certainly. As a judge, I continued to work to fight all the injustices, the discrimination, and the segregation that we saw around us. One of the things I really pushed when I went on the superior court was a better approach to bail. We put together a task force to work on that, and we got going a pretrial release program.

Then in 1965 you were appointed chair of the Oakland Economic Development Commission (OEDC).

Actually, I had been approached, and I had told Clint White that I wouldn't accept the chairmanship. White told the mayor, John Houlihan, "He's afraid you're going to try to run the show and he won't serve under those circumstances."

What had happened was that the mayor had called me one day and said that there were no blacks on any important boards or commissions. He said he wanted to correct that and asked me for recommendations of blacks whom he could appoint. I said fine, and I called together a committee of about 15 community leaders, a real broad representative group. The names we suggested were unacceptable to Houlihan. We had words about it, and I had to tell him off. He wanted us to simply rubber-stamp a couple of people he already had in mind.

I didn't want to go through that again on the OEDC, but Houlihan committed that he would not interfere with the operation of the committee, and I agreed to take the chairmanship. That commission was the antipoverty program, under the federal Economic Opportunity Act. I had hopes that it was going to provide some jobs and some training programs for many of the people who needed it so they could ultimately get jobs.

Earlier, we had had a program to stabilize the Castlemont area of the city. The Ford Foundation put up several million dollars for that, and I had been on the policy committee. [Senator] Bill Knowland was active in the group that submitted the proposal to Ford, and Evelio Grillo wrote the proposal.

The first thing I did as OEDC chairman was to move the board meetings out of city hall. We organized the city into seven districts, each district with its own organization and district council. Those community councils exist today. Then we began to hold meetings each month in a different part of the city so as to involve more people in the decision-making process. For six years, I can't remember a meeting that wasn't packed. Some of those meetings got pretty controversial. [*chuckles*]

When did you start thinking of running for mayor of Oakland?

Well, it didn't originate with me. Some people came to me in 1972 and suggested that I consider running for mayor the next year. I looked at it and informed them that I wasn't interested. I was thinking more in terms of a future on the bench.

Four years later some of the same people and a few others came to me again. By then, I had presided over various phases of the court, so I suppose I had reached a point where the idea of running for mayor was more appealing. And John Reading, who was mayor then, was considering not running, which made a significant difference in terms of being able to win such a campaign.

There was support for a black person as mayor, and there were other potential candidates. One of them was John Williams, a friend of mine who headed up the city redevelopment agency. He had talked about approaches that had been made to him from time to time, from the Republican side. We would have worked very closely together. He was a very charismatic personality.

John decided not to run, I think, because there was a lot of talk [by Republicans who said Williams should run for mayor, but no one wrote any checks to pay for the campaign]. My major opponent was the president of the school board, Dave Tucker. The business community supported him, the *Oakland Tribune* endorsed him, and he had a lot of money for his campaign.

Later on, Edgar Kaiser, head of probably the biggest employer in town, from time to time said how sorry he was that he did not support me in my first campaign. I had worked with him and other business leaders in the antipoverty program and when the Black Panthers became active and announced to the press that they were thinking of going after white businesses on the basis of integration and employment.

At that point a group of leading businesspeople got together and formed an organization called the New Oakland Committee. They wanted to have in it business and labor and minority representation. When they got to the minority representation, there was a group called the Black Caucus, which was pretty political. They said they had to be the exclusive representatives of the black community. That was unacceptable to the business community, so everything stopped.

I was asked if I could put together the minority caucus for the New Oakland

Committee and get things moving. I said I'd do it on one condition: that top business executives would continue to be active in the organization. They made that commitment, and so I told the Black Caucus, "You ought to be a part of the minority caucus, but you can't call the shots." And that's how the New Oakland Committee was formed. It still exists today, helping get things started here that are needed like jobs and housing.

Did you see the Panthers as a threat to the future of Oakland?

Well, I saw it from a dual perspective. One, I have never condoned violence and confrontation as the solution to social problems. On the other hand I saw the Panthers as a catalyst to bring about some meaningful change. Doing the same things that the NAACP was doing, but in a different way. When I ran for mayor in 1977, the Panthers were active in my campaign.

How did you organize your campaign?

Oakland was just a big blob then. There was no real organization other than the East Bay Democratic Club. There were people willing to help once I indicated I was interested in running, mostly pretty moderate Democrats: black, white, and Hispanic. There were labor people, and a black lawyer who was on the school board. Ron Dellums, who was already in Congress, let a young fellow named Sandre Swanson have leave from his staff to work for me. I raised much more money than I anticipated.

We put together an organization by district, and we had pretty broad support in the flatlands. I put together committees of doctors and lawyers and teachers and groups like that. And I spent a lot of time in neighborhood meetings and in churches talking to people.

I always thought I was going to [win,] from the time I decided to run. The governor [Edmund G. Brown, Jr.] had offered me an appointment to the court of appeals, and his office said to me, "Have you decided whether you're going to run for mayor or move to the court of appeals?" And I said, "Yes, I have. I'm going to become the mayor."

How did it feel to go from the bench to running a city the size of nearly half a million people like Oakland?

Well, I had chaired the antipoverty program for six years. While I was chairman, I put together the first antidrug program in the Bay Area and the first on-the-job training program for the city of Oakland. I had been involved in many different ways in city activities, so it was not a new world for me when I moved into the mayor's office.

As mayor, one of the first things I did was call George Vukasin, a member of the city council who was also on the antipoverty board, and ask for a meeting. He said, "Fine. Mayor Reading never talked to me." And I never had any quarrels with George while he was on the board, although John Reading and I had constantly been fighting over the antipoverty program. So I moved in with a much stronger position than a new mayor normally would have because I had Vukasin supporting me, and he brought with him three or four votes from the middle-of-the-road business community.

Let's talk about some of the things that have gotten a lot of public attention while you've been mayor, like the Port of Oakland and the Raiders football team going from Oakland to Los Angeles.

Well, those subjects are very involved. It is hard to do justice to them in a few words. As far as the Raiders were concerned, there was a lot more to it than most people understand. The manager, Al Davis, simply made up his mind that he was going to move. He thought Los Angeles was a better opportunity for bigger attendance and more money, and that was it. He won a lawsuit in a fight with a major stockholder, and the court found that his contract gave him complete power to do anything he wanted to with the Raiders.

Later there was a plan to try to bring the Raiders back to Oakland. We could never get the message across to the media or the public that the money that would have been made available to the Raiders would all have come from ticket sales, not from the schools or other social programs. That not a dime from any tax funds would have been spent on the Raiders.

When you're trying to deal with all the other city issues, there is only so much time and energy that you have to put into any one thing. I knew that the plan was going to make people vote against me in the next election, but I believed that it would be good for the city.

How about the Port of Oakland? Would that be more important to the city's economy than the Raiders?

It certainly is the single most important economic factor in the city. Some years back there was a farseeing port director named Ben Nutter who foresaw that the then wave of the future was going to be container shipping. He moved the port into that area before all the other ports on the West Coast. The Port of Oakland became very busy, and there were lots of jobs. Then other ports, like Seattle and Los Angeles, began to put freight on ships in big containers too. Some ships began to have trouble docking at the Port of

Oakland [because the Bay needed to be dredged], and business was not so good.

It's not that the Port of Oakland did anything wrong, it's just the facts of life. Things keep changing. Many people think that Oakland should be the center of transportation in the Bay Area and that we are all one big region that should work together. Instead, there seems to be a continual rivalry between San Francisco and Oakland and Richmond and even Redwood City.

What would you tell a young person about how to become the mayor of a major city?

I think a young person should understand that politics is not a dirty word, that politics is part of every facet of life—the very air we breathe, the clothing that we wear, the way the coffin is made. Every facet of life is influenced and determined by political decisions somewhere.

Politics is so important to life. I think that Oakland has become one of the cities where citizens have become more and more awakened to what an important part politics plays in their lives. Citizens' participation is probably far more active here than in almost any city in the country.

If you're interested in becoming mayor, you have to find some way to get in there and become active in what's going on. You can't just say, well, I want to be a candidate. Technically, anyone can file to run for office, if you come up with the fees and live in the city and are of minimum age. But in terms of ultimately winning many factors come into play during the period from one election to another.

8

MARVIN POSTON

Making Opportunities in Vision Care

Marvin Poston was born in St. Louis, Missouri, in 1914. The family moved to Canada when he was a small boy and in 1928 to Oakland, California, when his father became ill. His mother became an agent for Golden State Insurance Company, and Marvin also worked for the company while he was in college to help his mother support the family and to pay his college expenses. He enrolled at the University of California at Berkeley in 1935 and was the first African American to graduate from its School of Optometry. He built a successful interracial vision-care practice in downtown Oakland and went on to become a leader in the county, state, and national professional societies in the 1960s and 1970s. He also became a consultant to young doctors in starting up an office and a winegrower.

When I was between one and two, my parents left Missouri and went up to Canada. I had an uncle who was up there already, working on the railroad. He encouraged all of his family, his brothers and sisters and their families, to come to Edmonton. He felt it was a better life.

My father had a degree for school teaching from Lincoln University in Missouri. So he did some teaching up there. Canada at that time didn't have many Americans, so there was total freedom where racial discrimination was concerned. We participated in shows and went skating and to churches and all of those things.

I don't recall running across discrimination until I hit California. I'll take that back. I had one incident when I was growing up. A family came from

This chapter was adapted from Marvin Poston, *Making Opportunities in Vision Care,* 1984 interview with Gabrielle Morris (Berkeley: Regional Oral History Office, University of California, 1989). The volume appendix includes additional information about Poston in Louis B. Crouchett [sic], "Black Visionary," *California Monthly,* March–April 1982, 87, and Lawrence P. Crouchett, "Dr. Marvin R. Poston, Pioneering California Optometrist," *Boule Journal,* February 1980, 82.

the states and moved into our neighborhood. They used to call us names and so forth. There were very few blacks in Canada. That may have been one of the reasons why they didn't have a lot of discrimination. Secondly, blacks all thrived economically in Canada.

People could find work, and they lived in comfortable homes. The plots of land were big enough so everybody grew gardens during those years, and there were vacant lots where you could grow vegetables. My father owned two lots. On one he grew vegetables in the summertime, and in the winter he built an ice rink for us to skate on.

All you had to do was pile up dirt around the perimeter and, for fifty cents or a dollar, the city would come out and give us the first flood. Of course, it would freeze overnight. You may have a few weeds, and we would go along and chop them off. All during the wintertime we would scrape and water it. My father would take a hose and flood it from the house, and it would be just like glass.

My dad was there supervising us most of the time. Our friends came over, and we all skated and played ice hockey. My mother used to skate. My dad tried it once and went down, so he wouldn't skate. We played hockey purely as recreation. The schools didn't have any teams there, at least not at the level I was in. Edmonton had its own professional hockey team. They played every week. They would let all the children in at halftime to see the rest of the game. You can be a very dirty player in ice hockey. But if you play it as we played it, it's a fast, vigorous, and very skillful game.

I did play ice hockey for the University of California when I attended Cal. The university had an ice hockey team at that time. I went out just to practice with them for the exercise and ended up on the team. But that was later.

My father developed heart trouble. The physicians in Edmonton told him it was too cold for his condition, and they recommended he come to California. He sold out everything he had and came down here, mainly because he had a classmate who was a minister in Oakland, Reverend Prater.

Did you go to his church when you moved to California?

We went to church there, at the First AME [African Methodist Episcopal] Church in Oakland. My two brothers and I were active in the youth groups, in the youth choir, and that sort of thing.

Following Prater, there were some very interesting ministers. They had one named Scott, who was a well-educated man. And they had another one named Daniel Hill, who got a Ph.D. from Berkeley while he was here. After I graduated, he was very instrumental in helping me move forward in the practice of optometry.

Once when the pressures were very heavy on me, I talked to him and his wife about my problems. They said, "Well, it matters not how long it takes you to acquire something. The important thing is that you have acquired it at the end."

What was it like attending school in Oakland in the 1930s?

Oakland Tech High was one of those institutions that had very few blacks. I was not an athletic student per se. I tried out for football, and after the first game I quit.

Of course, I worked nights too. When I got into the ninth grade, I got a job at the Oakland Athletic Club. I worked there from four o'clock in the afternoon until one o'clock the next morning. I did that from ninth grade all the way through my last year in college. I was a bellhop. The first part of the evenings were very heavy as far as work was concerned. After ten o'clock, things quieted down and we could study.

Was your father able to work after the family came to Oakland?

In fact, I had gotten a job because his heart trouble made it difficult for him to work. And my mother was trying to find work. Because she only had a high school education, mother started out cleaning up houses behind contractors. That was pretty heavy.

Then she decided to go into insurance sales, and she went to work for a black company, the Golden State Life Insurance Company. Golden State was started in the twenties. Two of its founders were from Oakland. The others were from Los Angeles. You remember those days were not what we have today, so all they could serve was the black community.

In the summer months later on, I started to sell for the company. That helped with my college expenses. I sold under my mother's name at first. Eventually the company issued a license under my name. My younger brother did the same thing. He ended up by getting a degree in actuarial science from Harvard as a result of that exposure.

I was learning the insurance business while I was still working at the Oakland Athletic Club, which employed a lot of blacks. All the menial jobs were African Americans: the waiters, busboys, dishwashers, janitors, maids were all black. I used to insure them when they came on the job. Then on payday, which was the fifth and twentieth of the month, my other would come in with enough money to cash checks. She couldn't go into the club, but I could go into the employee quarters and cash checks and collect the insurance premiums.

They used to give me a bad time. They would say, "Here comes Marv. He's going to take your money away from you." But it was good experience for me. How to do business and be with people.

Of course, at the time companies like Metropolitan, Pacific Mutual, Golden State, and Washington National, as I recall, were the main ones that were after the black market. Washington and Metropolitan both upgraded. In other words if I was 30 years old and I took out a life insurance policy with them, they figured the risk was greater so I paid a higher premium like an older man.

Then Golden State came out with a policy that used national actuarial tables, so that regardless of who they insured, the premium would be the same if you were the same age. Liberty Mutual and some other companies that were out in the East Coast did the same thing and were able to survive during the depression.

When I used to go out and sell in Oakland, I would have to deal with the competition of this basic psychology that existed that [if] it's a white man's insurance, it's better insurance. Even though it cost more. It still exists today to some extent. Many people who came out of the South were taught that the only person who could do something was the white man. And that everything that he did, regardless of what it was, was better than what a black man could do. You still have that, but not near as bad as you had back in those days.

The one thing it taught me when I got out of school and I was going to practice optometry was that I wasn't going to cater to a limited market. That I was going to cater to the whole market. So I came into downtown Oakland and opened an office right in the heart of town. I was the first black to have any kind of office in downtown Oakland. Money's green and it doesn't see color. [chuckles] None of my friends were game enough to come into downtown Oakland with me.

That took a lot of courage back in the 1940s.

There were several things that I think may have contributed to that. My parents and having lived in Canada, not having been brainwashed as some young blacks have been brainwashed in the United States. So I would approach everything with an open mind and no fears.

I did that when I first got ready to buy a house. I decided I was going to buy where I wanted to buy, so I went up and bought a house in the East Oakland hills. And I bought it by looking at it at nighttime and by double-dealing through a white person.

Did your mother and father encourage you and your brothers to think about going to college?

That started way before we got into high school. I can remember as far as I can go back, both my parents used to say, "You're going to college." As the end result, my oldest brother became a veterinarian. My younger brother got his Ph.D. from Harvard. And I graduated from Cal in 1939 in optometry.

I started out as a math student. One day, I was thumbing through the catalog for an elective course in one of the sciences, and I happened to hit optometry. The requirements were all the courses that I enjoyed taking: physics, math. I went up to the department and there was a secretary.

She said, "Let me send for your transcript." The next day, I came back and she said, "Oh, you would make a wonderful optometric student." She was so enthusiastic about it that I signed up to transfer majors right then. Of course, after I got in, that's when all hell broke loose.

There was a professor who didn't want a black student in optometry?

Frederick Mason. He was a very difficult professor, I think, for anybody. He was very hard on students. I guess when he saw a black face, that stimulated him to be harder and be more difficult. When he saw black, he saw red. First of all, he got very hard on me in class. I don't know why he did it that way, but he allowed me to get good grades all semester. Then when I got to my final exam, he failed me.

I didn't think that was fair, so I went to see Walter Gordon and a fellow named George Johnson. Walter Gordon was practicing law and was head of the NAACP. Johnson was working for the State Board of Equalization and was a lawyer too. Then Walt Gordon talked to Harry Kingman, who ran the University YMCA. Kingman and Gordon made an appointment with [University Provost Monroe] Deutsch. Then he wanted to see my notes, all the records I had kept. He turned them over to the people in physics, and they changed my grade. Of course, when that happened, I guess I irritated Mason more.

Deutsch did another thing. He created a whole new class, and put other students in there, so I would not be in contact with Mason. Then he took another course Mason gave and made it an elective.

When I got to practice in the school's optometry clinic, something else happened. The way they did it then was they had spots for students to sign up for appointments. And Mason took my spot and put "reserved" on it for the whole semester, so I wouldn't receive any students.

So then Deutsch came in again and made them remove all that. But Mason came up to me and told me they didn't think a black person could be an optometrist. He wanted me to go out in the black community and solicit students to come to the clinic.

I sometimes felt as if anything I did would be an excuse. For example, in those days we examined a student, wrote up the findings, and then a clinician would come in and check the statement. There was one clinician who would get a student in there and he would start talking about "Niggers this" and

"Niggers that." I think what he was trying to do was to make me do something that would justify throwing me out. But I kept my mouth closed.

Actually, the people who were most receptive to me were Jewish students. I used to study with some of them. I think because they had suffered racial discrimination or had families who were suffering, they were very sympathetic. We would discuss the lectures, and they would ask Mason questions that I wasn't clear on, because he would not answer my questions.

When I got ready to take the state licensing exam, which was given at Cal, he walked in the room and started talking to the state board examiner and pointing at me. So you knew he was saying something about me. But there was a Jewish fellow on the state board. I learned later that he had taken the position: if I fail, I fail; if I pass, I pass.

Did you take part in any extracurricular activities—join one of the black fraternities or things like the NAACP?

Working 60 hours a week and going to school, I really didn't have time for much social activity. I played ice hockey.

There was an NAACP youth group that was active when I was on the campus. Either Walter Gordon was president, as I said, or maybe C. L. Dellums. I guess Walter Gordon, in essence, kept an eye on students to see if they needed help. He certainly was a direct influence on my coming out of school.

We got a little radical so they took the student charter away from us. We had learned that the restaurants that refused blacks service could be sued and we could get money from it to increase our treasury. So we started out with a group of white kids to go in restaurants and not get served. Then we would take them to court. Around 1937 or 1938 we won a couple of cases.

The power structure in Oakland got ahold of Walt Gordon and said, "You'd better stop those radicals." And so we had to stop. I don't know who the people were that got to Walt and C. L. Dellums, but then they came to our meetings and told us we had to cool it for a while. After I graduated, I would get involved once in a while sitting in on a political meeting. But I'm not a political animal.

Then sometime in the 1940s I got appointed to the YMCA board of directors, Northwest YMCA, which was the black branch at that time. It was not long before I became president of that branch, and then I got optioned to the Oakland Central YMCA. Of course, I was the only black on that board. I remember I used to go play handball with a classmate of mine.

One day, we went to the Y, and the fellow at the desk said, "Just a minute. What are you here to do?" I knew what he was getting ready to do was to tell me I couldn't play. But somehow the name Poston rang a kind of bell. Then he goes in another office and he calls Fred Dyer, the executive secretary of the Y. And he says, "Fred, I got a—" he didn't call me a black then—"I got a colored fellow here. He says his name is Marvin Poston. He wants to play handball."

Fred says, "Is that Dr. Marvin Poston?" So he came back and he said, "Are you Dr. Marvin Poston?" I said yes. He said, "Well, come right in."

The next morning I called up the executive secretary of the North Oakland branch and said, "You mean to tell me that I'm on the board of directors of an organization that's discriminating against blacks? Well, you tell me when you're going to change that." I didn't have to raise a fuss. When I got to the board meeting, they had had an executive committee meeting and the whole policy of the Y had been changed.

How did you go about setting up your optometry practice?

When I got out of school, I went to all the cities for 40 miles around here looking for a job. At that point I felt I'm a graduate of optometry school, now I can get a decent job. They told you in school the first thing you should do is go work for somebody. I found that wasn't possible.

After I couldn't get a job as an optometrist, I applied to an employment agency. I had all my credentials with me. This fellow was all enthusiastic, and he had just the job for me. When I got there, the job was to be a valet for a retired lawyer.

I was broke, so I said to myself, "OK, I guess I'll have to crawl before I can walk." He'd had a stroke. My job was to dress him, make his bed, and then drive him around San Francisco and entertain him until four o'clock. Then I could clean up the dishes after dinner. I decided that I wasn't going to do that long.

So I went to San Francisco and talked to a fellow who worked with American Optical Company. He said he would let me have some equipment and gave me 90 days before I started to pay. I went to Gross Brothers furniture store here in Oakland. They let me have some furniture, let me start paying in 90 days. Then I went to see a fellow named Berkovich, who owned an office building. He called a black real estate man and that man gave me an excellent recommendation.

Mr. Berkovich said, "I'll let you have the place. Do you have any money?" So I paid him a little bit. I took $25 of the $50 I had left and got some young people whom I knew, young ladies, to write notices and send them out by mail announcing I was in practice. Then Reverend Hill got up at church and gave a very nice little speech about I was a member of the church and they should support one of their own.

That's how I got started. There was no referral, nothing from the school of optometry. They didn't even teach you the economics of practice. The first patient I had—one of the people that came in because of the announcement—broke her glasses.

She said, "How much is it going to cost?" I said, "Three dollars and fifty cents." When I got the bill from the lab, it was seven dollars and some cents. My first lesson in economics was when I lost money. Then I went out and talked to a couple of friends who had exposure, and they began to educate me about the economics of optometry.

One other thing to show you what Mason did. After I got started, I tried to join the local optometric society. When I put my application in, Mason appeared and got five people to vote against me. And so they wouldn't let me in. I went out and talked to Dr. Minor and Dr. Stoddard from Cal and talked to a couple of Jewish optometrists here in town. At the next meeting they reopened discussion of my application and had arguments from eleven o'clock at night until midnight. And then I was voted in.

When I was voted in, Mason resigned. I decided I would go to every meeting so they would never bring it up again. So I went to every society meeting for seven or eight years.

Why do you suppose it was not until 1963 that a second black optometrist graduated from UC?

I really don't know. I recognized that there was going to be a problem after I graduated, that the doors would close behind me. So then I started a personal campaign of going to high schools and talking to counselors and talking to high school students to try to get some other blacks to follow me. But I found either I was not very effective or the exposure optometrists had to African Americans was so limited that it was like looking for a needle in a haystack.

I recognized that here's a wide-open field for black people. And it still is. When you talk to young blacks today about going into a profession, all of them are headed for law or medicine. They seem to have a little fear of the math and science that you need for background.

When did you begin to have time for community activities?

I began to get active in the local optometric society in the late 1940s, early 1950s. There was a fellow in the society named Henry Peterson. Henry had a project he wanted to put on. This was a screening process to check for glaucoma and to see whether or not you had a refractive error.

In order to do this project we had to raise some funds. I became the treasurer, and he was the president, and we set out a strategy. We created a public relations project here in Alameda County and Contra Costa County. In one night we raised about $12,000 and got a commitment for about

$21,000. That was the first time anything like that had been done in the state. We had a trailer, and we did visual screening and we referred people. We just did this for the general public, because statistics showed that Americans just took eyes for granted.

A few years later some of us got together and put together what we called the Children's Vision Center—for children who are not covered by any programs for eye care. So we went out into the community and we got an attorney to let us use the third floor of his building, which was vacant. Then we went to the various optical companies and got them to donate equipment to us. We went to banks and got desks and other furniture. The electrical union came up and did the electrical work.

All this was donated. We even got some of the optical companies to fill the prescriptions free of charge. We put the Children's Vision Center together, and it was very effective for many years.

California Vision Services was an outgrowth of the first program. This was also Hank Peterson's idea. Hank had a patient who was head of the hod carriers [laborers who used a portable trough to carry bricks, mortar, etc.]. They had talked about prepaid care for the union members. And so Hank talked to the same group about changing the vision center over to a prepaid program. They would have one visual examination a year, one complete set of glasses if they needed them, one complete frame. I was the treasurer. I think later on I became the president. What we did was we wrote a two-year contract and hoped that we would come out even financially. We arranged it so that if we didn't make it, the optometrists' society would suffer the loss.

It was quite a thing. We then got the bricklayers, masons, plasterers, and a few others. And then we got big eyes, and we signed up the Masters, Mates, and Pilots Union. They wanted optometrists in Seattle, Los Angeles, San Diego. And the East Coast. After it got too large for us, the state association took it over. If you look at the figures, you'll see it's a $10, $15, $20 million organization.

And then I got active on the board of directors of the Alameda County Optometric Association and later on became president. I instituted a lot of public relations. I invited schoolteachers to meet optometrists. I invited school nurses. The local society gave me an award; the state society gave me an award. I ended up becoming man of the year for the whole United States. That was quite an honor.

When did Governor Pat Brown appoint you to the State Board of Optometry?

It must have been about 1960. I was on the board, and then Pat reappointed me. Then Governor Ronald Reagan appointed me again. I tell you, the interesting thing, I had met with the state board almost six months before I was appointed. I looked at those fellows and said to myself, "I wouldn't sit in your shoes for anything in the world. That board's a whipping boy. I don't intend to be a whipping boy for anybody." They didn't have control of anything.

I was president of that board for four years until I got tired of it. By that time I had turned it around. When it came up for the third term I was prepared to resign.

I said, "There may be a conflict of interest with my being on the board because I'm setting up an organization to help young people get started in practice." And they said, no, that would not be a conflict, I would be able to stay. I said, "OK, I'll stay if you give me the right to resign when I'm ready to." And so after two more years, I resigned.

While I was on the board, one of the questions that most of the students would come up and ask was, "Do you [know] where I can get a job? Do you know how I can open a practice? Do you know the best place to practice?" One fellow said he was thinking about Monterey, and did I know where he could go to get some help. So I said, "I'll help you." I didn't realize how much work it was.

I wrote the chamber of commerce and called real estate people and did what limited research I knew to do, just guessing. We sent him down to find locations. And then I went and looked at them, decided which one was the best location for the price. Then, of course, I had to sit down and work out a budget, what it was going to cost him to open. I ended up making a list of all the equipment and inventory he would need.

Then I decided to go over to the bank and see about financing. I found who was the head of the loan department at Bank of America in San Francisco. I went over there, up to the twenty-seventh floor in the Bank of America building, and told him what I was going to try to do.

He said, "I'll tell you what we'll do. We'll set up one person for you to work with." That was the first one. Then he told me about two or three others. Then fellows started coming to me. That's when I decided that I couldn't do it for free. At that time I charged them $85 an hour for my time.

We take the young fellow just out of school. First of all, we want to know where he's going, whether or not there's going to be a possibility for his success. Second, we will supervise or do part of his layout work for him. We will expose him to the various types of furniture that are available for his reception room, carpets, we will do that. We will set up his filing system, his appointment system, his record and collection system.

As far as I know, no one else is doing this sort of thing. I've set up several physicians—a pediatrician, an ophthalmologist, gynecologist, a general practitioner. They don't have any greater sense of business than anyone else.

Was this how you got involved with the West Oakland Health Group?

That was different. That was the federal government. Do you remember when the black people were putting all the pressure on the federal government, and they were worried about the cities burning up and all this sort of thing? Well, my own analysis is that the federal government decided they would spend a little money in the black community. And they looked on this as a good project to quiet Oakland down.

So they sent people from Washington out here. They got somebody from the University of California to write a proposal for the money. They sent an organizer out here to organize the community group and set up a board of directors. This is the federal government doing all this. They said there was no group in West Oakland who was pushing for a health center.

When they got ready to fund it, they asked me to set up the eye clinic. So I met with the architect, and I arranged for the purchase of the equipment. I got the personnel for the clinic. I got it all organized myself.

And then they set up the board of directors to run the thing. But some of the people they put on the board of directors didn't have a fifth-grade education, and here they were running a million-dollar clinic. There was talk that when they wanted to hire a janitor service, a couple of guys on the board set up a janitor service and paid them pretty well.

People saw an opportunity; some of them were smart enough where they saw a chance to make some money. And some of them were just ignorant about what was happening. They had a guard service down there and while it was on duty, they lost all kinds of equipment. But as far as I was concerned, the federal government was to blame. You can't take somebody who can't manage $50 a month, or $200, and expect them to manage a million-dollar place.

When these people were busy with the clinic, they were no longer unhappy with the federal government. They threw a couple of million dollars out there, and they quieted the whole community down. But the clinic has been able to survive, They've gotten through their problems, and they've done very well. The directors have changed. I think it's well-organized now. I don't think they have near the problems they had. I think they went through those growing pains and saw that it wasn't going to work. So now the whole thing has been changed.

9

LLOYD FERGUSON

Personal and Professional Opportunities in Chemistry

Born in 1918 and raised in Oakland, Lloyd Ferguson is a third-generation Californian. Starting with a schoolboy's backyard laboratory, he became in 1943 the first African American to win a Ph.D. in chemistry at the University of California at Berkeley. He has been an honored teacher at Howard University and California State University at Los Angeles; at both institutions he was department chairman. With the assistance of the American Chemical Society and National Institutes of Health, he developed national programs to encourage and support minority students in pursuing science-based careers.

My parents often worked away from home, so I was raised by my grandparents probably until my high school days. When my parents did buy a home, it was just a block and a half away from my grandparents' place, so I could run back and forth. I am an only child.

I always liked school; I couldn't wait for summer to be over to begin again. Around eighth or ninth grade I bought a chemistry set and fell in love with chemistry, particularly when I learned how to make gunpowder and other exciting substances.

My chemistry teacher in high school was Ruth Forsythe. She was very inspirational. After school, I would help her set up the next day's experiments and earned 25 cents an hour. I also built a little shack in our backyard where I could do experiments as soon as I learned things in class. I had four products that I made up and sold to the neighbors. There was Moth-O, a packet to hang in the closet to repel moths, and Clean-O, which was a spot remover for fabrics. Prest-O was a silverware cleaner. Even now I sometimes use it. The fourth was Lem-O, to which one added water to make lemonade. I

This chapter was adapted from Lloyd Noel Ferguson, *Increasing Opportunities in Chemistry, 1936–1986*, 1992 interview with Gabrielle Morris (Berkeley: Regional Oral History Office, University of California, 1993).

wrote a leaflet in which I described lab experiments. It included a chemical crossword puzzle and advertisements of my products. I had a lot of fun with Ferguson's Chemical Laboratory. From there, when I got the chance in 1936, I started in chemistry at Cal.

My father lost his job because of the depression, and I started working while going to high school. I had a large paper route. After I graduated, I worked as a laborer on the start of the Berkeley marina for the federal Works Progress Administration.

Later I started redcapping [portering] for the Southern Pacific Railroad, handling baggage for travelers back and forth across the bay from Oakland to San Francisco. The hours were flexible and enabled several of us to attend college. Myron King, who was the captain of the redcaps, did a lot to help young fellows who wanted to go to college.

Were there many other African-American kids in high school with you?

Not really. Before the forties, there weren't many African Americans in the Bay Area, perhaps 10,000 all together, maybe most of them lived in San Francisco. In junior high I had a lot of white friends, but by the end of junior high our friendships had fallen off.

I might point out that I have never had a black teacher. It was just a white world. I noticed in my Cal yearbook there were only eight African Americans in the class of 1940, which had 1,874 members.

Did you join one of the black fraternities at the university?

I did not participate in any of the social activities. All my time through undergraduate school was taken up with working morning and night and going to school during the day. Occasionally, I might go to a Cal football game, but I missed out on parties that black students might be arranging.

I did join a fraternity, Alpha Phi Alpha, after I got my Ph.D. When I was going to take a job at a black college, friends who had gone to black colleges urged me to join because fraternities and sororities play a prominent role in those schools.

Did you have any problems enrolling at the University of California?

There wasn't any particular problem. You just came up here and registered. Of course, since none of my adult relatives had been to college I had to find out all of the routine for myself.

One thing I did discover: I really didn't know how to study. All through school I had been getting good grades without any unusual effort. But during my first or second year at Cal, I joined a study group with three or four fellows. One of them was Pat Fuller, who I had known in high school. He was very well organized, and we are still close friends after some 55 years.

There were a couple of times when I got into a tight spot in the lab. One time, something went wrong with an experiment and I got a strange-looking yellow compound. So I had this bucket full of stuff that I should have poured slowly down the commode. But what I did was take it out and throw it in the gutter. That yellow stuff ran all the way down the street across the campus. Did I catch it from the professors!

Another time, I had just learned to make a material that is safe as long as it is wet, but when dry it easily explodes. I made a big batch of this and set it up on the shelf while we went to have lunch. While I was away, some of it dried and something set it off. I was told how the professor came dashing in and wanted to know what was going on.

Gradewise, I had closer to an A than a B average. As a result of the grades, I guess, I was invited to the rushing luncheon of Alpha Phi Sigma, a national chemistry organization. When I got there and they saw that I was African American, they didn't follow through with an invitation to join. I didn't think too much about it until later in the year when I found out all of the other candidates had been initiated.

Did you have any problems with the chemistry faculty or feel left out?

They were very friendly and helpful. It was exciting in the thirties and forties because the research done then at Cal led to more Nobel prizes than any other two decades. Quite a few of them were my professors: Melvin Calvin, Willard Libby, William Giauque, Glenn Seaborg, and E. O. McMillan. All of the graduate students had an idea of what they were doing in the secret area of the lab where they were working on the atomic-energy project. What we learned in our classes was right at the forefront of what was known in chemistry and physics.

I always thought in terms of teaching and therefore I would need a Ph.D. My counselor had told me that it was very unlikely that I would get a professional position in industry when I graduated, because of my race. That was one of the reasons I prepared for teaching. I knew of the work of George Washington Carver, the eminent agricultural chemist. He was phenomenal in developing products from peanuts. With that in mind, I asked myself, "I wonder what I can get from rice?" After a few experiments, I produced a combustible gas and some oils, but nothing very valuable.

When I graduated, I wrote to Dr. Carver and asked him if I could study with him. He advised me to go to graduate school. I then inquired about applying here at Cal, and Dean Gilbert Lewis thought about it briefly and soon accepted me. I was very pleased about that.

At first I worked in the cyclotron, upon an invitation from Glenn Seaborg. After a few months, Melvin Calvin asked me if I would be interested in working on a new national defense project he was directing. I switched over to that group, and so I became an organic chemist instead of a nuclear chemist.

The purpose of the wartime project on which I assisted Calvin was to find a reversible source of oxygen for the armed forces. Up to that time, battleships going into a skirmish would throw their oxygen tanks overboard, because if the tank was damaged, it would become a missile itself with the power to go right through the side of the ship. Having done this, there would be no oxygen for welding and so forth after the battle. We eventually developed a compound for providing the oxygen as needed. The process was later taken over by industry.

I learned a lot from Calvin as far as aggressively attacking research problems. He would come look over my shoulder and ask how things were going. One night, I was working late in the lab on an equation that conceivably could produce a new class of compounds. Calvin came by and said it looked good, "What will we call it, Fergusonobenzene?"

The next morning, I prepared the solutions needed and started the reaction process. I had stooped down to watch the temperature as the reaction proceeded, when the mixture blew up showering chemicals over my head. That was the end of my new type of compound, but it was very exciting while it lasted!

When I was about to get my Ph.D., I noticed that none of the recruiters set up interviews with me. I realized that it was going to be difficult to get a job, as my counselor had said. Fortunately, an announcement came in for a teaching position at North Carolina Agricultural and Technical College. I found that A&T seemed to be a good institution, so I applied and got appointed assistant professor. Being a black college, they were looking for African Americans. This was 1944, a war year, so there weren't many applicants.

By that time my wife, Charlotte, and I were married. She grew up in Arkansas and graduated from Wiley College in Texas. She came out here during the war years after she graduated, and lived with her brother and sister-in-law about a block from my home. We met through them.

After a year, I moved on to Howard University when a job opened there. It was a larger school, and the chemistry department was stronger, so the opportunities were better for professional growth. And I was glad to get the chance to supervise some students in graduate-level research.

Howard attracted some of the cream of the available black students. Many of the top black professionals were on the faculty—people like Nobel Prize winner Ralph Bunche, Supreme Court Justice Thurgood Marshall, and the physician who developed the blood bank, Charles Drew.

How did it feel to be at A&T and Howard, in primarily African-American communities, for the first time?

My wife had prepared me for it. The only thing that shocked me was that during that year at A&T, the students had a strike against the cafeteria food. I just couldn't understand a strike by students! I enjoyed Howard even more because the students were a bit more mature and there was an opportunity to consult with the physics department and the medical school, which were very strong, on problems overlapping chemistry and their fields.

Also we were able to take advantage of a sabbatical at Howard. My first sabbatical was in Copenhagen, Denmark, and the second was in Zurich, Switzerland. In both places I was able to increase my professional knowledge by working with distinguished scientists.

Another benefit of sabbaticals, I would point out, is the opportunity to travel with one's family. All of our children became aware of different cultures by living and traveling extensively in Europe, Africa, and Asia. In Denmark we made friends with several Danish families with whom we have kept in touch over the years.

Then in 1971, after I was at California State University, Los Angeles, I spent a sabbatical in Kenya. I had written to the Ford Foundation to see if they had any openings in programs in East Africa and learned that the University of Nairobi was looking for an organic-chemistry teacher. So Ford and the university got together and awarded me funds. After I got there, I was asked to visit several universities in East Africa to see what they were doing in science and engineering, with the possibility that the Ford Foundation would provide them some financial support.

At the University of Nairobi virtually all of the students were either Indian or black Kenyans. They were pleased to see a black professor. At that time the professors there were white, so my coming gave the students some inspiration. I didn't think that the professor who headed the department was right for the position because his opinion was that the black students couldn't learn enough to go to graduate school and become professionals.

In fact, when I left I wrote a strong letter to the administration. By coincidence he didn't stay there much longer.

When did you become active in the American Chemical Society (ACS)?

I guess that was after publishing my first book.[1] Books in chemistry only last three or four years before they need to be updated. The book and some articles drew considerable attention, which started a fortunate cycle for me in chemical education. Opportunities opened up to participate in various activities, leading to my becoming chairman of the Division of Chemical Education and later of the Southern California Section of ACS.

I was also invited to be a visiting lecturer in a number of professional programs and was eventually appointed to advisory boards such as the ACS Petroleum Research Fund, the Chemistry Graduate Record Examination Committee, and the National Cancer Institute Cancer Chemotherapy Advisory Committee among others.

What made 1965 a good time for you to join the faculty at California State University at Los Angeles?

I had spent three summers as a visiting professor at the University of Oregon in Eugene, and spent several weeks here in California at the end of each summer. So my family and I were partial to California living. Then in 1965 I applied for a visiting professorship at Cal State LA. We became interested in each other; they offered me a full professorship with tenure, so we stayed.

There wasn't yet an aggressive action to get African Americans or other minorities, but shortly after my arrival, which coincided with the social revolution of the sixties, there was a strong program at Cal State to increase both minority students and faculty members. When I became chairman of the department, we added another African American, and a couple of years later we added an Hispanic and a female Asian, and later another female. So we were one of the leading departments in the California State University system in terms of percentage of minority faculty members. At the same time the department is distinguished among the CSU campuses for receiving the largest number of systemwide Trustee Outstanding Professor Awards.

For a number of years, I had been talking at different places trying to interest minority youth in going into science as a career. Then the National Institutes of Health (NIH) started a program called Minority Biomedical Research Program (MBRS), and in 1973 our chemistry department at Cal State was successful in getting a grant to participate. At one point CSULA had one of the largst MBRS programs for Hispanics, African Americans, and Asian/Pacific Islanders. We became the first school with a majority of white students to get an MBRS grant. The program is responsible for hundreds of students going into science-based careers. In addition to becoming university professors themselves students in the program have gone on to become physicians, dentists, pharmacists, veterinary scientists, and medical technicians.

You see, MBRS provides funds for undergraduates to do research—say, 15 hours a week—during the school year and full time during the summer.

Graduate students get a larger stipend, plus their graduate school fees. Students get inspiration from the faculty members and also good recommendations for graduate school. The program has been located at between 50 and 60 schools around the country and it has been very successful in getting minorities into science careers who otherwise did not have the academic and financial opportunity to do so.

Earlier, after the Watts riots in 1965, the American Chemical Society wanted to do something to help. They called an informal group of professors and staff together to plan a program which they named Project SEED, Support of the Educationally and Economically Disadvantaged. ACS was the largest and first of the major professional societies to organize some civilian support for that type of activity. ACS set aside a certain amount of money for the program, and in future years they prodded industry and corporations to support it too.

It's now primarily a summer program, and the name has changed to Summer Education Experience for the Disadvantaged, still called SEED. The program gives quite a few students an opportunity to see whether or not they like chemistry and gives them some inspiration to do their best.

How do young people get into the program?

Faculty members have to be involved. We go to high schools in the area and talk with students and teachers. We ask the teachers for recommendations of students to participate because they know the students' potential best. There is a screening committee at the colleges which reviews the students' applications.

The college faculty are usually impressed with the enthusiasm and ability of the high school students. You find out they have inquiring minds; they ask questions you don't expect, and sometimes they even challenge you. And they follow directions well. Quite a few of the SEED students who have gone on to college have received support from MBRS. The statistics show that MBRS has been a success. It has to be in order to continue to get funds from Congress. Periodically, we wrote letters to congressmen urging continued funding for the MBRS program.

A sister program is the MARC program, Minority Access to Research Careers. Its goal is to get students into doctoral programs. To qualify for either program, a student applies jointly to the campus NIH program and to a faculty member participating in the local program.

In recent years the chemistry faculty has spent a lot of time thinking of ways to attract more students to the department. The number of students has been down, perhaps because the public tends to think of the hazards of chemistry instead of the good things, the beneficial things that derive from chemistry. For example, if it weren't for chemistry, agriculture could not have developed as it has. Even though there are concerns about toxic chemicals, we have to balance the benefits against the risks.

Looking back, what aspects of your work have pleased you most?

I enjoyed teaching and research. I was particularly interested in the biological effects of organic chemicals. One example is the taste of substances. What are the molecular properties of compounds that elicit a certain taste? The same thing with cancer chemotherapy. How do the chemicals react to lead to a cure of cancer? We also want to know why certain chemicals produce cancer. There is a lot of research being done to understand these processes. Progress is slow but moving in a forward direction.

As far as any contributions that I might have made, I think most of my concern has been with getting minorities into science careers. With respect to my own career, I have had good fortune. My family encouraged me to go to college even though no one else in the family had been to college. Then I was lucky in having a job so I could meet my expenses while going to college. I had good teachers, both in high school and at Cal. Also my wife and children were very tolerant, because I was away from home a lot on speaking trips, and panel and society meetings.

My wife, who went into teaching and became a resource specialist in Los Angeles, and I to a certain extent saw ourselves as setting an example for our children and for other minority kids too. We didn't go out saying, "Here we are as role models." But we were always emphasizing the need and the benefits on the job of a college education. Also to go to college for the sake of learning, in addition to earning a living.

I think that the opportunities for minorities and women to go into science as a career are quite good nowadays, mostly because of the help that is available from national minority organizations. Almost every fraternity, sorority, and professional group, like the the Society of Black Physicists, the Society of Black Engineers, and the National Organization of Black Chemists and Chemical Engineers, has a social-action program directed at getting students to go to college and stay in college. Other examples are the Links, a women's organization, and the Hundred Black Men, an organization of professional men. All of these organizations provide role models, tutors, mentors, funds for elementary and high school students to visit libraries and laboratories; and they offer help in preparation for college and graduate school entrance exams. I think these academic support programs have a big impact on minorities and women going into science-based careers.

I am quite proud of the National Organization of Black Chemists and Chemical Engineers. Back in 1972, about eight or ten of us met in somebody's living room to lay out plans for the organization and some of the activities that it might be involved in. We received funds from the Hass Community Fund and Drexel University for expenses, and we added some of our own funds.

Twenty years later, 600 or 700 people attend the annual national meetings, which provide a forum for discussing important issues, hearing technical papers, and holding college fairs. NOBCChE provides graduate fellowships for African Americans and is a clearinghouse for professional job openings. More recently, there is a similar Puerto Rican organization and one among Hispanics and Native Americans in chemistry.

Some of your students have said you were a tough taskmaster in the classroom.

I think all organic chemistry teachers are reported to be a little tough. Perhaps it is because organic chemistry involves a lot of memory work. That calls for considerable individual effort from all students—fast learners as well as slow learners. And organic chemistry is required for a wide range of careers in the medical and biological sciences—pharmacy, medicine, dentistry, veterinary science, nursing, botany, zoology, biology, and on and on. It is also needed for certain engineering sciences. Thus students with a broad range of backgrounds and interests take organic chemistry, many against their will.

As advice to my students, I tell them to study with one or more other students. Instead of just reading and using sight for study, one speaks and hears the material. The more senses you use, the longer you remember things. Many organic teachers give frequent quizzes, too, often unannounced, so that the student has to study continuously rather than hoping to cram just before the midterm or final exam. The repetition in frequent study helps retain the information.

Another point about studying with a group is that someone in the group may have caught some point that you missed. They may ask questions that make you think. So you get some breadth in your studying. That, again, helps the student to succeed.

I tried to impress on my students that I wanted to see all of them do well. "Even though I post office hours," I'd say. "I don't mind if you drop in. Any time I'm in the office, come in and ask, if you have a question."

Over the years have there been some students you've been particularly proud of?

Oh, yes. One of my students has served as president of the National Association of Orthopedic Surgery. He is now dean of medicine at Howard University. Quite a few went on to get their Ph.D. degrees. Almost any place I go, I run into physicians or dentists who took organic chemistry with me.

You see, for years black parents directed their students into medicine, a smaller number into dentistry, because those were among the few fields where African Americans could prosper. Up until the forties or fifties, there just wasn't much job opportunity in science or in the professions in general. Minority college graduates could only think in terms of teaching or businesses for primarily African-American clientele.

When Jackie Robinson came along and signed with major-league baseball, that opened up the opportunities for African Americans in professional sports. But not until the Soviet space capsule *Sputnik* in the 1950s were there opportunities for minorities in science. When the country needed scientific personnel, then it began to give minority men and women a chance to go to school, with financial assistance.

Then the social revolution in the 1960s opened up opportunities for minorities to get jobs in business, in science, engineering, and to hold political office. Equal-opportunity legislation increased minority employment in industry. Once the minorities were able to show what they could do, then there was further interest by industry in hiring them. Unfortunately, it slacked off a little in the 1980s because the administration didn't exert pressure to continue to hire minorities.

When the question of reverse discrimination came up, that raised some barriers to increasing the effort to get minorities and women into corporate-executive jobs. But I think that the Los Angeles riots in the summer of 1992 opened up the conscience of America to ask just where do we stand as far as racial attitudes are concerned. Like the Watts riots in 1965, I think more people were affected positively than negatively. Those who were affected negatively may have been those who were competing for jobs with minorities, and so they felt threatened.

What advice do you have for young people today?

I strongly recommend that the students and young graduates coming through get into a field they enjoy. That is one major factor [in success], to enjoy your work. And I hope, as minorities do well in their careers, that they do not close the door of opportunity for other youth who follow them.

In the last few years more black professionals are doing a lot to help the youth go to college—even the professional athletes are putting money into some of these programs. There is a lot of opportunity for minorities to go out there and help. The main thing is for these [programs] to be brought to the youngsters' attention, especially in the ghetto or in the barrio, where the area doesn't have any outlets. Some of them don't have movies, don't have job opportunities: the youth are really just closed in and isolated.

One of the things that happened is that up until the 1960s some professional people or middle-class blacks lived in those areas. So that was sort of a network holding the community together and giving it some hope and aspiration. But then quite a few of the persons who got to college and into a career moved out. That left nothing but the hard-core, hopeless, husbandless, fatherless children in those neighborhoods.

These minority organizations are aware of that now and are trying to find a way to get back to those areas so that the students do become aware of what the opportunities are. Especially by setting up centers where youth can get not only recreation but advice, tutoring, encouragement, big brother associations.

There are people like Kevin Johnson, the basketball star, who has started the Good Hope Academy in Sacramento where young minorities can get some tutoring and advice; and the Hundred Black Men, who have started these Saturday academies in places like Atlanta. These are the kind of things that are beginning to penetrate these areas and help inner-city youth.

It's awfully tempting for youth in the ghetto to get involved with drugs, when they see they can make so much money right there. A few of them are beginning to learn that it is shortsighted and are trying to get out of it. But once they get into that cycle, it is hard for them to break out.

The Bridge Builders, 1944–1960

10

IVAN HOUSTON

From Buffalo Soldier to Corporate Executive

Ivan James Houston is a third-generation Californian. A 1948 graduate of the University of California at Berkeley, he saw combat with the 92d Division of the 370th Infantry Regiment in World War II and later was president of Golden State Mutual Life Insurance Company, co-founded by his father in 1923, one of the early businesses created to serve the black community. Like his father before him, Ivan Houston has been a leader in developing innovative insurance practices and, through his extensive community activities, in working for better race relations.

I was born in Los Angeles in 1925, and my mother [Doris Talbot Young] was born there too. Her mother came from Canada with her family, the Talbots. They came about 1886, when the railroads came to LA. Her father had come from Tuskegee about the same time.

Mother's people had gone from Jamaica to London, England, before they migrated to Canada. In Los Angeles they lived in the Furlong Tract on 54th Street, where most of the black people lived. Mother graduated from Los Angeles High School in 1916. She went to millinery school and took some courses at the University of Southern California.

My father [Norman Oliver Houston] was born in San Jose in 1893. His father was a waiter who used to work for Paul Masson, the wine maker. Apparently there was a liking between the two of them, and so they gave my father Masson as a second middle name. When we were children, we always used to stop and visit the winery when we drove to Northern California.

His mother was born in San Francisco; her father was from Connecticut. His mother's mother was born in Richmond, Virginia, in 1854. She was not

This chapter was adapted from Ivan J. Houston, *Interview with Ivan J. Houston*, 1986 and 1987 interviews with Ranford B. Hopkins (Los Angeles: Oral History Program, University of California, 1989), with the permission of the Oral History Program.

121

a slave. She left Virginia to sail around South America and reached California in 1869.

My parents met in 1919, after my father came back from World War I. He was a second lieutenant in the all-black 92d Buffalo Division, the same division I was in in World War II. He served in France and was the company adjutant. He always wanted to get into business and felt that the opportunities were greater in Los Angeles.

Before the war, he was a clerk in an insurance agency—white, of course. He also played semiprofessional baseball for the Shasta Giants and attended the University of California for a few years, taking courses in business administration. When he and my mother were married in 1920, they lived for a while with my mother's mother, who was the prime breadwinner for the household after her husband died.

She was a clerk in the county department of vital statistics. She started working there, I believe, in 1907, and was the only black person in a nonmaintenance position until she retired in 1940. Before then, she had a haberdashery shop in Bakersfield. My great-uncle by marriage, who was a big Republican, used his political influence to get her this position in the Hall of Records.

In 1928 we moved to our own house on what is now Central Avenue, which was about as far west as blacks had come. There were Jewish and other people around there, but most of the people we associated with, and all of our social friends, were black. I went to John H. Francis Polytechnic High School. It had a large number of black, Japanese, Chinese, Korean, Hispanic, and so forth students, and it had a very good academic rating.

For many years, my goal was to go to the University of California at Berkeley. I knew that I had to have so much math, so much science, so much foreign language, so much English, and grades no less than B to go to Berkeley. I never ran into anything in high school where they discouraged me from taking college preparatory courses.

How did your father become involved with Golden State Mutual Life Insurance Company?

He was always involved in trying to get something off the ground. In fact, he was one of the people that started the very first savings and loan in Los Angeles, Liberty Savings and Loan Association, in the very early 1920s. Louis M. Blodgett and Charles Matthews were involved in that. Angelus Funeral Home was also started about that time [by black businessmen].

In 1923 or 1924 he met William Nickerson, Jr., a black man who had worked with American Mutual Benefit Association in Texas. He was a very political person and had to leave Houston because he was too strong for the white power structure.

So he knew what a life insurance company was all about. My father was an excellent administrator and accountant, and he knew a lot about the law also. Then there was George A. Beavers, Jr., who was involved in a number of churches. I think he had his own maintenance business here at that time. So with Mr. Nickerson's guidance, the three of them got together and started this company.

Not long after the company was founded, we opened up an office in Oakland, and my father used to drive up quite frequently to visit the office there. Soon there were offices in Bakersfield, Fresno, Sacramento, and one in San Diego. My father was always on the go and wanting to open new offices.

Through the 1920s and 1930s and even most of the 1950s, we were mainly there to service the black community. So each office was opened where we felt there was a significant number of blacks to do business with.

We were the only black insurance company in California at that time. We were sort of isolated from the companies in the East and the South. My dad was determined that our company should become a member of the major insurance trade associations.

There was still segregation, and some of the insurance trade associations up until the early 1950s would not let a black company join. The Life Office Management Association [LOMA] would. My dad made sure that all our company people would take their training and examinations to improve ourselves. He took them himself. He didn't want anyone to do anything that he wouldn't do.

Up until the early 1950s, most of the people we employed were either college graduates or had completed some college. One gentleman had graduated from Cal Tech in the middle 1930s with a mining degree. Well, what was a black man with a mining degree going to do in those days? He couldn't go to work for anybody in mining, so he came to work for Golden State Mutual.

The company through its history has had largely a black clientele. Were there efforts to serve the Asian community and the Hispanic community?

Yes, there were. Not long after the company started, we had a Mexican-American staff which was devoted mainly to developing business in that community. There has always been that outlook. We've had outstanding Mexican-American agents, but we have not done as good a job as we might of developing that business.

Did your father ever talk about his years at Berkeley?

Oh, yes. He always followed the Berkeley football team. One of his good friends, Walt Gordon, was an All-American football player and later a football coach at Berkeley.

When I was in high school, my father was secretary-treasurer of Golden State Mutual Life Insurance Company. I worked part-time for the company, and it was always in the back of my mind that I would go to work for them.

Did you participate in extracurricular activities?

Sports I've always been active in. In the fall it was football, and in the spring it was track and field. By the time I got to the twelfth grade I was a varsity letterman.

Other than sports, I did become an elected officer of the Boys League, I was president of the High-Y at the 28th Street YMCA, which was all-black at that time. We had a great rivalry between the High-Ys, and a whole lot in athletics between Poly and Jeff and Manual Arts high schools.

How did you support yourself when you got to Berkeley?

My brother, Norman Houston, had gone to Cal before me. So it was determined that I should live in the student co-ops like him. I think the monthly rental was about $27.50, and that provided not only your room but also your board. In return for that you waited tables or cleaned up to contribute to operation of the house. My father paid the $27.50 per month, and we did odd jobs to earn a little spending money. The house where we roomed was very integrated. At one time my roommates were white; we were all friends.

This was 1942, so the war in Europe had started. I found out that if I enlisted in the army before I turned 18 I could get deferred for six months. So I did that and was able to complete three semesters before being called up. I was really somewhat excited about going to war, which probably seems strange in this day and age. But my father had been an American Legionnaire, and my brother and I had marched in many of their parades.

When I went to Berkeley, I had to take ROTC, and I became a corporal, although they did not let any blacks become officers. I was called to active duty in January 1944 and I took all their tests. Then I asked, "Listen, how do I get into the air corps?" And they said, "You're going to Fort Benning, Georgia, for infantry basic training." What can you do about it? Not much.

I was assigned to what was called the Army Specialized Training Program. The ASTP was made up of young men who had achieved a certain score on their general army classification tests and were to be sent to college to study engineering. When I got to Fort Benning, Georgia, there were only about six blacks in the whole ASTP company of roughly 200 men, so we were sort of an oddity. The six of us were assigned to a squad with six white fellows.

Basic training was an indoctrination into segregation for someone coming from California. Initially, they even gave the blacks the worst duty—KP, kitchen police, you know. The army cooked on coal fires at that time, and we were supposed to do nothing but keep the coal fires burning. We were also segregated at one table where we ate, but we protested that and then we could eat wherever we wanted.

In March of 1944, I guess, they were getting ready for the invasion of Europe, which happened in June, so all of us in ASTP, the whites and the blacks, were sent to infantry divisions. There was only one black infantry [outfit] in the United States at that time, the 370th Infantry Regiment of the 92d Division, and we went there. As I understand it, roughly 400 to 500 black college students who were in ASTP came into the division then.

We were called the Buffalo Division, and I later read something about that.[1] Back in the days when there were black troops in the cavalry in the western part of the United States, the Indians thought that their hair was like the hair of a buffalo. But we were not told that. In fact, I think the army made a great error in not giving the black troops any kind of history of the unit. We were just the Buffalos, period.

There had been some discussion during World War I that the soldiers of the 92d were not up to snuff with some other soldiers. Did you feel that somehow maybe your division was substandard?

I think we felt that the unit was well trained, although those of us who were fortunate enough to have a decent education knew that there were a whole lot of men in that outfit who had not had a good education. In fact, I heard that one of the reasons we were all sent to the 92d was to raise its general IQ level. A division had to have a certain score in order to be ready for combat, as I understood it. So when we were sent in, it helped to raise their general intelligence score and consequently helped the division get ready to go overseas.

I was assigned to the headquarters company. As soon as I got off the truck at my unit, the commanding officer asked if anybody on the truck knew anything about reading maps. "I do," I said. "You stay with me," he said. "I need somebody like you to assist the operations sergeant in combat intelligence, preparing maps, keeping records."

Late in June my regiment was designated the first black unit to go into combat. We were supposed to be the best trained and with the best leadership and the best men in the 92d. We had been on maneuvers in New Orleans, back to our home base at Fort Huachuca in Arizona, then to Virginia, and sailed from there for North Africa. From there, we went on to the port of Naples, which was just a rubble. We encamped nearby, and a Brazilian company arrived. We saw immediately that within all their ranks there were blacks and there were whites and that was interesting to us.

Just before we went into the combat line, I was promoted to corporal, still assisting the operations sergeant. Our objective was to cross the Arno River and retake a series of fortifications that was called the German Gothic Line. Our initial surge took us to hills that were designated X, Y, and Z that were part of the line. We reached them near the end of October 1944. Time after time, we would capture them, only to be chased out by a German counterattack.

As we crossed the Arno, we were liberating Italians from the Germans. The Italian people were extremely excited and happy, but they were also extremely hungry. They don't seem to think racially. We got along very well with them.

But it was a very demoralizing operation. We lost a lot of seasoned combat troops, especially all of our combat officers, in attacking these hills. Most of the officer replacements in our regiment were white because there just weren't that many black infantry lieutenants. As we began to lose leadership, the unit became less effective.

The final attack in April 1945 focused on a city called Massa just north of hills X, Y, and Z. We had just occupied a house that the Germans had apparently been in only minutes before because there was food there that was still warm. And once again the Germans counterattacked. A mortar shell fell right near the doorway and blew me halfway through the room.

I was what you would call "walking wounded," with a piece of shrapnel stuck in my shoulder. Our medic had a roomful of casualties, so he pulled out the shrapnel, poured some sulfa drug on my shoulder, wrapped it up, and asked if I was OK. I said yeah and went on back to my unit.

A few days later I was sent on leave to Rome. A couple of guys asked me if I wanted to go with them to the Vatican, and we saw the pope [Pius XII]. I think he talked in 12 different tongues. He talked to the Polish soldiers and he talked to the Italians and the French, and then he talked to us in English and gave us his blessings.

I caught up with my unit about the time the war ended in Italy. I left Italy in November 1945 and was discharged from the service in San Pedro, California, which is where I had gone into the army.

I've thought a fair amount about our outfit's impact on the war. We were the first black combat infantry unit to go into action in Europe. I think we made a contribution by holding German armed forces in place there in northern Italy. I believe we showed that we could fight. And I believe that it did show the army that it was not good to have a segregated unit in action because as we began to lose men in combat there were no trained replacements for us. Very briefly in the Korean War, segregated combat units did fight, but after that the army in its wisdom saw that it would be better to integrate the whole armed forces.

What did you do following your discharge?

My main goal was to go back to Cal and get my college degree, which I felt would be in business administration, and then probably work at Golden State Mutual. I had met my wife, Philippa Jones, who was going to UCLA, just before I went overseas, and we got married in July of 1946.

Come to think of it, I was on the track team at Cal. I was a long jumper and a varsity letterman. I was always in the University of California rooting section at football games. Very, very profane rooting section. A lot of drinking going on.

I was also a member of an organization that few people got into called the Order of the Golden Bear. It was made up of student leaders and so forth. I am still a member. They meet monthly and discuss what's good, what's not so good that's going on at the university, how to make it a better place. The only other black who I knew had ever been a member was Walter Gordon, Sr. There was always a concern at Berkeley, in my opinion, that blacks and other minorities should be represented in important groups.

At that time I was the only black letterman. There were some who were coming along in football. I was also involved in the Kappa Alpha Psi chapter when that was organized at Berkeley.

There was one racial incident that I remember. Married students at Cal supposedly lived at one place on San Pablo Avenue called Albany Village. But it turns out that if you were black and married, you had to live in Richmond in the housing projects among the black shipyard workers. They were sort of an interesting group. A lady upstairs used to chew tobacco and spit it out. It struck me as a bit ironic, but, you know, what the heck. I'm too busy trying to get out of there and carry on my own activities to mount a protest.

Did you ever feel as though you were receiving different treatment from other students?

No. At the time I went there it was purely a matter of academics. If you had taken the right courses and had achieved the right grades, then you were pretty much entitled to go there. As far as I knew, it was pretty cut and dried.

There was probably only one other black guy in the School of Business Administration, and I had a lot of good friends among the white guys there. New England Mutual Life Insurance Company did make an effort to recruit me. It's very likely that I could have gone to work for them, but my goal was still to work at Golden State.

After I graduated in February 1948, the company wanted to send me to school to learn about actuarial science; so I applied, and in September of 1948 I entered the University of Manitoba in Winnipeg, Canada. They had a very famous teacher at that time, and Canada was known for having a number of actuaries. Winnipeg is very cold, you know; not much you can do in the winter except lay up in your room and study math.

Not too many black people live in Winnipeg, probably only those people who used to run on the railroads, like the people we stayed with there. The railroad has been very interesting, I think, in dispersing black people around this whole nation. But I never did see any overt signs of discrimination while we were in Winnipeg.

I came back to work at Golden State as an assistant actuary in charge of settling life insurance claims and determining premiums and reserves.

In my personal life I began to do a lot of religious reading, and in 1954 I decided that I would become a Catholic. Since that time I have been involved in a lot of church activities. In the sixties there was a question on the state ballot dealing with fair housing.[2] I wanted to really know where the church stood on this issue—could a person really not sell his house to a black person? So I went and talked to the cardinal for about an hour and a half about the whole subject of discrimination. He felt that it was a moral issue, too, but I didn't think he wanted to come out overtly and tell the Catholic population that they were sinning if they failed to sell their house to a black person.

I don't think he knew too much about the black community. He did see people like Dr. Martin Luther King, Jr., challenging laws. I think he was concerned about where challenging the law would lead us. I felt that a person like the cardinal should take a leadership role in trying to overturn these unjust laws that we had in our land at that time.

I was involved in the Catholic Interracial Council here in Los Angeles too. That was a group of Catholics, black and white and Oriental and all others, who were doing their very best to try to break down racial discrimination. At one time some of them actually picketed the cardinal's office.

You mentioned you were assistant actuary for Golden State. Were there other black actuaries?

There were probably only two or three in the whole nation at that time. Even today, there are not too many actuaries in the whole U.S. You have to have a liking for mathematics.

Later on, I was also in charge of the sales force and all of the marketing. I took quite an interest in the sales function, analyzing where we were good and where we were not so good. In 1957 we had a strike of our company agents in California, so I got involved in negotiating with the union.

By 1970 I was a member of the executive committee and my father, who was 76, decided he was going to retire. So it became a question of who would become president of the company. I was senior vice president and actuary and my brother, Norman, was senior vice president and investment officer. After some discussion with my father and Mr. Beavers and Mr. Johnson, with whom he'd founded Golden State, it came down that I should be the president and chief executive officer and my brother would be chairman of the executive committee and chief investment officer.

My brother resigned as an officer about six months later and became a business consultant. Then he was appointed a deputy secretary in the Department of Health, Education and Welfare by [President Richard] Nixon. But he is still a member of our board of directors and on our investment committee.

Norman is older than I am and was a year ahead of me at Berkeley. After his army service, he came back to UCLA instead of to Berkeley. I graduated in February 1948, and he graduated in June. I'm certain that both of us felt—I guess as all younger people feel—that there should be some change in leadership at Golden State, but we never really discussed who should do what.

Norman has always been very active outside the company, in the NAACP and other community activities, and was appointed a member of the San Francisco Federal Reserve Board. As an offshoot of being a consultant, he was sort of a troubleshooter for companies in difficulty. People always get minorities involved in companies that are on the verge of going bankrupt. He is currently executive director of the Stovall Foundation, which runs housing for senior citizens.

What kind of changes have you been responsible for at the company?

I really like to see good data before we make decisions, so I did generate reports that we should analyze before we make decisions. If management doesn't have the right information, it really doesn't know what to do.

Around 1970 Golden State was one of the first black life insurance companies to press for a percentage of the group-insurance business if a major company had a certain number of black employees. We got companies like Ford, Chrysler, Pacific Bell to place part of their employee coverage with Golden State. The first one we signed up was Crown Zellerbach Corporation in San Francisco.

The country was more concerned about affirmative action then—about righting things that were wrong. Once we did sign them up, many companies publicized the fact in the business press as a part of their public relations. After we got started, Jesse Jackson and his Operation PUSH [People United to Save Humanity] joined in this effort, and I believe the NAACP and other civil rights organizations did also.

In the late 1970s we began to study our market very seriously and determined that still our most successful market was the lower- to lower-middle-income black population in the central cities where we operated. Another big market is funeral insurance. Right now in the eighties, when there's not as much financial aid as there was several years ago, our current biggest seller is our education-at-18 policy.

I find that—and this has always been there—no matter what their circumstances, black people are very concerned over the education of their children. This policy grows as you continue paying for it and when the child reaches age 18 you can have a substantial sum—whatever amount of money has been set aside—available for educating the child. The interest we pay on the fund is pretty good, and it is not subject to income taxes until it is taken out of the policy.

In the 1980s we also have had computers do more and more of our record keeping. This relieves the agents of all that accounting, so they can do more selling and servicing of clients. Often they take care of other business for people at the same time they collect their insurance premiums. Many people don't have bank accounts; they deal only in cash.

It's a social thing too. A lot of times people have other questions they might like to ask an agent. We try to have our agents keep up on welfare, Social Security, Medicare, things of this nature, so that they can give an answer if a client asks.

When an agent doesn't go out to collect for some reason, the phones ring like crazy. Clients call because they expect the agent to go out. Middle- and upper-income people don't go for the agent coming out. They think that's back in the Dark Ages.

How did the Golden State Minority Foundation get started?

Our company became 50 years old in 1975, and we wanted to do something that would have a lasting impact. We looked around and we decided that we would start a foundation. The main purpose would be to provide scholarships to blacks and other minorities and also to get more black businesses involved in the community, as Golden State has always been in the chamber of commerce and trade associations.

We had our first fund-raising dinner in 1976 and raised substantial funds. We've been doing these dinners ever since. Each year we raise nearly a couple hundred thousand dollars, which we pump back into minority scholarships.

How did the civil rights movement in the 1940s and 1950s affect the company?

I think our company was in the vanguard of helping to open up housing, certainly here in Los Angeles, by providing mortgage loan money for blacks who wanted to move, especially to the west side where they could not move before. When we built a new headquarters in 1948, it was pretty far west. Some people thought we were leaving the community. At first we had a few bomb threats from, I presume, white individuals who did not like the fact we were here.

As a person, I've always supported the cause financially, and we did support Dr. Martin Luther King, Jr. Following the Watts riots in 1965, he came to Los Angeles and held a meeting with a lot of community leaders here in our offices. People were very frustrated and angry because nothing seemed to have been accomplished in civil rights.

That was quite an amazing time. We had three offices in that area where many of the buildings were burned. All of our offices were spared. I guess we all knew that we had been through an historic event, but we were surprised and shocked that it had taken place. I don't think it was planned at all, but I think certain events can trigger something like that. You still have a lot of frustrated people there.

Unfortunately, even today a lot of vacant stores still stand in the Watts riot area. However, it did bring the existence of racism to the attention of the whole nation and that this problem had to be dealt with. Certainly, a lot of attention came from the government to the black community in the 1960s and 1970s as a result of trying to solve the problems. Many of those programs have gone now, so I really wonder how lasting it was.

And yet nowadays, in the western part of the city, you have some white families moving back because this is a very good place to live, and there are a lot of historic homes in this area. Racism may still exist, but the opportunities for blacks are there. I think anybody would have to say that there has been a marked change from the 1940s and 1950s and 1960s. Blacks have integrated housing throughout this area quite well. Blacks are employed now at many companies: they're managers; a few are even officers. Prejudice still exists in some of the private clubs in Los Angeles, but it's not nearly as broad or as acceptable as it used to be.

Curiously, in my father's day there were proportionately more black businesses than there are now. One way to account for that is that then blacks couldn't work for white businesses, so some smart, energetic, industrious blacks started their own businesses. We used to have our own hotels. Well, there's no need for a black hotel if you can go to the Hilton.

And there are now fewer black insurance companies than there used to be. We're very much a reflection of how the black community goes. As it becomes more integrated, we're going to be more integrated. If it prospers, we will tend to prosper. But in this day and age all companies have to look out or we might get gobbled up by someone.

Black companies are not showing much growth because there are so many blacks working for white companies. In the future it would be very nice to say that Golden State was still black-owned and -controlled, but it would be even better if it were prospering and growing even if it were completely an integrated outfit.

You and your wife have been involved in a long list of civic organizations, haven't you?

My wife, Phillipa, is a member of the board of directors of the World Affairs Council here in Los Angeles and also of the public television station, KCET. At one time she was on the board of the Otis Art Institute. I'm not sure how well she likes those boards, because it means we go out an awful lot, since I have a number of outside activities too. I think her real liking, other than art, which she's been away from too long now, is her plants. She just grows all kinds of plants, even orchids now; I get to do the moving of the heavy plants in pots.

As the company succeeded, I became involved in a number of major company boards. They were at the time, I presume, seeking black representation. Being a UC Berkeley man and all, several of them sought me out, and I did accept the offers of Kaiser Aluminum and Metromedia and Pacific Bell and First Interstate Bank.

They are all very good companies when it comes to dealing with blacks and other minorities. I think my presence there spurs them to continue to do the right thing. It's been very interesting to work with major companies and see how they handle things. It's amazing the number of people you have to deal with; Pacific Telesis had 122,000 employees when I went on their board.

Whatever the size of any organization that you head, you have to be involved with a whole lot of people. And I have found that you don't have too much control over your time. As I think about retiring from the company, I'd like to get on my computer and do some demographic studies of the black population. I'd like to spend more time playing golf and more time just reading, especially history.

I would like to see Golden State moving off in a profitable, growing direction. There are a lot of questions for minority businesses and still no real answers. Getting good people onboard is a major problem. We try to get good, solid college graduates and bring them through the organization so that they experience the goods and the bads of it. Such a person may in the long run be better than someone who is real brilliant but who may land with another company next year.

| |

EMMETT RICE

To Be Ready When the Door Opens

Emmett Rice was born in 1920 in Sumter, South Carolina. His father was a Methodist minister, and his mother became a teacher after his father's death. Emmett went north to live with an older brother and studied economics at City College of New York. He was a captain in the U.S. Air Corps during World War II. Next he went to the University of California at Berkeley to study for a Ph.D., where he was the first African American to become a member of the city fire department and, in 1952, received a Fulbright fellowship for graduate research in India.

His professional career has taken him from the faculty at Cornell University to the Federal Reserve Bank of New York, the U.S. Department of the Treasury, the World Bank, and other prestigious positions in central banking at home and abroad. In 1979 President Jimmy Carter appointed him to the Federal Reserve Board in Washington, D.C., where he served until 1987.

My father was the pastor of a large Methodist congregation in South Carolina, where he was born. He had gotten his divinity degree at Lincoln College in Pennsylvania. My mother was also born in South Carolina. Her father was a successful farmer. He had a fling in local Republican politics during Reconstruction after the Civil War. He was appointed superintendent of county schools by the governor. He was eventually forced out. My first horseback ride was up on the saddle with my grandfather. I was surely influenced by him. I had a great admiration for him.

We lived in the parsonage, a nice, huge old clapboard house. My father died when I was about seven. My mother had to support the family, so she took what savings we had and sent herself back to school and got her degree and started teaching.

This chapter was adapted from Emmett J. Rice, *To Be Ready When the Door Opens,* 1984 and 1992 interviews with Gabrielle Morris (Berkeley: Regional Oral History Office, University of California, 1995).

There was almost total segregation. I never knew a white person really well until I went to New York. I saw white people all the time. You see them in stores. You talk to them in stores. But if you didn't work for a white person as a maid or cook or something like that, you didn't get to know them. Every once in a while, a white boy would come over and play baseball. I'd say [that] after nine years old, you'd never play with a white boy.

When my father died, my brother was already a big boy at Lincoln College. We couldn't afford to keep him in college, so he moved to New York and became a social worker. He was anxious to get me out of the South, because he was convinced that I couldn't be properly educated there. I was able to live with him when I went north.

What was it like to go to a big city college in 1937?

I was 17 when I entered New York City College. I don't remember feeling anxious, but I am sure there was such a marked contrast from what I was accustomed to that there must have been some culture shock.

The college was not segregated by any means, but there was a great deal of prejudice. White students, generally speaking, didn't have much to do with me. We estimated that there must have been around 100 black students at City College, and there were some at Columbia and New York University, but we were so scattered that I never had another black student in class.

The YMCA was the gathering place of black middle-class kids in Harlem at the time. That was our social life and also where we did sports. There were no white members of our Y. Whenever a black boy tried to join a white Y, he was always referred to the Harlem Y. They wouldn't let us use their facilities. We accepted that as normal; that's the way it was. We didn't like it and were upset about it, and constantly wringing our hands about it.

Why did you decide to study economics?

I was a child of the depression. There was a great deal of unemployment and a lot of suffering as far back as I could remember. I wanted to understand the workings of an economic system where this kind of thing happened. I wanted to see if there was anything that could be done to alleviate some of the poverty and pain and social unrest that I saw. I think that was the thing that drew me to economics.

But the dominant influence that I felt on my life at the time and for a long time after was the impact of racial prejudice. It was always a tremendous burden that had to be adjusted to—everything that happened to you was influenced by your color, in New York as well as South Carolina. The impact was more complicated in New York. Residentially, all black people were pretty much segregated in one part of town, which was horrid. They were beginning to break out when I left.

As a matter of fact, the Republicans were strong in the North, where things were somewhat easier; one could think of them as somewhat better on racial matters than the Democrats. This was in the process of changing during the Roosevelt years, but not much. [President Franklin] Roosevelt was not known as somebody who was interested in civil rights for black people. He really didn't lift a finger about racial segregation in the armed forces during World War II. So while I was sympathetic to many of the things that Roosevelt was doing in the social arena, it did not address my problems. I was not political.

At CCNY I didn't have a great deal of contact with professors. Even in small classes the relationship was very formal. There was nothing in the way of rosy college life. Everybody commuted from home to school, so one didn't build up strong college ties.

What about military service?

During World War II, I was in the air corps. I went to Tuskegee Institute, where we turned out the first black fighter unit, the 332d Fighter Group. That unit distinguished itself in combat in Italy. I was not a fighter pilot. I was taught how to fly an airplane, but not officially. Some people insisted on showing me a thing or two when I was riding with them.

Before that, we learned soldiering and military leadership. Then the air corps took people like me who had some statistics and accounting and sent us off to the Harvard Business School. They had developed a course for the air corps that was a first attempt at trying to apply quantitative management techniques in a military situation. After the war, these ideas were used at the Ford Motor Company.

In a wartime situation you didn't have time to do a lot of thinking about what you are going to do after the war. What you want to do is get through the war. Toward the end I decided I was going to go back to school. What was there to do? In those days people didn't hire professional blacks in business. Had I been white, one of my options would have been to work for a large private corporation. As I saw it, my only options were which kind of graduate school to go to.

My mother was still trying to get me seriously to consider medical school. She said being a doctor was a sure way to get ahead. She asked me what could I do with economics? She was absolutely right.

How did you happen to come to California?

During the war, at Tuskegee, I had met some people from California; so some of my friends were from the University of California. I knew that Berkeley was an excellent university. I had been at Harvard and knew I didn't like it. While I was there, I found it extremely formal, and I just didn't see myself enjoying life there. So I decided to take a longshot. And from my point of view Berkeley was a longshot.

The first time I saw it, I was already a student at Cal. They were very generous to veterans. I was told by my friends in the service that things were more open out here. I just couldn't believe it, but they were right. I sensed that they had an enthusiasm and a sense of identity with California that I did not have with New York.

A number of professors took a personal interest in me at Cal and encouraged me. One of them was Robert Brady, who taught the history of economics. He was a great iconoclast. He criticized everybody. He felt nobody was honest; everybody was trying to get away with something. It's very challenging when somebody is a total iconoclast. Nothing's sacred.

There was a professor named Leo Rogin. I walked into his class totally unprepared for the kind of course he was teaching in economic theory. He picked out four economists whom he dealt with in great detail. They were the Austrian school of the last half of the nineteenth century. We had to read everything they had written. I didn't realize it was going to be as rigorous as it was.

Even though I struggled in that class, I learned a lot. It was highly useful to me. The question he used to ask was, "What is his strategic factor? What is it that causes him to see things as he sees them?" Unless you can isolate that strategic factor, you are not going to understand what he is getting at. The strategic factor is always in the person himself. It's a very useful way of approaching someone's thinking, even somebody who is not an economist.

Why did you decide to live at International House?

I lived in International House because I wanted a pleasant place to live and I wanted to be exposed to people from different countries. Those were two enjoyable years. It was very broadening, stimulating. Something like 100 American students lived there and 200 foreign. The majority were from Europe. There was a liberal sprinkling of Asians—more Indians, I think, than Chinese. And one African.

Now, that's not surprising, since in those days the African countries were not independent. Even so, Stanford attracted some students from Kenya. I got to know two of them. One was in the medical school and one was in political science. I got to know the graduate student in political science pretty

136

well, and then I persuaded him to transfer to Berkeley to get his Ph.D. Within 10 years after they finished their graduate work, they both became ministers in the Kenyan government.

You were also a firefighter while you were at the university, weren't you?

I was a city fireman for two years, bona fide. I had always wanted to be a fireman, ever since I was a little kid. I never wanted to be a fireman forever, you know. But it seemed like something I could do and at the same time continue studying. There were notices in the newspaper and a lot of word of mouth. So I just went down and took the examination. The physical was kind of tough. You had to take a mental test, too, but that was not too hard.

I was the first black in the department. Quite a bit was made of it when I first joined. They did not make me feel particularly welcome, but they also did not freeze me out. They were not happy that this barrier had been broken. It was a big thing. It was not easy for Chief Meinheit to do.

I do not know if there was any pressure on him to move at that particular time, but he wanted to do it. I have to say that nobody really took it out on me personally. They would just as soon not have any black people to be bothered with. They seemed to take the view that it was not my fault. After all, they couldn't blame me for trying to get a better job.

I was primarily concerned with getting a job. If I could do some good in the process, so much the better. I never saw myself as a world savior. I am always glad to try to make things better in the ordinary course of business.

What was it like being a graduate student in the 1950s?

In those days professors did invite us to their homes for a hamburger or whatever. It was a great experience for me. I enjoyed it very much, looked forward to it. I wished I'd experienced it earlier.

The university at Berkeley was the first time when I felt almost free. It was the first living experience—extended over time—where I did not feel the constant pressure of being black. And the first time I had the experience of people relating to me not as a black person but as another *person*. Previously, it was a matter of preconception about blacks.

Relationships are limited to what kind of relationship the white person thinks it is possible to have with a black person. That is really what you mean by prejudice. You have already prejudged what you are going to experience. You've already made up your mind in advance what kind of person you are going to be dealing with because of the color of his skin or some other characteristic. This is the way it works in its worst form.

Anybody who physically conforms to certain characteristics, you assign certain attributes to the person. Once you do that, you have already structured the relationship; you have set its limitations and possibilities. And that is the way it always was with me and, I think, with all black people in their relationships with white people.

As I was saying, the first time I experienced anything different was at Berkeley. Therefore, it was, again, a terribly broadening and developing experience. Again, black students were widely dispersed, and things were so easy around here that there was nothing pushing us together. There was no reason to organize. As far as I recall, there was no black club.[1] I wouldn't be surprised if you didn't have 200 black students around when I was here.

I don't want to give the impression that there were no racial problems around at the time. There were some off-campus; some restaurants where black students were not welcome. While things were relatively open socially as compared to the East, there was more difficulty with respect to employment. It was much harder to get a job on the West Coast than it was on the East Coast.

When I finished my doctorate, it was possible for a black person to get a job teaching at a major university in the East, and I went to Cornell. But I could not get a job at San Francisco State or at the University of San Francisco. I could not get a job at the Federal Reserve Bank of San Francisco. It was a matter of public policy changing faster in the East than in the West. There was a great reluctance to pass laws in California governing fair employment.

When I was a graduate student, there were great debates over long years about fair-employment practices. Most people were saying no. I made a speech at International House one time to a student group there and the need to do this. It was a debate, with some white American students taking the position that we don't need fair-employment legislation.

I know how that sounds now, but back then it was pretty common. I took the position that we needed to have these kinds of laws. Some people thought this was a way-out position. In fact, one of the administrators sat by me one day at mealtime. And he did that to say that he thought I was wrong and should not be making statements like that to foreigners, who might not understand.

Byron Rumford was the assemblyman for Berkeley then, and he was working to pass fair-employment legislation. Did you get to know him?

Byron Rumford was on campus at the time, taking courses in political science while he was in the legislature and while he was running his drugstore. He was kind of a father and advisor. When you had a problem, you went to

Byron. This was because he gave good advice. And he was older than the rest of us, so we looked up to him.

How did you decide what to study for your Ph.D. dissertation?

I got to know some Indian students when I was living in I House and got interested in their economy. I decided I was going to do my dissertation on India. And a Fulbright fellowship came along at just the right time, so that I could go there and do the research.

Right after their independence, India made a decision to develop what they called a mixed economy. They proposed to combine a large public sector with a large private sector and make them harmonize. The Indians were very optimistic that they could solve a lot of the problems that they had suffered with.

They had their eyes set on the right kinds of problems, but they were overwhelmed by other, larger problems like population growth, like the capacity to train people properly. Those things do not lend themselves to easy discussion and planning documents. But you have to overcome some of these practical problems of how do you create a skilled workforce: how do you develop a sense of responsibility in workers so that they will do the best they can, be less wasteful, so that they will try to improve their efficiency and their own productivity.

Professor Norman Buchanan helped me a lot with my dissertation. When I finished a chapter, he would look at it and tell me what he thought. I remember his comment on one of my earlier chapters, on taxation. "Good stuff," he said. "But dry as hell."

The oral committee is a confrontation situation. Even if the committee is basically sympathetic to you and hopes you will get through, they are trying to satisfy themselves that you really know what you are talking about and that this is a creditable piece of work. You have to defend your work. They have to ask good questions, and you have to try to answer them.

I came through feeling that I had made it. When I went outside to await the verdict, I felt good. No one can be absolutely sure. Everybody is nervous until this guy comes up and calls you "doctor."

Black Enterprise *magazine quoted you as saying, "It is always better to act, to work and to perform as if there is no such thing as discrimination."*[2] *How did you develop that philosophy?*

I cannot pinpoint when I reached that conclusion. It was not an idea that came full-blown to my head one sunny afternoon. It was something that gradually evolved. I had been struggling with the problem of how a black person performs in a competitive world where there is a lot of prejudice and where people try to have it both ways—that is, pretend that no prejudice exists in a particular situation, but on the other hand expect black people to behave in a model way because, after all, it is a privilege to be in this position, like Jackie Robinson, et cetera; it is a privilege for you to have this opportunity to do this especially important job.

And you are unusual. For example, I was unusual as an assistant professor at Cornell. There were not any other black assistant professors at Cornell. And I suspect that certain people looked at me harder than at other assistant professors. And they were judging me more constantly.

I had struggled with this problem for a long time. What do you do? Are you always a good boy? Do you always try to be a model person so that nobody can say anything bad about you or use you as an excuse to be prejudiced against other black people? And I concluded that I am only one person. I am only human, and I cannot carry the burdens of the world around on my shoulders and at the same time function. So I was just going to be myself, and I was not going to be constantly minding my p's and q's because people expected me to. If my being black caused a problem, it was not going to be to me; it was going to be to the other people.

I never had any clear, strong signal as to what the black community expected of me. I still do not. I would assume they want me to do a good job. The message I get from articles about me in *Ebony*[3] and *Black Enterprise* is that they are glad I am doing what I am doing. That is all I get. There were people who thought that I should see myself as a representative of blacks on the Federal Reserve Board. But there is no such job. It was quite a number of years between the time the first black member [Andrew Brimmer] served on the board, and when I came along, so there may not even be a black seat in that sense. There is nothing for a black person to do as a black person. You cannot make monetary policy from a black point of view.

Carrying around the consciousness of being black continuously is a psychological burden. You cannot bring your best performance to bear as long as you have this additional drag on you. You have to free yourself of this drain on your energy and your creative power in order to work to your full potential. You have to get rid of this burden so that you will be able to compete fully.

In 1960 you went on from Cornell University to work in government and international banking.

I was teaching the money and banking course at Cornell, which was a popular course, very heavily attended. After five years or so, I wanted to have more practical experience, so I took a sabbatical and arranged to go to the Federal Reserve Bank in New York.

They treated me very well. I was doing research and working on some papers, seeing how things operated. Gradually, I became integrated into the bank operations until I was doing a regular article for the bank's monthly publication and had other responsibilities. After two years, they offered me a permanent position. By then, I had gotten married, and I decided not to return to academic life.

How did you happen to go to the Central Bank of Nigeria?

Nigeria had just achieved its independence from Great Britain and it had asked the United States for assistance in setting up its central bank. That is one of the first things that a colonial country does when it becomes independent, so it can issue its own currency and get control of its monetary system.

Over the years central banks have developed a kind of fraternity, because they do the same thing in every country in the world. They recognize their common responsibilities, and they cooperate on many things. So when the Federal Reserve asked for volunteers to go to Nigeria, I volunteered. I was curious, and I wanted to do whatever I could to be helpful in Africa.

I worked there for two years and had a very interesting and productive time. In the process of operating the central bank we created the institutions by which it would continue to operate and trained Nigerians where that was necessary so they could take over positions previously held by British civil servants.

Before I finished my tour, the U.S. Treasury Department offered me a position in their international finance division. I went there not expecting to stay permanently. But as usual, things don't seem to happen the way you expect them to.

In those days there was a European office, a Latin American office, and the Office of Developing Nations—or the rest of the world. I became deputy director of that office. As a result of our foreign aid, we were beginning to have relations with many of the countries in the Third World. Our responsibility was to see that the U.S. government's overall financial interest was looked after.

We looked at everything that was happening in our financial relations with these countries. It had to make sense to the Treasury, which had to, in a sense, raise the money to pay for the loans. Up until the mid-1960s, we were earning more money abroad than we were spending overseas. But then we became a country that spent more abroad than we earned. That meant we had a balance-of-payments problem and had to be very careful about what we did.

Some of the work of the Office of Developing Nations related to reviewing activities of the World Bank. Thus I had some familiarity with the operations of the bank and was appointed by President Lyndon Johnson and confirmed by the Senate in 1966 to the World Bank to represent U.S. interests.

How did that work differ from what you'd been doing?

The function of the World Bank, of course, is to lend money to developing nations. We established policy for lending rates, approved the loans, and took part in raising special funds for what we called soft loans. At first World Bank policies would only permit lending for railroads, highways, bridges—infrastructure things that would generate revenue to pay back the loans. While I was there, we made a policy decision to start lending for education purposes, population control—social lending, so to speak.

I was at the World Bank for four years. Then in 1970 the District of Columbia decided it wanted to have a development bank and that I was the fellow they wanted to come and work on setting it up. So I did. President Nixon thought it was a good idea as well and submitted a bill to create the bank, but it got bogged down in Congress.

The next year, I became a senior vice president for the National Bank of Washington, where I stayed for eight or nine years and got to be a pretty good commerical banker. We did some inner-city lending; not as much as we wanted to. People would come in with ideas, but without the kinds of plans and resources that were necessary to push them through. But we did some of the first private housing renovation in D.C.—really trying to be socially responsible.

When did you learn that you were being considered for appointment to the Federal Reserve Board?

In 1979 [a senior economic adviser to President Jimmy Carter], whom I had known for some time, asked me to come in and see him. After about an hour of talk about what was going on in the world, I asked him why he asked me to come in.

He said, "Oh, my goodness. No one told you you were being considered for the Federal Reserve?" It turned out that people within the administration had been talking about it for some time. They all assumed that one or the other of them had asked me if I was interested.

I took a few days to think it over, and I decided I could do it. I was sworn in at the White House by Vice President [Walter] Mondale. He had a special interest in economic matters, and I think he was the man who really pushed for my appointment.

I hate to seem to stress this, because it seems like I'm being defensive on the black issue, but I was the right man for the job at that time, regardless of color. There were not many people around who had commercial-banking experience, who had the academic qualifications to fit in with other members of the board, who had been in the government and in international institutions. I would have been a good appointee even if I had not been black, and I insist on that. [*chuckles*] Even though it might have been politically convenient at the time to appoint a black person.

But you resigned after eight years, even though you were appointed for a longer term.

Yes. I had the feeling that I had paid my dues, so to speak. It was a terribly demanding job, and still is. There were always deadlines. Preparation for the Open Market Committee meetings ate up entire weekends because of the volume of material you had to get a grip on before you could even think about making a judgment as to monetary policy. That committee met every five weeks.

There were meetings almost every day on different responsibilities of the board, with long agendas. If you could not find time during the day to work on the agenda, then you had to do it at night at home. You had to do it before the meeting or you were not doing your job. Then there were meetings about things you hadn't anticipated, meetings with other agencies—there were a lot of things going on.

Every governor has a special set of hands-on responsibilities, although everybody is responsible for voting on all matters when they come to the board. I was in charge of two research departments at different times—a division for domestic research and one for international research—and later I became the administrative governor in charge of running the establishment.

For about two years, I was in charge of the Division of Consumer Affairs of the Federal Reserve Board, which had been delegated by Congress certain responsibilities for a number of laws concerning consumer credit and fair-lending practices. The division was in charge of writing the regulations for these laws and for oversight of their implementation. One of them was the act which required banks to demonstrate that they were actively lending in the communities where they are seeking depositors and being what I call socially sensitive. We didn't want to do that, but Congress didn't trust any other agency to do it.

I reached a point where I felt I had done a yeoman job on all these duties for long enough. I think I could have survived it another three years, but it is demanding work, and after a point I decided that my important work had been done. The reason I thought my job was done was that I believed, and do believe, that the most important thing we did during the time I was a member of the board was that we broke the back of the raging inflation that occurred in 1981.

We had a serious inflation problem when I joined the board, but we didn't recognize how really bad it was going to be. As the inflation gained momentum, it seemed less and less responsive to the traditional measures we were taking. We had to be more and more restrictive in our policy on the growth of the money supply and allow interest rates to rise to very high levels. We hated to see them there because they were hurting a lot of people and industries. We were criticized and threatened; the anger that was directed at [the] Federal Reserve was a symptom of what people were feeling out there in society.

It took about two years to break the back of inflation, and it took us another two years to stabilize the economy. It was 1984 or '85 before things were getting back to normal, from a central banking point of view. It was the Open Market Committee that really took the tough decisions. That committee was the seven of us who were on the Federal Reserve Board, plus five of the presidents of the 12 Federal Reserve banks around the country. I consider it a privilege to have been a member of the committee that did so much to bring inflation under control.

There continued to be a lot of problems throughout all of this. On some of them we had an impact. For instance, we made, I think, a contribution in the Third World by lending money at critical times to countries in critical need. The United States has become much more part of the global economy than we were.

What do you think of current economic policy?

We're not following sensible economic policy in the United States and haven't for some time. Many places in the world also are not using the best economic knowledge that is available to make conditions better. That's usually because the political imperatives are inconsistent with what needs to be done in the economic field.

For the most part, people understandably follow their own interests as they see them. Often they're governed by short-run rather than long-term interests. Sometimes they are slow to recognize what their interests are, and sometimes they never do see them right. What actually happens is a result of all these often competing interests working themselves out.

Regardless of what economic policy is changed or what political decisions are made, it usually takes a year or more before you are able to see real results. The most important thing is to establish national priorities to achieve sensible economic and social goals. That's a problem, but it's a problem in political courage.

12

ALLEN BROUSSARD

Working for Equality in Society and the California Courts

Born in Louisiana in 1929, Allen Broussard came to California with his family as a teenager. Graduating from the University of California at Berkeley in 1950 and its Boalt Hall law school in 1953, he entered private practice in Oakland and became a key figure in creating a viable African-American political presence in the city. He began 27 years as a judge in 1964, rising to the state supreme court, where he served from 1981 to 1991.

A leader on the court and in judicial education and administration innovations, Broussard has been called "a great role model for blacks and whites [with] a sophisticated understanding of the struggle of blacks for recognition in law practice and the judiciary."[1]

The first Broussards came to the Carolinas in 1695. My parents were both reared on farms in small communities near New Iberia, Louisiana. When they were married, they moved to Lake Charles, where I was born and lived until I graduated from high school in 1945. My father was a weekend barber and a longshoreman.

During World War II, my brother served in the Army Transportation Corps in several West Coast cities. He interested my dad in coming out to San Francisco because of better working conditions and better pay on waterfront work here. My dad came out in 1944, and my mother, sister, and I joined him the next year. We lived in apartments or flats in San Francisco until we were able to acquire a single-family home in South Berkeley, and [we] moved there in 1948.

My family never really pushed me, but they always supported me. Going to college was probably more my idea than theirs. I had one male instructor

This chapter was adapted from Allen E. Broussard, *Working for Equality in Society and the California Courts*, 1991 and 1992 interviews with Gabrielle Morris (Berkeley: Regional Oral History Office, University of California, in press).

145

in the Catholic high school I attended. I talked with him and he said, "Well, Allen, you've got a fine mind. I think you can do anything you want to do, but I think you'd make a good lawyer."

When we came to San Francisco, I was told that I had everything I needed to get into the University of California at Berkeley except that I had to make up a D I'd gotten in algebra. I credit that D with saving my life academically. I still feel that if I had gone to Cal as a freshman, I might have gotten lost.

Instead of going to summer school to make up algebra, I went to City College of San Francisco. That campus was only 5,000-plus students, unlike Cal which was larger than Lake Charles. Even City College was a very large transition for me, but I was able to handle it, eventually functioning on the campus and getting active in student government.

Did you experience racial discrimination at City College? How did it compare with Lake Charles?

Louisiana law at that time required segregation, even in the Catholic schools which I attended. In California the law didn't require segregation. But, remember, there was a tremendous influx of blacks during the war years. Segregation maybe was still expected, both by us and by the dominant white community.

In Lake Charles five of us worked in retail stores. Every morning before school we'd ride our bicycles downtown and sweep the lobbies, wash the windows. We used to carry broom handles to defend ourselves, because by the time we rode back the white kids would be coming out to go to school and they would sic their dogs on us or chase us. At noon as we would be going home for lunch, the black kids from the public high school would be walking in the opposite direction, and we used to have turf battles, who was going to walk on the sidewalk or in the street!

Our home in Lake Charles was right at the end of the pavement, and then you had a few blocks of dirt streets with black families' homes. Beyond that you had a little section of relatively poor whites we called Fisherville. When they would come with their roller skates to skate on our sidewalk [*chuckles*], we'd put on our skates and run them back to Fisherville. So it was an environment where there was a lot of hostility between one group and the next. Some of it was between fair-skinned and dark-skinned blacks, some of it was between blacks and whites, and then some of it was between Catholics and non-Catholics.

At City College black students used to sit together in one section of the cafeteria, which I guess was a comfort zone. I remember the dean used to try to get us to mix with others; but as you began to venture out, you began to get opposition. We formed a student chapter of the National Association

146

for the Advancement of Colored People, and I was the perennial president. That was a very important chapter in my life because, being president, I was ex officio a member of the senior NAACP executive board, which was then in the forefront of integrating San Francisco.

The nucleus of the NAACP in the late forties was the great leaders like Carleton Goodlett, Cecil Poole, William McKinley Thomas, Josephine Cole, Noah Griffin—so many others I can't recall—Terry Francois, Joe Kennedy, Audley Cole. Whenever they needed assistance in passing out leaflets, doing door-to-door work, or picketing, or whatever, they'd just call in the younger people in the college chapter.

When the World War II jobs started closing down, we started running into lack of job opportunities, lack of housing opportunities. A lot of the craft jobs were union, and in San Francisco those unions were closed to blacks. The NAACP started negotiating with the Downtown Merchants Association to get them to open up retail selling jobs to blacks—with no success. Finally, we had to picket to get the first two blacks hired in downtown San Francisco. The first was at Macy's and the next two African Americans to be employed were at Emporium, which had been one of the stores most resistant to hiring minorities.

We had to bring political pressure, threaten to strike and bring lawsuits, to get the first black high school teacher, the first black police officer, and then later on to get a job as auto salesman or waiting tables or in the craft unions and on and on. All of those barriers had to be broken.

My college work with the NAACP was a large factor in my deciding that I wanted to be a lawyer. And it played a large part in my commitment to being involved in community organizations and trying to make a difference. I'm just grateful to have been a part of the change that we were making.

What was it like in the late 1940s when you transferred to the University of California?

I made some good friends there, both black and nonblack. A very small black enrollment; almost all the black students got to know each other. When I realized that Berkeley has one of the finest law schools in the country, I looked into what it took to get admitted to Boalt. And I said to myself, "Broussard, you better start making some better grades." Once I had a specific goal and started pushing my studies, my grades went up almost a grade point.

During the school year, I worked at C. H. Baker Shoe Store, always in shipping and receiving and stock. When I went to law school, I spent most of my summers working at the Del Monte cannery and saved as much money as I could. I'd give it to my parents and have them give me back so much a month. I wanted to help them as much as I could. But I would take a little out for a trip to Los Angeles when Cal would be playing UCLA, and I managed to get a little car.

Everything was new and strange the first year of law school. We started with three blacks in my class, out of 106, and one woman. It was the first time there had been three blacks at Boalt at one time. The whole concept of special admissions or support programs hadn't developed yet. I was admitted competitively and had to perform competitively. I had to operate pretty much on my own. And there was so much self-doubt because I didn't know whether I was learning what I was supposed to learn.

The saving grace was to get into a study group and not try to get through alone. A study group requires that you keep up with the work and that you articulate the concept that you're studying. If you can't explain a concept to your study group, you don't understand it well enough to do well on an exam. At the end of the first semester I was number six in the class.

When I graduated from Boalt in 1953, I didn't even realize that the law firms were interviewing my classmates. I couldn't join the American Bar Association. I didn't get any job referrals from law school until after I came back from the army and began private practice.

After law school and before the army, I was the research attorney for Ray Peters, a presiding judge of the First Appellate District. I think I was the first black attorney in that district. Peters was a great judge and a true liberal. While I did have law-review experience and a pretty good class standing, I think that was an instance in which he reached out to give me that opportunity.

It was a great experience to work for him. He really helped to shape and develop some of my judicial philosophy. He taught me not to just coldly and objectively analyze a case but to think of the impact you were having on people and society.

How did you go about starting a private law practice?

What I did was join a black law firm in Oakland. Through my NAACP work, I knew most of the black lawyers in the area by the time I graduated, because the traditional way for a young black lawyer to become known was to get involved in what was going on in the community.

In 1959 I went in with Lionel Wilson, Carl Metoyer, and Wilmont Sweeney as an associate and became a partner in 1961 when Lionel was appointed to the Oakland Municipal Court by Governor Pat Brown. Lionel was the first black muni judge in Alameda County and the first black superior court judge. I was the second.

We both came out of the East Bay Democratic Club, as did a lot of other appointments. We also had an organization called Oakland Men of

Tomorrow, to which most of the black business and professional men belonged. I met my wife through Men of Tomorrow. Odessa was working for a radio station in San Francisco that offered us some free air time; we started dating and got married in 1959.

Within Men of Tomorrow, we developed a sense of obligation to be involved in the various organizations that served the community. We built the kind of relationships that carried over into business. It got to the point where many organizations would contact Men of Tomorrow and ask for recommendations for people to serve on various boards and commissions.

Out of that we built the East Bay Democratic Club, which included Evelio Grillo, Don McCullum, Lionel Wilson, Viola Taylor, Dolly Hughes, Ruby Bims, and others, and we began to build a political base in the East Bay. We were the group that elected Byron Rumford to the assembly in 1948.[2]

We had a modicum of white membership in the East Bay Democratic Club, but our goal was to be able to select our own black candidates and deliver the votes within our own district and not be spoon-fed by Democrats from outside of the district. In 1958 our members chaired the campaigns of all of the Democratic candidates on the ticket in the Eighth Congressional District, and Democrats won all the top statewide jobs except one.

We started agitating at the local levels, too, and that led to the election of Wilmont Sweeney to the Berkeley City Council in 1961 and Barney Hilburn, who was a Republican, to the Oakland school board. At that time the key to getting a black elected in Oakland was to get someone who had good, basic support in the black community but who could also get some white support.

In the early 1960s you also had the Afro-American Association, which was developing race and cultural awareness and black pride. Don Warden was the head of that initially. Then came Bobby Seale and Huey Newton and the more militant Black Panthers. The Panthers were a very positive influence for a long time. Later on, when some of them were tried in court, the Panthers created a problem for the establishment because they would stand there with their weapons in front of the courthouse door.

That was a new experience to a lot of people and really shocked them. But they never presented a real problem within the courtroom. I'm sure that the Oakland police and others paid that matter a lot of attention, but as a judge you go in and try to do the best job you can with your cases and try to ignore what's going on outside the courtroom.

There was a lot of uncertainty as to what their motivation was at the time, but it developed that they were expressing their concern about the whole law-enforcement mechanism. They were making a statement and, in the main, doing it peacefully. Although obviously they did have other contact with the police that was not so peaceful.

There were people saying that Oakland was a powder keg. "Don't buy there, don't live there," you'd hear or read in the newspaper. But for some reason, there was always a cohesiveness in Oakland that just prevented riots from ever happening. As members of the Men of Tomorrow, we do think that because of what we and a lot of other people were doing in the community, it never did blow.

Oakland was just as often a city with potential, that's the way I viewed it. The Ford Foundation, with input from Evelio Grillo, put money into Oakland for the first antipoverty program in the nation.[3] Then along came the War on Poverty, and Lionel Wilson chaired all that work of urban renewal and rehabilitation through the Oakland Economic Development Commission.

What did you think when Governor Pat Brown wanted to appoint you to the municipal court?

I was 34 years old, just was beginning to make money. If I'd had my druthers, I would have wanted to wait 10, 15 years. But I talked it over with my wife, my parents, and with Lionel and Byron and others and decided that it was an opportunity that I shouldn't pass up.

When I went on the bench, there were several of us newer judges, and we learned the work together. I enjoyed the muni court because I like people. On the municipal court you're handling misdemeanor matters and civil matters with a cap on what you can recover, and preliminary examinations of felonies.

It's a whole different ball game on the superior court: less volume but more substantial matters, and the possibility of complex legal issues. When you're a superior court judge, you look to the supreme court and its cases to tell you what to do. You worry about whether you're doing what the supreme court told you ought to be done in a given situation. And up here on the supreme court, when you're deciding a case, you're trying to determine how it is going to impact upon all those lower court decisions that are going to be made, that affect the lives of so many people.

In 1981 you were appointed to the California Supreme Court. What was the appointment and confirmation process like?

There were actually two vacancies on the court. Bill Clark had resigned to go to Washington with President Reagan, and Wiley Manuel, the first African American on the court, had died. The governor, Jerry Brown, knew that whoever replaced Manuel would have to run again in eight years, but the person who got the Bill Clark term would get a full 12-year term.

The then attorney general, George Deukmejian, had set his sights on the governorship and was already making a political issue of Brown's judicial appointments. So the governor deliberately appointed me to the Bill Clark vacancy. During the hearings on the confirmation of my nomination to the California Supreme Court, the attorney general asked me if I was going to be an activist judge.

I said something to the effect that I frequently think that judicial activism is in the eyes of the beholder. I don't think he liked that answer, and when the vote was taken he voted against me. So I was confirmed by a 2–1 vote and, of course, it created a big furor. Then I think he realized that it would be too political to vote against just me, and in subsequent hearings he voted no on a number of other Jerry Brown nominees.

Fortunately, I knew all of the justices on the court, so it was not too difficult to learn how the institution operates. It's a very unique institution; there's nothing like it in the whole country. It's not only the size of the state and the complexity of the issues, but we generally managed to be very much in the forefront of state supreme courts and very much on the cutting edge of the law as it developed.

Rose Bird, the first woman on the California Supreme Court, was chief justice when I went on. There were a lot of people who were not happy with her appointment, but I always found it easy to work with her. Until 1986, when there were a number of changes in the seven members of the court, I was generally in the majority in the decisions of the court and wrote the opinions on a number of significant cases.

Some supreme court cases raise a lot of issues. We would wrestle with the legal issues and the analysis and case precedent. And we did a lot of reasoning among ourselves to try to get the justices to agree. Sometimes you can overcome differing views and persuade people to sign onto an opinion; other times you can reason with people and not agree. Then you have dissenting opinions.

At that time the court was getting approximately 5,000 petitions for review of lower court decisions per year, plus automatic review of all death-penalty cases, which was a much-publicized issue at that time. Being a justice is a very demanding job. First of all, the work is never done. There are always more cases to be dealt with. And the work doesn't go away. Even if you take a vacation for two weeks, when you come back you have to review everything your fellow justices have done while you were gone.

After Rose Bird left the court in January 1987, I served as acting chief justice for three months. One of the things that was very challenging for me was that I sat on the confirmation hearing for Malcolm Lucas, who became the next chief justice. He was nominated by George Deukmejian, who by then was governor. Since Deukmejian had voted against my appointment on the view that I was a judicial activist, I was tempted to comment that if I were to do what Deukmejian had done I would vote against Lucas simply because I had a different judicial philosophy. There was some testimony against Lucas, largely on the basis that he had minimum contact with people of color and their problems and situations in life.

One of the reasons I believe that a court is well served by having some diversity in its membership is so that people who have different experiences and views, and are competent and professional, can impact on each other's thinking and conclusions. We judges sit around the table and discuss cases so that we can all give input to the ultimate work product. If there's no diversity, there's very little give and take. If you all have the same attitude and philosophy, the results are rather predictable, and the court is not going to expand its thinking.

I enjoyed saying, "Wait a minute. Let's stop and take a look at this." In some instances I was able to turn the direction of the court around by the power of analysis and persuasion. I will not be specific on this because it would be a violation of confidence.

You've been active in judicial administration as a presiding judge and in a number of judicial organizations. What interests you about this kind of work?

Well, that's just the sort of person I am. I thought I could provide some leadership, effectively administer the business of the court, motivate some of the judges to maybe be a bit more efficient in terms of the way they applied themselves to their work.

I have tried to work effectively for individual fairness and justice and equality. I have a tremendous admiration for people like Thurgood Marshall who took the tools that society provided to try to improve the society for people of color. He worked within the system in a most effective way.

Sometimes I wonder why I never grew up to be a hater. There were many things in my background which could have caused me to hate white people. Growing up in Louisiana where everything was segregated in law and, in fact, I had a lot of personal conflict because of my race and my religion. It would have been easy for me to hate people who were different from me, but for some reason that has not happened. I have race and ethnic pride, but I don't have bitterness and animosity.

When you think of it, we have moved rapidly, even though things seem to move so slowly. In January 1992 Governor Pete Wilson appointed three blacks to the bench in Alameda County or elevated them to a higher court; one of them, a woman, became president of the county bar association and then went on to the federal court. And all three of them replaced judges who were black. Compare that to 1964, when I was appointed to the municipal court and Lionel Wilson was the only other black judge in the county. There were just one or two in San Francisco then and maybe half a dozen in Los Angeles.

There were so few black judges in the sixties that I was aware that many judges were seeing or working with a black judge for the first time in their lives. That helped motivate me to get involved in judicial education and judicial organizations. Over a long period of time I was in essence setting an example for a lot of people. I belonged to the California Association of Black Lawyers, which had a section for we judges. In addition CABL was very involved in encouraging the appointment of blacks to the bench.

In the 1980s Chief Justice Lucas appointed a Commission on Race and Ethnic Bias in the Courts. I became co-chairman of that, and I hope to continue on that now I'm retired. It's important to study people's attitudes about race and ethnic discrimination, and the existence or appearance of racism in the courts. We've had a good response in hearings around the state—some very poignant testimony from Native Americans and other ethnic groups, as well as African Americans. Much of the testimony related more to police-citizen contact than to the courts. The seminal point is that you can't separate police work from court work. In the eyes of the average citizen it all starts with the police.

Now that you've returned to private law practice, do you see any unfinished business for the courts?

We have a lot of wide-ranging problems facing the judiciary in California and a number of things in the works to try and solve them. As a judge, I was involved in matters bearing on equal treatment for our diverse population, and I spoke out on these issues.

What I'm concerned about now is that, more than any state in this nation, California has racial and ethnic diversity. It is increasing rapidly and presents a major problem of two dimensions. One is to really assure that all of the ethnic diversity that comes before the courts is being dealt with fairly and, secondly, to assure that, assuming fairness, there's also the appearance of fairness. Because people's perceptions are as important as the reality.

Stop for a moment and contemplate the differences that people come to California with: some monied, some poor, some with skills, some without; different religious, cultural, social, educational, and language backgrounds. Yet we have one court system. It is a tremendous challenge to maintain what we call a system of justice and to apply it equally to all people.

13

CHARLES PATTERSON

New Horizons: The Peace Corps and Corporate Leadership

Charles Patterson (1925–1994) was born and raised in Indiana, where his father worked in the steel mill. After army service in World War II, Charles received a B.A. from Antioch College and an M.A. from Case Western Reserve in sociology. He worked for the Urban League and other civil rights and social research organizations in Ohio and California. In 1958 he began work on a doctorate in sociology at the University of California at Berkeley, which led to research in England and Africa.

From 1964 to 1966, Patterson was deputy regional director of the Peace Corps for African programs and later associate director, following which he came to Oakland, California, as coordinator for federal economic development programs. As senior vice president for public affairs for World Airways (1968–85), he was in charge of affirmative action, corporate social responsibility, and administration. In 1985 he became general manager of the Oakland Convention Centers. With his wife, Dorothy, a leader in health education, he was active in many civic, cultural, and philanthropic organizations.

The formative thing in my life was race. I grew up in a time when lynchings were quite common—every week you'd open the black newspaper and there were pictures of lynchings. In my hometown, Fort Wayne, Indiana, you had to sit in the balcony of the movies. We couldn't eat in the restaurants.

We lived on the outskirts of town, next to the Romanian and Hungarian immigrants who came to work in the steel mill. My father's life was full of prejudice and discrimination. He was trained as a mechanic and yet he worked as a janitor in the mill.

This chapter was adapted from Charles Patterson, *Working for Civic Unity in Government, Business, and the Community,* 1992 interview with Gabrielle Morris (Berkeley: Regional Oral History Office, University of California, 1994).

There was no union or anything like that. And there was real illness—my second-oldest brother died at 16 of tuberculosis; premature death was another thing that one was very much aware of.

As a kid, I loved going to church. We went to the African Methodist Episcopal Church on Sunday and we stayed. We'd maybe go home for dinner about two in the afternoon. Then about 4:30 be back for Young People's Christian Endeavor. The thing that stuck years later was the whole Christian notion of ethics and helping other people.

That overwhelming awareness of being black and surrounded by racial prejudice and discrimination was probably sharpened because I did go to an integrated school. But I think that was only because there weren't enough African-American children to have separate schools.

My grandfather, who fled from Alabama ahead of a lynch mob, had been a teacher. He set great store by education, so that's probably why I took to school. Some teachers were encouraging, but in general we were just not welcome, and we knew it. I found myself in a very marginal position because of my interest in school and because other black kids were less interested in school. And marginal because I was not part of the white student groups.

One of the great discoveries in my life was reading and libraries. Out in this disadvantaged neighborhood of ours, the library truck used to come every Saturday. I would be there and get five or six books every week. I still remember the truck was a marvelous, shiny apple green.

I got good grades in high school and was president of the high school Latin Club and French Club. So I wound up a lonely black kid in the high-achiever track. I grew up with this great awareness that there was something quite wrong and something needed to be done about it. But I was never able to articulate these feelings until years after I came out of World War II.

Tell us about your military experiences.

First, I was encouraged to take this test for the Army Specialized Training Program. The ASTP was intended to find all these bright kids and send us off to college, after which we would be trained as officers. I was drafted when I got out of high school. Here again, everybody else was going in one direction and I was on a train by myself going to ASTP. When I got to Fort Benning, Georgia, I was one of four blacks out of a training company of 250. But the first sergeant and the captain told me that if anybody gave us any trouble, we should let them know.

Interestingly enough, it was a setting into which I was able to fit very well. We had young fellows from places like South Dakota, many of them had never seen a black. Others from the North had gone to integrated schools. Mostly, guys from the North outnumbered the guys from the South. The military learned that the way you integrate is that if you have good discipline, soldiers take orders, and nobody would give us a hard time.

They wiped out most of the ASTP programs when things got bad in Europe, and I was sent to Fort Huachuca, Arizona, for training with the famous 92d Division of African Americans that had fought in World War I. I became a rifleman in the Jim Crow infantry. I went overseas, and I did a lot of shooting and killing. I got a Silver Star, a Bronze Star, and a Purple Heart all between the age of 19 and 20.

I came out of the war having been wounded and feeling this overwhelming sense that the wrongs of the world needed righting. My first impulse in terms of wanting to do good was I thought I'd like to be a minister. That's what I thought of as a fit role model. It never occurred to me that I could be a teacher. All my teachers were white. I got disillusioned with the church because our minister at that time was giving these sin-and-howling-death sermons that pushed me right out of any inclination to be a minister.

I knew I wanted to go to college, so I started in at the Indiana University Extension Center. By this time I'm thinking I'd like to do something about discrimination against Negroes—I wanted to save the race. I didn't have the faintest idea how one went about this, but I embarked on the study of sociology because it looked to me like that was most relevant.

Somehow I found out that the only race-relations committee in town was at the YWCA. I went to one of their meetings, and this white man stood up and started saying we need to organize an Urban League here and an NAACP to do something about prejudice and Jim Crow. I could have fallen through the floor, because here is a person talking about the kind of things that I want to do! He was Aaron Gilmartin, a Unitarian minister, and he really took me under his wing. He and Paul Jacobs, who was a radical journalist.

So we organized the first NAACP in Fort Wayne, and this white minister became the first president. Gil started giving me things to read, and we talked—I guess I made my unhappiness with Indiana University known, the Jim Crow dormitories and stuff like that. He started talking about Antioch College in Ohio, which I had never heard of. And he and Jacobs decided that Antioch was the place for me. They helped me apply, and I was accepted.

I had a great time at Antioch. There weren't many blacks, but I found these great New York, Jewish intellectual friends; those were my spiritual people. I found myself in a situation where I'm free for the first time, in terms of social relationships. There was a great deal of ferment at Antioch: students were boycotting barbers who didn't cut blacks' hair and generally were active in annoying the neighboring small towns about Jim Crow practices. I loved that and was very much involved.

In a very real sense Antioch delivered me from a sense of hopelessness based on my early Fort Wayne experiences. Antioch was a community that believed in the ethic of change and progress; their teaching and attitudes were about how to improve this world we're in. I'm still following those directives.

Antioch sends you out to work part of the year, you know. That was a problem because you weren't always welcome in the jobs available. I found my own job working for Paul Jacobs, who had gone back to New York to work for the American Jewish Committee. AJC was working with the Fellowship of Reconciliation and the Congress of Racial Equality [CORE] opposing discrimination in the military.

What I didn't know was that I was expected to raise the money for them. I didn't know anything about that; it was my first experience with looking for philanthropic funds in order to get something done. In those days CORE was heavily integrated and dominated by Bayard Rustin and the pacifists. They were the ones who took the first freedom rides in 1949. I remember the blacks and whites that did that got beat up and threatened and almost killed. I began to understand that it would take a lot of hard work to save anybody.

My first full-time job was with the Cleveland Urban League, from 1951 to 1957; I'm in my late twenties by then. While I was there, I went to Case Western Reserve and worked on my master's degree. The Urban League was primarily fighting job discrimination. We had this pilot program to create jobs for qualified black people in nontraditional settings. Every day I went with my portfolio of resumes under my arm, hammering on the doors of business and industry to try to persuade them to hire some of our people. Years later that experience was relevant when I got involved in the Private Industry Council jobs program.

I remember I called on some of the big defense contractors. I read up on government-contract requirements and decided that they were a much better weapon than the usual Urban League–type persuasion. My biggest success was when we persuaded the federal authorities to come in and take a look at contract compliance. That immediately led to a breakthrough, and three major corporations began hiring Negroes for something other than janitor jobs.

How did you get from Ohio to California?

What happened was that I had become interested in the whole area of intergroup relations, which was then expanding. There were more and more jobs in civil rights agencies, [and] fair-employment-practices commissions were coming into being. The National Association of Intergroup Relations Officials, in 1957, got a grant from the Fund for the Republic to establish some internships. I applied and received one of those spots, which was a fellowship with the San Francisco Council for Civic Unity.

Again, I think it was mentors looking after me. I think they decided it was time for me to leave the Urban League and work in a different intergroup setting. The people that I came to know there I have worked closely with in different organizations over the next 35 years. Interestingly, this was my first major contact with the unique quality of Jewish philanthropy. Many of the people active in the Council for Civic Unity were part of the Jewish community, which plays such a unique and positive part in philanthropy in the Bay Area.

The council had a broader base than the Urban League and was interested in housing legislation and things like that. I was quite impressed to see that their board had some very heavy hitters, in terms of white people at the senior corporate levels. They were very active in taking on committee assignments and raising funds. They had been instrumental in getting a city FEPC. They were people who had the capacity to open doors and get things done.

After my one-year internship, I went to work for Paul Jacobs again. He had also come to California, to work for the Center for the Study of Democratic Institutions. [Even though the center was in Santa Barbara, we worked in Berkeley.] I got the feeling they were glad to have a black person like me on their staff. There I was surrounded by all these high-powered academics, and Paul, again, was mentoring me. The job was part-time, so he said, "Hey, you can study for a Ph.D." So I enrolled at the University of California in 1958.

There were two other black students in the graduate sociology program, but at that time you could walk across the campus and if you saw another black student, it was a real surprise. It was a unique opportunity. I was well paid for my research job, and I had ample time to do the doctoral studies. I still wanted to devote my career to dealing with the problems that were being faced by black people.

I discovered that there was nobody in the department for whom race relations was a specialty, although I did find an adviser who knew a lot about it even though he had moved more into mass behavior. I was impressed by some courses I took on the development of the intelligentsia and on the concept of marginality, and I began to focus around them. I realized that I fit the definition of marginality myself: marginal meaning living with one foot in one culture and another foot in the other culture. Most of my life activity was in an integrated setting because that's where the opportunities were opening up.

A [white] faculty friend suggested that I follow up this idea by doing my doctoral research on Africans who had been educated in Europe, and he got me a fellowship with the Institute of Current World Affairs. Once again, I was the first black in a heretofore all-white situation.

First, I spent some time in England, where there were gobs of Africans finishing their education. I went to meetings about what was happening in

West Africa and elsewhere and wrote about them for the Institute of Current World Affairs. The whole notion was to develop expertise among Americans about Africa.

There were also all kinds of African leaders coming to London for meetings in the great ferment going on about Ghana and other countries becoming independent. I met many of them, including the prime minister of Nigeria, where I planned to do my research at the University of Ibadan. I became aware that shared color was a limited bridge in terms of understanding each other. Among educated Africans, there was much awareness of Negro Americans and their accomplishments, but in this country Negroes (I use the term "Negroes" because I'm talking about that period) tended to look down upon the Africans. All this looking to Africa came much later.

When I got to Nigeria, I had some terrific experiences. There were still a lot of British lecturers at Ibadan and a lot of American scholars, but I also dealt with a growing number of Nigerians who had studied in the United States. My wife, Dorothy, was there, too, and she was involved in nutrition and growth studies at the medical school.

About that time I came to the conclusion that my interest in the academic world was not as sharp as it should have been. We came back to the States and started checking out job possibilities. A friend in Washington was director of African programs for the Peace Corps and he talked to me about coming to work for them. That seemed exciting to me and consistent with the idea of being in a place where I could be effective and use the knowledge and insights I had been gathering in Africa.

When I took the job in 1964, the Peace Corps was at its height. I wanted to spend time actually running the program in one African country, but the program was expanding rapidly and instead I wound up as the acting associate director. That put me in charge of all the overseas programs, figuring out what was the best use you could make of volunteers and what kind of programs we were going to do. They were demanding projects, mostly in agriculture and education, sometimes organizing clinics and digging wells. Volunteers had to work hard and do their very best. My notion was to give them as much help as possible so they could do a good job.

Then you came to Oakland with the War on Poverty.

Yes, in 1966. I was hired to oversee the Economic Development Administration [EDA] program that invested in public works, business development, and technical assistance, and also to coordinate with all the other federal agencies that were giving aid to Oakland under the economic-opportunity legislation. This was not too long after the Watts riots in Los Angeles, and a lot of people thought that Oakland would be the next city to erupt. My EDA boss wanted to demonstrate to Washington that we could help the city and keep that from happening.[1] Basically, the goal was to create jobs.

The biggest pot of money was for projects at the Port of Oakland to develop a new terminal and an aircraft-maintenance facility. We were the first to require that whoever leased the new facilities commit themselves to develop a plan to bring in the unemployed or underemployed. World Airways was the biggest beneficiary because they leased the maintenance hangar.

Ed Daly was head of World. He did not start off thinking about working with the people targeted by the legislation, but he responded very quickly and strongly. He hired a man who was teaching aircraft-maintenance courses at a junior college to set up a training project. The beauty of it was that the project included funds to train people to work in these new jobs being created in the new airport facilities being built with project funding. That was the beginning of more than 20 years that I've been involved in manpower-training programs, from the War on Poverty through CETA [Comprehensive Education and Training Administration], and then the Private Industry Council and the National Alliance for Business jobs program.

I had gotten to know Ed Daly while setting this all up. One day, he said, "Why don't you come to work for me?" I said it would be a conflict of interest because EDA was still involved in building this hangar. But then there were some changes at EDA; Daly and I talked some more, and he decided he wanted me to develop a social-responsibility program for the company.

So I became head of public affairs for World Airways, which meant I dealt with the outside community. I was responsible for affirmative action and company giving and appearing before government bodies. We helped several Third World countries develop their own airlines, and I was always involved because of my experience in Africa.

It became clear to me that the World Airways was hiring people who looked and acted like the people already employed; there was downright discrimination. But Daly was strongly committed to affirmative action, so I was able to change those employment practices. While I was there, World Airways became one of the most integrated companies for its size. I was responsible for bringing in at least 300 minority people, including several vice presidents.

I got to be very visible around the community, and people would talk to me when they wanted support from World Airways. I would check out personal charities that Daly was considering, and I was also the company's representative at meetings and events and went on the boards of various organizations. I saw that in the Oakland–San Francisco metropolitan region, there was no other board member who was black like me. Gradually, I wound up on the board of the San Francisco Fine Arts Museums; the board of overseers of University of California, San Francisco; KQED; the San Francisco Foundation; and similar organizations, often because somebody was looking for someone to integrate that board somewhat.

I got the feeling that some of them heaved a sigh of relief when the "right" person appeared, someone like me who came out of the corporate matrix. I never felt out of place because I had a certain amount of self-confidence, which told me I could handle things on anybody's board.

When I came to World, I think Ed Daly probably relaxed because he didn't have to do so many community things himself. I could do it. The New Oakland Committee is a good example. It developed out of a long series of confrontations with the Black Caucus, which went after the business community, saying,"You've got to do more." Three or four of the top white businessmen in town agreed to put out some money to get it going, and just about every prominent black leader has been a member. It's one of the few urban coalitions that's still going.

Bill Knowland got heavily involved in the New Oakland Committee [after he left the U.S. Senate]. He used to say, "We dared. We got a dialogue going and we got black and white people talking to each other." The critical change in Oakland had to do with the growing number of blacks, who became the dominant political group in the city, and the solid presence of middle-class blacks with education and training and jobs. A lot of them were in politics, although some of the younger ones continued to fight the power structure even when it was taken over by moderate blacks like Lionel Wilson.

But it is also important that there was this commitment to the city by these business leaders. The City Center development [with the big hotel and convention center] had its roots back in the early days of the New Oakland Committee. That has been the only place where white corporate leaders and black professionals and community activists have talked on a continuing basis.

In the committees and boards where you started out as the only African American, did you have ideas you wanted to introduce?

I developed this idea that you have to do things differently. One of my favorite words is "reconfigure." Reconfigure contains the notion that you don't tear something up, you reorder it. I feel that it is very important to reconfigure the kinds of people you have on all these boards. For one thing, if you have a different kind of life experience than they're used to, you can develop the notion, "Why don't we do it this way instead of that?"

In the 1980s, when I went on the San Francisco Foundation board and, later, the East Bay Community Foundation board, I was able to get into dialogue with other board members, saying, "You haven't got that quite right." To my thinking, on occasion they were not too understanding of what some minority groups proposed to do with the grant funds they were requesting.

I found that my fellow trustees wanted to do good but didn't necessarily understand fully what the problem was that people seeking support were trying to address. So my thought is that it's a good thing for public bodies to have someone there who has some personal experience about what's facing people in education, what's facing people who are homeless, what's facing people in the way of racial discrimination.

How did you happen to leave World Airways and become head of the Oakland Convention Centers?

Ed Daly died, and so did the spirit that made the company so responsive to the community and other people's cares. I decided it was time to leave. I mentioned that to my friend Lionel Wilson [who was the mayor at the time]. He suggested that the general manager had left the convention centers and they needed somebody to get things squared away, and that I should talk to the board chairman about it.

So I came over here, and I have rather enjoyed it, so I stayed until 1993. The convention centers have had a role in the continuing development of the City Center, which now includes two new federal office buildings, and we also sit in on the Oakland Metropolitan Forum, which is a University of California effort to help in resolving whatever problems the city faces.

In a very real sense Oakland has arrived, because people are leading good lives here. There is an awful lot of good housing and an awful lot of things to do. People talk about the slow pace of development, and I say, "If you had been around here in 1968, you would realize that the city has strongly turned around."

Some people say that if you didn't get this or that project, you blew it. That notion is all wrong. Nobody blew the development of Oakland. All the things that go into making this a better city take time, money, and effort. There has been a lot of movement and an awful lot of people working on things in the neighborhoods as well as downtown.

One of the ideas I've developed over the years is that increments are OK. This life will go on and on and on and certain things will still be totally unresolved. But there will also have been some continuing improvement and updating in the lives of more and more people.

The important thing, as Martin Luther King, Jr., said, is to help somebody! That's been very much part of my life, because I received a hell of a lot of help. People offered me a way to break through to new horizons I didn't know existed when I was floundering around after World War II. That's why I believe very strongly in efforts addressed to young people. They can't consider other ways to live unless they are aware that there are other possibilities.

Afterword

Change and Continuity for Black Students, 1950–1990

Since the 1950s when the African Americans whose oral histories are reported in the previous chapters completed their college educations, great social and political changes have created a very different experience for black students now entering the University of California from what their predecessors encountered. These changes fall into two phases that have had significant impact on African Americans at Berkeley and at other campuses in urban areas.

In the 1960s and 1970s, owing to the civil rights movement, affirmative-action programs, and sizable increases in the state's minority population, people of color became an established part of the campus scene. In the 1980s and 1990s economic recession and the expectations of large numbers of new immigrants have caused sharp pressures on admissions to the university that will undoubtedly affect who goes to college in the next century, regardless of ethnicity or race.

In this 40-year period the number of African Americans enrolled at Berkeley has risen from about 200 to around 2,000. But even as many of these students distinguish themselves academically, in extracurricular activities and professional careers, they continue to speak of feelings of exclusion and discrimination similar to those expressed by earlier generations.

1951–1968: ONLY AT THE MARGINS

For today's college students, it is difficult to imagine that higher education in America has almost always been characterized by nearly complete racial segregation. Until the late 1960s, a student body that was 97 to 98 percent white at the major colleges and universities was taken for granted. The traditionally black colleges were routinely at least 99 percent black.

The University of California was no exception. As late as 1968, blacks comprised only 2.8 percent of the students at Berkeley.[1] A few years earlier, when the African-American graduates interviewed by Gabrielle Morris were on campus, black undergraduates were an even smaller fraction of the students enrolled. This was true of other colleges across the country, public and private, even in urban areas, many of which had become more than 20 percent black in the post–World War II period. The Berkeley-Oakland community adjacent to the campus, for example, had grown from 387,710 to 498,380 between 1940 and 1950, and the black population from 11,857 to 60,851.[2] And yet the city of Berkeley was characterized by racial residential segregation and its public schools were segregated.

This typically white-as-normal pattern continued at the university as well. It was not until 1954 that the campus hired its first black professor, David Blackwell.[3] An important contributor to the field of statistics and a member of the National Academy of Sciences, Blackwell's appointment was delayed for five years by the department of statistics, in a social climate in which the wife of the department chair wondered, out loud, how he might fit in at faculty dinners.

The handful of young African Americans in the student body of approximately 12,000 during this period were, in effect, at the margins of the institution: they were made to feel unique, unusual, even freakish, or they were praised for having distinguished themselves from the rest of what was in that era called the Negro population. The few hundred blacks who were undergraduates during the 1950s recall being "congratulated" for "not sounding black" by their white acquaintances and peers.

While the numbers tell us that the African-American student was a rarity, these figures do not quite capture the often demeaning, apartheidlike quality of life for these students. In 1951 a young black freshman from Los Angeles named Thelton Henderson arrived on the Berkeley campus and was assigned to a room at Tyrone House, where most of the black students on campus were housed. He joined the baseball team and became friends with Donnie Walker, a white baseball player. The two decided to room together and went looking for an apartment. For several weeks, they followed up leads from the housing office, but wherever they went, they were refused housing.

More poignantly, Henderson remembers the day in 1953 when baseball coach Clint Evans called the team together to give them a pep talk. Henderson, now chief judge of the federal court of the Ninth District, recalls Evans's speech vividly: "This is the year in which we can beat Southern California [USC]. We have all the talent, but we need to be focused, purposeful, and in top shape. I am going to make sure you are in shape. Now, I want all of you to run around this playing field twice, and the last one back is a nigger baby."[4]

The Transition, 1964–1972

As the civil rights movement began to change the lives of African Americans in California and other parts of the nation, there was a strong impact on the ways in which black students experienced the University of California. In the early 1960s civil rights was a powerful and compelling topic of politics among students at Berkeley. Indeed, the Free Speech Movement (FSM), launched in the fall of 1964, was a direct outgrowth of the civil rights movement. Scores of students, mainly white, had gone south during the summer of 1964 to participate in campaigns to help black people register to vote. They brought back with them to Berkeley a fervor and excitement from working in the movement that quickly took on a local political flavor.

Insisting that blacks be hired for jobs from which they previously had been almost completely excluded, students took part in boycotts of local stores and sit-ins at automobile dealers and hotels in San Francisco. The protests and rallies, many of them mobilized on the campus, angered merchants, who wanted the university to put an end to what the business-men felt was unwarranted political intrusion. The administration, re-sponding to political pressure, attempted to shut off this avenue of political expression. Student activism, however, had been launched, and its insis-tence on a voice in campus decision making would have a lasting impact on the university.

The role of black students in the FSM, and in the early anti–Vietnam War movement, was at most marginal. All this soon changed when in 1966 Stokely Carmichael and others launched the Black Power Movement, which reverberated on college campuses around the nation in the next three years. African-American students mobilized for a black studies department at San Francisco State in the fall of 1968. A few months later militant black students at Berkeley joined Chicanos, Asians, and Native Americans to form the Third World Liberation Front, with some input from white radicals. Their demands for student-controlled minority programs led to months of confrontation ending in a campus strike in the winter of 1969.[5]

Three factors converged in the late 1960s and early 1970s to abet black students' demands for change. First, there were relatively small numbers of African Americans on campus in a context of a powerful civil rights movement (and the later moderately effective black-power spin-off). Second, admission to and enrollment at the university was available to anyone with a 3.25 grade-point average (GPA) who had fulfilled course requirements or supplemented somewhat lower GPAs with high SAT scores. Third, the state's relative affluence provided a higher-education budget large enough to enable the university to put in place special services, special programs, outreach, and support systems for its relatively small number of minority students.

In this climate affirmative action for a few hundred blacks was irrelevant in the larger context of general admissions. Moreover, in the larger political context it seemed the right thing to do. The social, political, and economic costs were manageable, and so an affirmative-action admissions policy was not a contentious issue for the campus in those years.

The Admissions Crunch Meets Affirmative Action

In sharp contrast by the mid-1980s the crunch at the admissions gate was so severe that both the presence of black students and their sense of entitlement to be on campus became the source of resentment in many quarters. This is in large measure attributable to the fact that by the end of the decade only 16 percent of all those applying and meeting the eligibility requirements were admitted.

Approximately 21,300 high school graduates applied to Berkeley in the fall of 1989. Only 3,500 spots were open in the freshman class, however. To complicate matters, more than 5,800 of the 21,300 students who applied had straight-A (4.0) averages. The median GPA of the black and Latino freshmen admitted to Berkeley that year was 3.5 (well above the 3.25 requirement), but the median GPA of white and Asian freshmen admits was 4.0.

The social consequences of this small 0.5 difference in median GPA between groups are far greater than could have been imagined by the students of the 1960s. Not only does the difference generate a sense of superiority among those with the higher average, but charges of racism, reverse discrimination, and a panoply of recriminations and sensitivities revolve around the meanings and interpretations given to this difference. Emotional statements about the fairness or unfairness of the current affirmative-action admissions policy come from all sides. Indeed, the admission of a single one of these "mere 3.5" students becomes the source of passionately told stories of resentment that enter the folklore and the conventional wisdom.

Moreover, the fierce competition using only the academic index has pitted whites directly against Asians, and the whites are losing. According to a

1980 national survey, 78 percent of Asian/Pacific Islander high school seniors expected to earn a four-year college degree, compared with only 46 percent of white seniors.[6] By 1986 33 percent of Calilfornia's Asian high school graduates were academically eligible for admission to the University of California, whereas only 16 percent of white high school graduates qualified.[7] By the fall of 1993 there were 7,656 Asian undergraduates and 7,219 Caucasians, in addition to 1,183 African Americans, 2,956 Latinos, and 239 Native Americans on the Berkeley campus.[8]

Continuities between the 1950s and the 1990s

Campus surveys and newspaper and magazine accounts report that America's college students segregate themselves by race and ethnicity on campus in the 1990s. While this appears to be a new development worthy of commentary, black students of earlier years also primarily kept the company of other African Americans. Justice Allen Broussard in an oral history for the Bancroft Library recalls that when he was an undergraduate at San Francisco City College in 1946 and 1947 "black students used to sit together in one section of the cafeteria, which I guess was a comfort zone. I remember the dean used to try to get us to mix with others, but as you began to venture out, you began to get opposition."[9]

Since Broussard's student days there have been profound changes in the status and roles of ethnic and racial populations in the United States. Issues of race have not disappeared in the 1980s and 1990s, but rather have taken new forms. In the 1950s when there was only a sprinkling of blacks on campus, the presence of a Negro, the term then generally used, in the college setting frequently aroused curiosity and suspicion. What was this person doing in this normally white setting? In the 1990s with an increasing black middle-class population and increasing ethnic and racial minority representation on campus, students of color still face questions concerning their presence on campus.

These doubts take two forms. In the classroom and residence hall blacks are often still seen as affirmative-action (read "perceived to be special action") admissions, and questions are raised about their intelligence, qualification, and aptitude. Walking around campus or in the surrounding community, these same students may be seen as part of the outsider population of teen "gang bangers" or the hangers-on, homeless, unemployed or underemployed, who have become part of the street culture of Berkeley and other nearby urban areas. Like other black persons, these students encounter passersby who treat them as high school dropouts, not doctoral candidates.

The Current Scene, 1989–1994

From 1989 to 1991, extensive survey research, known as the Diversity project, was conducted on the Berkeley campus. It involved all the racial groups present in the student body in order to gain some understanding of how members of each group perceived themselves and other groups.[10] These homogeneous focus groups revealed that African-American students feel that, despite their belief that blacks on campus are normal and appropriate and despite profound academic achievement and success in the workplace after graduation, they seemingly cannot escape from long-standing stereotypes about their race.

In these discussions black students said they thought that Berkeley would be a liberal, "ethnically diverse but socially integrated" environment in which differences would be accepted and respected. They also commented how much their actual experiences have diverged from these expectations. Instead, they have encountered an environment in which racial and ethnic segregation is "everywhere," as well as what they term subtle and pervasive racism. Moreover, many of them hold the view that students are "categorized," "labeled," and "stereotyped" according to their perceived group identity.

As with Asian Americans, Latino students, and Native Americans, the African-American students who come to Berkeley fall into two distinct categories: those who come from predominantly white high schools and those from overwhelmingly black or integrated urban high schools. It is counterintuitive that black students from white high schools experience the greatest tension about racial identity when they arrive on the Berkeley campus. Though race was important in high school, as part of a tiny minority in the school, most adapted by fitting in. While they had casual and comfortable friendships with whites and members of other groups, they were also conscious of their racial difference: "Teachers would make racist jokes. Like one guy used to always walk up to this other student and pat him on the head and say, 'Oh, Brillo pad,' or something like that. . . . [T]here were three black students in this class and the other two always got this. I never got that so it was a really difficult situation because I could escape it by being quiet."[11]

Peer Pressures

On arrival at the Berkeley campus these students were surprised to discover themselves no longer the "token black person," burdened with constantly explaining what it is to be black. Rather, as part of a significant population of African-American students, they were invited to join clubs and organizations that celebrate aspects of African-American identity and culture. Several said that the new salience of race was unanticipated. "OK, I went to private school my entire life until the tenth grade. Then I went to basically an all-white school. And I never felt any need to realize my African-American descent. Now I'm here, everybody puts such a stress and importance on it, I am realizing that I am black. . . . I never saw a colored world until I got here and people started stressing the importance of color."[12]

These students experience a new kind of pressure that comes from other African-American students on campus. It is experienced as pressure to make decisions about friends, social networks, even who you sit with at lunch, on the basis of race: There is "a kind of external pressure put on me to act a certain way, speak a certain way. Because always in high school you talk white, you act white, they think you're white, you're white. [*laughs*] So when I got here, it was just everyone running around trying to be blacker than thou and so I kind of gave in to that."[13]

This pressure can be detrimental to a student's ability to settle down to academic work. The majority, however, manage the situation remarkably well, negotiating unfamiliar opportunities as well as new and changing boundaries. Some retreat into their own worlds. Some gravitate to social groupings of blacks. A few consciously cultivate friendships and associations across racial and ethnic groups.

Most, however, even those who resent and resist pressures to conform, speak positively about the opportunity to discover and explore their racial identity with groups of other African Americans. Self-discovery is seen as essential before interacting on any meaningful level with another group. One woman described what it meant to her: "I know this is a real diverse school but where do I fit in and where are my people and what are my support groups? . . . You have to find out where you are in this big scheme of the picture before you start looking at the whole thing."[14]

The second category—African-American students from black or integrated urban high schools—is a substantially smaller proportion of the total. They actually find an easier adjustment to the social groupings at Cal.

Academic and Social Support

Many black students arrive at Cal with very successful academic backgrounds, having been A or A − students throughout high school. They are brimming with confidence about their abilities, but they are also sensitive to the potential stigma of being characterized as an affirmative-action admit. Rather than seeking out study groups or finding assistance from a teaching assistant or visiting the Student Learning Center, they may retreat to individual study patterns.

Other students come with an attitude that the university will be a new level of competition. They arrive knowing that they are going to have to reach out for help wherever they can find it. In subtle ways, however, the atmosphere around race and the implications of diversity in admissions policy reverberates even into such small crevices as the choice of study habits.

Asian-American students routinely study together in groups, even when they are doing relatively well, and apparently have little problem asking for help from an instructor or even going to the Learning Center. For a number of African-American students, their sensitivity to the potential characterization that they are "of course in need of help" makes them put up a barrier to help seeking or collective work that might otherwise be rewarding experiences intellectually and socially.

In the Diversity project research African-American students spoke starkly, too, about their academic adjustment at Cal in terms of their high visibility in classes: the sense that they were objects of scrutiny and silent discrimination by professors, teaching assistants, and other students, and the lack of other blacks who might provide a sense of support. Their experiences in the natural and physical sciences recall comments from the 1950s when black students were a rarity in all departments on campus. According to one student, "I'd say . . . there's maybe two or three other blacks in my [pre-med] field, and we know each other. We walk into the class and a lot of times you're the only black there, and the professor might mention something and, you know, I catch people looking over my way and making sure, do you understand what he's saying? I sensed . . . it was because I was the only black in the class."[15]

For all students, there is a need to develop social support groups that will assist in sustaining their progress through college and even into the world of work. Some African-American and Latino students describe race-based associations in engineering and the health sciences as a response by members of racially identified groups who found themselves to be small minorities in certain subjects and came together to gain social support and to get mutual aid in their academic studies.

Because it is a large institution, with large classes and relatively intense competition for academic rewards, Berkeley can be difficult for many students. This is heightened for anyone who experiences his or her situation as marginal socially or who, as is the case with some students, still needs to acquire study, writing, and other skills that are necessary to academic success. In asserting the need for more black faculty as well as more adequate social and academic supports black students seem to be saying that if the university makes efforts to recruit blacks to campus, they have a parallel responsibility to help provide the kinds of support services that will encourage academic retention and graduation.

A Multi-Ethnic Focus for the Twenty-first Century

African Americans, like Asian American and Latino students, often have their first encounters with campus ethnic and racial politics in high school. For some black students, the excitement and pride they experience upon learning that they have been accepted into Berkeley can be squelched when they share the news of their acceptance with high school friends and teachers of other ethnic backgrounds. They begin to hear stories about how Cal is not the most hospitable place for them.

Several students recounted the reactions of Asian and white friends when they were informed that a black student had been accepted into the freshman class at Berkeley. Instead of sharing in their joy, these friends found ways of alluding to white or Asian friends with 4.0 GPAs and high test scores who did not get into Cal. The African-American student's acceptance was invariably attributed to affirmative action. One student told the following story: "You know, I went to a teacher in high school and said, 'Well, I got into Berkeley.' And she like told me, 'Oh, you only got in under affirmative action. And I'm like, 'OK, thank you, bye!'

"Then I came up here and another white friend, he tried to water it down. [He said,] 'Most black people get in, you know, under affirmative action because they don't really get good grades, because they don't study' or stuff like that."[16]

In addition to adjusting to academic studies and college life the most visible and public choice incoming African-American freshman have to make is what kind of black they are going to be. One student notes, "My high school was 98 percent Mexican or Hispanic background. And so I had friends from all over, in terms of background and everything. So when I came here, I figured I'd find the exact same thing. Of course, I was wrong. . . . When I began the year, I felt like I was expected to join this group of blacks because I noticed that they were all sitting at the same table near one corner of the dining commons. . . .

"I had met my roommate, who was Asian. I had met all the guys on the floor and I was thinking to myself, OK, am I going to go sit with the guys from up on the floor or go sit with the blacks? And I felt this pulling in both directions and I was confused. I didn't know what to do and, um, I stopped and looked and they all looked up and saw me and I was just standing there. I didn't really know what to say, and my roommate said, 'Oh, we're sitting over here.' And I looked over there and they're sitting over there waiting for me and I'm standing there in the middle of the dining commons going, 'Great!' So I went and sat somewhere else," away from either spot.[17]

As the above quote illustrates, prior to their arrival at Berkeley, some African-American students have already had their hard work negated, and once on campus they have to continually prove that they "deserve" to be at Berkeley. One student stated that no matter how long he studied, his Asian-American roommate perceived him as "lazy" and not studying "hard enough." Another student said that he was told by an Asian student that African Americans and other minorities don't have to work hard because they know that they have affirmative action.

For many students, constantly having to justify their right to be on campus engenders self-doubt, defensiveness, and the desire to stick with their racial group and thereby be less likely to get hurt by the perceived color-coded stigma of affirmative action. One black student summarized the impact of negative stereotypes as follows: "I know there's a perception amongst black students that they, the Asian students, more so than even the white students, look down upon us or our capabilities or there's a kind of silent air against [us] at times, about them."[18]

In an environment of polarized race relations simple questions such as dress take on new meaning. Yet another African-American student commented on this topic: "The reverse stereotype is that blacks are normally big, loud, strong, forceful, musically inclined, athletically inclined, intimidating. It's kind of weird when, say, for instance, you're walking down the street and they have these stereotypes and certain things they can see that are true about you. You are big. If you happen to be wearing sweats and high-top tennis shoes, you look like you're athletic. And playing on those, they say, 'Well, you know, he must be coming from a basketball game or something like that.' "[19]

This suggests that within the student culture beyond the classroom, African Americans continue to have to justify their presence at the university. And, indeed, that failure to conform to expectations about their racial identity may cause confusion among other groups. The need to explain and define to each other the varied cultures that are increasingly large segments of the university population would seem to be an urgent and rewarding academic challenge.

For most of the nation's history, racial and ethnic relations have been primarily dominated by the relations between blacks and whites. For the last two centuries, blacks have been the largest single minority, although Latinos and Asian Americans have at various times played significant roles in California history. During the last two decades, however, Asian and Latino immigration and reproduction levels have come to occupy an increasingly important role in the nation's consciousness.

California and New York have for some years been the largest states in the nation. Approximately one in every five Americans now lives in one of these states. They are also among the most ethically and racially heterogeneous regions, with the heaviest concentration of Asian Americans and a large proportion of the Latino population. Indeed, African Americans now constitute the fourth-largest population group in both places. This development has remarkable significance for the transformation of consciousness about the meaning of race in these states and, ultimately, nationwide.

Until recently, a very circumscribed pattern of thought has dominated the American social landscape. The discourse between black and white has influenced most of the empirical research on race and ethnicity and has shaped the public debates about educational policy. The data from Berkeley in the late 1980s suggest the emergence of polymorphous interethnic relations on campus. As Asians and Latinos have become a larger part of this landscape, the old assumptions, the old dance of two, have been completely transformed. A trio, a quartet, and even a quintet of ethnic and racial groups mixing together changes vital and important conceptions of issues of race and ethnicity for both blacks and whites, as well as their newer partners.

For example, black students who come from suburban areas and have professional parents are sometimes accused of "acting white" by their urban peers. In a dually configured world in which "being black" is partially achieved by "not acting white" African-American racial identity is partly defined and framed in terms of this negative belief. In its extreme form this can take the shape of defining academic success (in grammar school and secondary school especially) as white behavior. This necessitates affirming black racial identity by avoiding behavior that would produce academic success.

When Asians and Latinos are a part of the matrix, all this changes. For starters, academic success, which was once regarded as dominated by, if not the province of, whites, has now shifted to Asians. Asians now have more than double the rate of eligibility for the University of California than do whites. Latinos, on the other hand, share with blacks the problem of lower rates of college eligibility and high dropout rates from high schools. African Americans and European Americans are thus no longer the sole audience for each other on matters of academic success. "Being black" becomes much more complex and may offer both problems and opportunities in identity construction in such a newly developed multicultural or multiracial situation. Indeed, the quest for identity must move from the negative of "not acting white" to the positive of some form of affirmation of a substantive identity. This, in part, may help explain the reemergence of African centrism in segments of the black community.

The entry of third and fourth parties into the ethnic mix requires rethinking the concept of academic success. Just as the arrival of academically oriented new immigrant Jews from Europe in the 1920s led gentiles to demand college admissions based on "individual merits and achievements," there now exists on the Berkeley campus an open questioning of the value of getting straight A's and having high GPAs as the definitive and only measure of entitlement to study at the university. Although many European Americans would like to continue to insist on this standard, they are faced with a contradiction. With Asian Americans excelling on existing scores and tests, arguments are being made for including other criteria on admission applications.

For African-American students at the University of California, the struggle on the road to a level playing field has been long, bumpy, and, even into the current era, extremely difficult. The contours have changed dramatically over the last half century, and yet the elusive issue of "equality" provides the continuity. As the oral histories of this book's earlier chapters remind us, until the 1950s there were only a few score African Americans on the Berkeley campus. Their narratives tell us that these pioneers were, and are, exceptional individuals, some of whom appear to have sought out a marginal life in which they would interact with other races. During this period, they were segregated by the housing policy of the university, the routine practices of landlords, and the expectations as to what areas of study and employment should be open to them. Although these students of the pre–World War II years distinguished themselves in varied academic and career fields, it is likely that they were, then as now, often seen as special cases, as atypical of their race.

In the 1990s the numbers of African-American students enrolled at Cal in a given year reached more than 2,000, yet most still appear to socialize among themselves, generating the characterization of "self-segregating." But rather than experiencing their sense of full acceptance, as legitimately entitled to be on campus (at least as they typically perceive how others see them), today's black students also speak of being marginalized, on the sidelines. The hope, of course, is that this is a period of transition—that no group of students feels "ownership" of the campus any more, that this might be a healthy development. If students can learn to adjust and learn to live and study and work together as time passes, then no one group needs to feel ownership; rather, campus life will be continually, mutually enriching.

Such increased consciousness of the richness and value of the diversity among us might, indeed, eventually be applied to the human and technical issues of the next century. As the testing ground for many key ideas of recent years, perhaps the way the University of California responds to the needs and abilities of its diverse students can be of use elsewhere in higher education and the nation.

TROY DUSTER
Director, Institute for the Study of Social Change
University of California at Berkeley

Methodology

The following remarks are presented for readers interested in the technical aspects of the oral history process. The book draws on material collected by Radcliffe College and by the University of California at Berkeley and at Los Angeles. Seven of the interviews produced by the Bancroft Library Regional Oral History Office are four- to six-hour narratives taped for the UC Black Alumni Project and focus on university experience; three are more detailed biographical memoirs from the Negro Political Leaders Series, completed in 1973–75; one is from the History of Bay Area Philanthropy project. The UCLA interview is one of a series on Negro Leaders in Los Angeles; the Radcliffe memoir is from their distinguished Black Women Oral History Project.

The interviews with Miriam Matthews and Ivan Houston and portions of the Byron Rumford interviews presented in Chapters 4, 5, and 10 were conducted by black interviewers. Comparison of the tone of questions, nature of responses, and interaction between speakers in these oral histories indicates little difference from those conducted by white interviewers.

A number of interviews were recorded in the 1970s and reflect the language and philosophical patterns of those years, as well as of the much earlier times they describe. Others taped in the 1980s and 1990s reflect the speech and attitude changes resulting from the later years of activism and reconciliation. Readers will therefore find the terms *colored, Negro, black,* and *African American* used by various speakers at various times. All these terms have been preserved in the dialogues in order to reflect and maintain the historical accuracy of changing language usage.

Narrators generally were responsive; they appeared to give thoughtful attention to questions asked and usually gave detailed responses. Each made a point of including some bitter or sad memories of exclusion, segregation, or more overt racial prejudice—a somber note among the numerous accounts of the satisfactions of accomplishment and recognition.

All adaptations of oral histories for this volume were made by or under the supervision of the editor. In selecting passages for inclusion, every effort was made to preserve the speech patterns and rhythms characteristic of each narrator, and also to preserve the dynamics of the experiences related. Each narrator is presented in a separate chapter to maintain the integrity of the full oral history.

These shortened versions are in the narrators' original words, although occasionally verb tenses have been changed to maintain continuity and purely local references rephrased to be understandable to a larger audience. Occasional clarifying phrases added by the editor are enclosed in brackets. Interestingly, as passages were gathered together a consistent story line continued to emerge in each narrative. A number of interviewer questions have been deleted where they interfered with the dramatic impact of the telling.

Each adaptation drawn from the Black Alumni Project was read and approved by its narrator, in addition to the usual interviewee review of the full oral history transcript. Comments received in this process assured greater accuracy and also the narrators' satisfaction with the results, thus strengthening their authorship of their own oral histories.

These individual voices are a joy to listen to as they echo each other—one chapter adding detail to an event sketched in an earlier account, someone giving another side to an event that was vividly recalled by a long-ago rival. Occasionally, a footnote refers to further information in another chapter, but aside from clues in the Index, the challenge of following all the threads of the story is left for the reader to discover and enjoy.

The focus of these adaptations is how the narrators got to college, what they experienced there, and how they made their way in the world. The archival volumes from which they are drawn contain much additional rich material on the substance of their work in business, politics, and community activities that will reward scholars in those fields. The extended oral histories will also refer readers to other interviews awaiting study, as well as to numerous other men and women whose experiences should also be documented in oral histories.

Notes and References

Preface

1. Ida Louise Jackson, *Overcoming Barriers to Education*, 1984 interview with Gabrielle Morris (Berkeley: Regional Oral History Office, University of California, 1990), 2.

2. Ibid., 76.

3. HUAC refers to the House Un-American Activities Committee, known for its rigorous, sometimes punitive investigation of reputed Communist activities in the entertainment industry and in labor unions; many beatniks, some of the first literary counterculturists, lived in the Bay Area; *Sputnik* was the Soviet Union's first spaceship; Elvis is the pop singer Presley; SNCC is the Student Nonviolent Coordinating Committee; SCLC is the Southern Christian Leadership Conference; Wisconsin Senator Joseph McCarthy was a vociferous anti-Communist.

Introduction

1. Gwendolyn Etter-Lewis, *My Soul Is My Own* (New York: Routledge, 1993).

2. Ibid., 65–67.

3. Ruthe Stein, "Split Personalities: Anna Deveare Smith's Amazing One-Woman Show," *San Francisco Examiner*, 2 January 1994, Datebook section, 19.

4. Werner Sollors, Caldwell Titcomb, and Thomas A. Underwood, eds., *Blacks at Harvard: A Documentary History of African-American Experience at Harvard and Radcliffe* (New York: New York University Press, 1993).

5. Jackson, *Overcoming Barriers in Education*, 76.

6. Charles Patterson, *Working for Civic Unity in Government, Business, and*

Philanthropy, 1991 interview with Gabrielle Morris (Berkeley: Regional Oral History Office, University of California, 1994), 58.

7. Troy Duster, et. al., *The Diversity Project: Final Report* (Berkeley: Institute for the Study of Social Change, University of California, 1991), 3.

8. Lawrence P. Crouchett, Lonnie G. Bunch III, and Martha Kendall Winnacker, *Visions toward Tomorrow: The History of the East Bay Afro-American Community, 1852–1977* (Oakland: Northern California Center for Afro-American History and Life, 1989), 26.

9. Delilah Beasley, *The Negro Trail Blazers of California: A Compilation of Records from the California Archives in the Bancroft Library, University of California* (Los Angeles: Times Mirror Printing and Binding House, 1919). A typescript that appears to be part of Beasley's text, including bibliography, is included as an appendix to Miriam Matthews, "Library Activities in the Field of Race Relations," Library School, University of Chicago, microfilm, 1945.

10. Rudolph M. Lapp, *Afro-Americans in California,* 2d ed. (San Francisco: Boyd and Fraser Publishing Co., 1987), 3–4.

11. Lapp, *Afro-Americans,* 21–24; Kenneth G. Goode, *California's Black Pioneers: A Brief Historical Survey* (Santa Barbara, Calif.: McNally and Loftin, 1974), 85.

12. Lapp, *Afro-Americans,* 27.

13. Ibid., 35–37.

14. Librarian Phyllis Bischoff memo to faculty and students in African and African-American Studies, University of California, Berkeley, January 1992.

15. Office of Student Research, "Undergraduate Statistics," University of California, Berkeley, Fall 1993, 5.

16. Jackson, *Overcoming Barriers in Education,* 2.

17. Patterson, *Civic Unity,* 26; Emmett J. Rice, *To Be Ready When the Door Opens,* 1984 interview with Gabrielle Morris (Berkeley: Regional Oral History Office, University of California, 1991), 39.

18. Marvin Poston, *Making Opportunities in Vision Care,* 1984 interviews with Gabrielle Morris (Berkeley: Regional Oral History Office, University of California, 1989), 7.

19. Crouchett, *Visions,* 30–31.

20. Lloyd Noel Ferguson, *Increasing Professional Opportunities in Chemistry, 1936–1986,* 1992 interview with Gabrielle Morris (Berkeley: Regional Oral History Office, University of California, 1993), 17–21.

21. Poston, *Vision Care,* 49–50.

22. Archie Williams, *The Joy of Flying: Olympic Gold, Air Force Colonel, and Teacher,* 1992 interview with Gabrielle Morris (Berkeley, Regional Oral History Office, University of California, 1993).

23. Patterson, *Civic Unity,* 27.

24. Quoted in Troy Duster, "Marginality and Political Consciousness," Institute

for the Study of Social Change, University of California, Berkeley, unpublished manuscript, n.d., 1–2.

25. Ibid., 2.

26. Rice, *To Be Ready When the Door Opens*, 69.

27. Allen Broussard, *Working for Equality in Society and the California Courts*, 1991 and 1992 interviews with Gabrielle Morris (Berkeley: Regional Oral History Office, University of California, in press), 274–375.

28. Patterson, *Civic Unity*, 104–105.

29. Ibid., 214.

30. Ibid., 286.

31. Ibid., 239.

32. William Byron Rumford, *Legislator for Fair Employment, Fair Housing, and Public Health*, 1970 interview with Joyce A. Henderson (Berkeley: Regional Oral History Office, University of California, 1973), 52.

33. Williams, *The Joy of Flying*, 31; Ferguson, *Increasing Professional Opportunities in Chemistry*, 21–27.

34. Poston, *Vision Care*, 17, 19, 21.

35. Rice, *To Be Ready When the Door Opens*, 60.

36. Williams, *The Joy of Flying*, 29.

37. C. L. Dellums, *International President of the Brotherhood of Sleeping Car Porters and Civil Rights Leader*, 1970 and 1971 interviews with Joyce A. Henderson (Berkeley: Regional Oral History Office, University of California, 1973).

38. Marilynn S. Johnson, *The Second Gold Rush: Oakland and the East Bay in World War II* (Berkeley: University of California Press, 1993), 56.

39. Ibid., 169–70.

40. Rumford, *Fair Employment*; Lionel Wilson, *Lawyer, Judge, and Oakland Mayor*, 1976 and 1990 interviews with Gabrielle Morris (Berkeley: Regional Oral History Office, University of California, 1992); Broussard, *Working for Equality*.

41. Wilson, *Lawyer, Judge, and Oakland Mayor*, 26–27.

42. Broussard, *Working for Equality*, 178–79.

43. Ibid., 112.

44. Patterson, *Civic Unity*, 415–19.

45. Quoted in Teresa Moore, "Civil Rights Movement's Next Phase," *San Francisco Chronicle*, 17 February 1992, A1, A4.

46. Jackson, *Overcoming Barriers in Education*, 75.

Chapter 2: Ida Louise Jackson

1. A few more details of her student experiences are included in the chapter Miss Jackson wrote for *There Was Light,* Irving Stone, ed. (Berkeley: University of California Press, 1968).

2. See extensive interview with Louise Thompson (Patterson) recorded ca. 1988–89 by Margaret Wilkerson of the Afro-American Studies Department, University of California, Berkeley, forthcoming.

3. Jackson's work with the summer school is described in detail in James Willis Jackson, *The Search for Something Better: Ida Louise Jackson's Life Story* (Dallas: JWJ Enterprises, 1994).

4. See Dorothy Boulding Ferebee, *Interview with Dorothy Boulding Ferebee,* Black Women Oral History Project, 1979 interview with Merze Tate (Boston: Schlesinger Library, Radcliffe College, 1979–84).

Chapter 4: Miriam Matthews

1. Miriam Matthews, "Library Activities in the Field of Race Relations" University of Chicago Library School, 1945. The copy available at the Bancroft Library, University of California, Berkeley, contains an excellent bibliography of Negro historical materials that appears to be the same as Delilah L. Beasley, *The Negro Trail Blazers of California: A Compilation of Records from the California Archives in the Bancroft Library at the University of California* (Los Angeles: Times Mirror Printing and Binding House, 1919).

2. Matthews has donated a number of items from her collection to the African American Museum and Library of Oakland.

Chapter 5: Byron Rumford

1. Beasley, *Trail Blazers.*

2. The *Oakland Independent* reported in 1929 that three young African-American women had been accepted for nursing training at Highland Hospital following a five-year campaign by the Alameda County League of Colored Women Voters.

Chapter 6: Archie Williams

1. A wordplay on *Luftwaffe,* the name of the German air force in World War II, and 1940s military slang for an African American.

2. J. Alfred Phelps, *Chappie, America's First Four-Star General: The Life and Times of Daniel James, Jr.* (Novato, Calif.: Presidio, ca. 1991).

3. Charles E. Francis, *Tuskegee Airmen* (Boston: Branden Publishing Co., 1992).

Chapter 7: Lionel Wilson

1. Gibson was a crucial figure in developing minority political consciousness and organizations in Oakland from the 1930s to the 1970s. For further information, see Evelio Grillo, "D. G. Gibson: A Black Who Led the People and Built the Democratic Party in the East Bay," in *Experiment and Change in Berkeley: Essays on City Politics, 1950–1975,* ed. Harriet Nathan and Stanley Scott (Berkeley: Institute of Governmental Studies, University of California, 1978).

Chapter 9: Lloyd Ferguson

1. Lloyd N. Ferguson, *Electron Structures of Organic Molecules* (Englewood Cliffs, N.J.: Prentice-Hall, 1952).

Chapter 10: Ivan Houston

1. Hondon B. Hargrove, *Buffalo Soldiers in Italy: Black Americans in World War II* (Jefferson, N.C.: McFarland, ca. 1985); William H. Leckie, *The Buffalo Soldiers: A Narrative of Negro Cavalry in the West* (Norman: University of Oklahoma Press, 1967).

2. Proposition 14 on the November 1964 ballot, an initiative measure to repeal the Rumford Fair Housing Act of 1963. See Assemblyman Rumford's narrative in Chapter 5.

Chapter 11: Emmett Rice

1. The first fraternities and sororities for African-American students had been organized in the 1920s, and at least one additional fraternity was established in the 1940s. See chapters by Ida Jackson, Tarea Pittman, and Ivan Houston.

2. Isaiah J. Poole, "Emmett Rice: New Man at the Fed," *Black Enterprise*, October 1979, 50.

3. "Money Men: World Bank Post Requires Extensive Travel for Rice," *Ebony*, September 1967, 65.

Chapter 12: Allen Broussard

1. William Rodarmor, "A Conversation with Allen Broussard," *California Monthly*, February 1993, 32.

2. Grillo, "Gibson."

3. Ibid., 2.

Chapter 13: Charles Patterson

1. Amory Bradford, *Oakland's Not for Burning* (New York: D. McKay Co., 1968).

Afterword

1. University of California, Office of the Vice President—Planning and Analysis, "Summary of the Fall 1968 Ethnic Survey," 14 February 1969.

2. Johnson, *Gold Rush*, 35, 53.

3. Blackwell was actually the first African American to be hired as a professor in the entire University of California system.

4. Duster interview with Judge Henderson, 17 January 1994.

5. W. J. Rorabaugh, *Berkeley at War: The 1960s* (New York: Oxford University Press, 1989), 84–85.

6. Bob H. Suzuki, "Asian Americans in Higher Education: Impact of Changing Demographics and Other Social Forces," paper prepared for National Symposium on the changing Demographics of Higher Education, Ford Foundation, New York City, 1988.

7. For a more detailed analysis, see L. Ling-Chi Wang, "Meritocracy and Diversity in Higher Education: Discrimination against Asian Americans in the Post-Bakke Era," *Urban Review* 20 (1988): 1–21.

8. Office "Statistics," 5.

9. Broussard, *Working for Equality,* 16.

10. Diversity, 1991.

11. Ibid., 28.

12. Ibid.

13. Ibid.

14. Ibid.

15. Ibid., 29.

16. Ibid., 30.

17. Ibid.

18. Ibid.

19. Ibid, 30–31.

Bibliography

Oral Histories

Broussard, Allen E. *Working for Equality in Society and the California Courts*. 1991 interview with Gabrielle Morris. Berkeley: Regional Oral History Office, University of California, in press.

Dellums, C. L. *International President of the Brotherhood of Sleeping Car Porters and Civil Rights Leader*. 1970 and 1971 interviews with Joyce A. Henderson. Berkeley: Regional Oral History Office, University of California, 1973.

Ferebee, Dorothy Boulding. *Interview with Dorothy Boulding Ferebee*. Black Women Oral History Project. Interviewed 1979 by Merze Tate. Boston: Schlesinger Library, Radcliffe College, 1979–84.

Ferguson, Lloyd Noel. *Increasing Professional Opportunities in Chemistry, 1936–1986*. 1992 interview with Gabrielle Morris. Berkeley: Regional Oral History Office, University of California, 1993.

Gordon, Walter. "Athlete, Officer in Law Enforcement and Administration, Governor of the Virgin Islands." In *Walter Gordon Oral History Project*. Vol. 1. 1971 interview with Amelia Fry. Berkeley: Regional Oral History Office, University of California, 1980. Includes 1976 interview with Elizabeth Fisher Gordon conducted by Anne Hus Brower.

Houston, Ivan J. *Interview with Ivan J. Houston*. 1986 and 1987 interviews with Ranford B. Hopkins. Los Angeles: Oral History Program, University of California, 1989.

Jackson, Ida Louise. *Overcoming Barriers in Education*. 1984 interview with Gabrielle Morris. Berkeley: Regional Oral History Office, University of California, 1991.

Matthews, Miriam. *Interview with Miriam Matthews*. Black Women Oral History Project. Vol. 40. 1977 interview with Eleanor Roberts. Boston: Schlesinger Library, Radcliffe College, 1981.

Patterson, Charles. *Working for Civic Unity in Government, Business, and Philanthropy*. 1991 interview with Gabrielle Morris. Berkeley: Regional Oral History Office, University of California, 1994.

Patterson, Louise Thompson. Interviewed extensively ca. 1984–86 by Margaret Wilkerson. Berkeley: Department of African-American Studies, University of California, in press.

Pittman, Tarea Hall. *NAACP Official and Civil Rights Worker*. 1971 and 1972 interviews with Joyce A. Henderson. Berkeley: Regional Oral History Office, University of California, 1974.

Poston, Marvin. *Making Opportunities in Vision Care*. 1984 interview with Gabrielle Morris. Berkeley: Regional Oral History Office, University of California, 1989.

Rice, Emmett J. *To Be Ready When the Door Opens*. 1984 interview with Gabrielle Morris. Berkeley: Regional Oral Office, University of California, 1991. Additional interview, conducted in 1992, in press.

Rumford, William Byron. *Legislator for Fair Employment, Fair Housing, and Public Health*. 1970 and 1971 interviews with Joyce Henderson and Amelia Fry. Berkeley: Regional Oral History Office, University of California, 1971.

Williams, Archie F. *The Joy of Flying: Olympic Gold, Air Force Colonel, and Teacher*. 1992 interview with Gabrielle Morris. Berkeley: Regional Oral History Office, University of California, 1993.

Wilson, Lionel. *Lawyer, Judge, and Oakland Mayor* 1976 and 1980 interviews with Gabrielle Morris. Berkeley: Regional Oral History Office, University of California, 1992.

Books and Parts of Books

Beasley, Delilah L. *The Negro Trail Blazers of California: A Compilation of Records from the California Archives in the Bancroft Library at the University of California*. Los Angeles: [Times Mirror Printing and Binding House], 1919.

Bischof, Phyllis. *Afro-Americans: A Research Guide to Collections at the University of California*. Berkeley: General Library, University of California at Berkeley, 1984.

––––––––––. *African American Theses and Dissertations, 1907–1990: University of California*. Berkeley: University of California Press, 1992.

Bradford, Amory. *Oakland's Not for Burning*. New York: D. McKay Co., 1968.

Crouchett, Lawrence P. *William Byron Rumford: The Life and Public Service of a California Legislator: A Biography*. El Cerrito, Calif.: Downey Place Publishing House, ca. 1984.

––––––––––. *Bibliography on Negro History*. Concord, Calif.: Diablo Valley College, ca. 1967.

Crouchett, Lorraine Jacobs. *Delilah Leontium Beasley, Oakland's Crusading Journalist*. El Cerrito, Calif.: Downey Place Publishing House, ca. 1990.

Duster, Troy, et al. *The Diversity Project: Final Report.* Berkeley: Institute for the Study of Social Change, University of California, 1991.

Etter-Lewis, Gwendolyn. *My Soul Is My Own.* New York: Routledge, 1993.

Francis, Charles E. *Tuskegee Airmen.* Boston: Branden Publishing Co., 1992.

Goode, Kenneth G. *California's Black Pioneers: A Brief Historical Survey.* Santa Barbara, Calif.: McNally & Loftin, Publishers, 1974.

Grillo, Evelio. "D. G. Gibson: A Black Who Led the People and Built the Democratic Party in the East Bay." In *Experiment and Change in Berkeley: Essays on City Politics, 1950–1975,* edited by Harriet Nathan and Stanley Scott. Berkeley: Institute of Government and Politics, University of California, 1978.

Hargrove, Hondon B. *Buffalo Soldiers in Italy: Black Americans in World War II.* Jefferson, N.C.: McFarland, ca. 1985.

Jackson, James Willis. *The Search for Something Better: Ida Louise Jackson's Life Story.* Dallas: JWJ Enterprises, 1994.

Johnson, Marilynn S. *The Second Gold Rush: Oakland and the East Bay in World War II.* Berkeley: University of California Press, 1993.

Lapp, Rudolph M. *Afro-Americans in California,* 2d ed. San Francisco: Boyd & Fraser Publishing Co., 1987.

Leckie, William H. *The Buffalo Soldiers: A Narrative of Negro Cavalry in the West.* Norman: University of Oklahoma Press, 1967.

Matthews, Miriam. *Library Activities in the Field of Race Relations.* Chicago: University of Chicago Library School, 1945.

Phelps, J. Alfred. *Chappie, American's First Black Four-Star General: The Life and Times of Daniel James, Jr.* Novato, Calif.: Presidio, ca. 1991.

Rorabaugh, W. J. *Berkeley at War: The 1960s.* New York: Oxford University Press, 1989.

Sammons, Vivian. *Blacks in Science and Medicine.* New York: Hemisphere Publishing Corp., 1990.

Sollors, Werner; Caldwell Titcomb; and Thomas A. Underwood, eds. *Blacks at Harvard: A Documentary History of African-American Experience at Harvard and Radcliffe.* New York: New York University Press, 1993.

Stone, Irving. *There Was Light.* Berkeley: University of California Press, 1968. Chapters by Ida L. Jackson and Lionel Wilson in university centennial volume of alumni reminiscences.

Articles

Boschken, Irene H., and Ralph G. Craib. "Illustrious Californians." *California Monthly,* March 1968. Thumbnail sketches of Archie Williams, Walter Gordon, and Byron Rumford.

"Colored Girls In Training." *Oakland Independent,* 21 September 1929, 1.

Crouchett, Lawrence P. "Dr. Marvin R. Poston, Pioneering California Optometrist." *Boule Journal,* February 1980, 82–85.

Crouchett, Louis B. [*sic*] "Black Visionary." *California Monthly,* March–April 1982, 87.

"Money Men: World Bank Post Requires Extensive Travel for Rice." *Ebony,* September 1967, 65.

Moore, Teresa. "Civil Rights Movement's Next Phase." *San Francisco Chronicle,* 17 February 1992, A1, A4.

Poole, Isaiah. "Emmett Rice, New Man at the Fed." *Black Enterprise,* October 1979, 50–52.

Rodarmor, William. "A Conversation with Allen Broussard." *California Monthly,* February 1993, 32–36.

———. "A Conversation with Troy Duster." *California Monthly,* September 1991, 40–44.

Stein, Ruthe. "Split Personalities: Anna Deveare Smith's Amazing One-Woman Show." *San Francisco Chronicle,* 2 January 1994, Datebook section, 19.

Wang, L. Ling-Chi. "Meritocracy and Diversity in Higher Education: Discrimination against Asian Americans in the Post-Bakke Era." *Urban Review* 20 (1988): 1–21.

Miscellaneous Publications

Bischoff, Phyllis. "Memo to Faculty and Students in African and African-American Studies." Berkeley: University of California Library. January 1992.

Duster, Troy. "Marginality and Political Consciousness." Berkeley: Institute for the Study of Social Change, University of California, n.d.

Jackson, Ida. "Rate of Development of Negro Children in Relation to Education." Berkeley: University of California, 1923.

Matthews, Miriam, "Library Activities in the Field of Race Relations," Chicago: University of Chicago Library School, 1945.

Office of Student Research. "Undergraduate Statistics." Berkeley: University of California, Fall 1993.

Office of the Vice President–Planning and Analysis. "Summary of the Fall 1968 Ethnic Survey." Berkeley: University of California, 14 February 1969.

Suzuki, Bob H. "Asian Americans in Higher Education: Impact of Changing Demographics and Other Social Forces." New York: National Symposium on the Changing Demographics of Higher Education, Ford Foundation, 1988.

Index

Note: Entries in which the last name of the narrator is capitalized (as in BROUSSARD, Allen) refer to their testimony; lower case references (as in Broussard, Allen) refer to instances in which others mention the individual.

The Author

Gabrielle Morris is a senior editor at the Regional Oral History Office, University of California at Berkeley. Since 1970 she has interviewed more than 200 Californians, including former governors Earl Warren and Edmund G. (Pat) Brown, Sr., Secretary of State March Fong Eu, and Assembly Speaker Willie L. Brown, Jr. She has planned and directed projects that include the history of philanthropy in the Bay Area, the Ronald Reagan gubernatorial era, and black pioneers at the University of California, among others.